Details Are Unprintable

Also by Allan Levine

Nonfiction

THE EXCHANGE: *100 Years of Trading Grain in Winnipeg*
YOUR WORSHIP: *The Lives of Eight of Canada's Most Unforgettable*
  Mayors (editor)
SCRUM WARS: *The Prime Ministers and the Media*
FUGITIVES OF THE FOREST: *The Heroic Story of Jewish Resistance*
  and Survival during the Second World War
SCATTERED AMONG THE PEOPLES: *The Jewish Diaspora in Ten*
  Portraits
THE DEVIL IN BABYLON: *Fear of Progress and the Birth of Modern*
  Life
COMING OF AGE: *A History of the Jewish People of Manitoba*
KING: *William Lyon Mackenzie King: A Life Guided by the Hand of*
  Destiny
MIRACLE AT THE FORKS: *The Museum that Dares Make a*
  Difference (co-author)
TORONTO: *Biography of a City*
SEEKING THE FABLED CITY: *The Canadian Jewish Experience*

Fiction: Historical Mysteries

THE BLOOD LIBEL
SINS OF THE SUFFRAGETTE
THE BOLSHEVIK'S REVENGE
EVIL OF THE AGE
THE BOOTLEGGER'S CONFESSION

DETAILS ARE UNPRINTABLE
Wayne Lonergan and the Sensational Café Society Murder

ALLAN LEVINE

LYONS PRESS

Guilford, Connecticut

An imprint of The Rowman & Littlefield Publishing Group, Inc.
4501 Forbes Blvd., Ste. 200
Lanham, MD 20706
www.rowman.com

Distributed by NATIONAL BOOK NETWORK

British Library Cataloguing in Publication Information available

Library of Congress Cataloging-in-Publication Data

Names: Levine, Allan Gerald, 1956- author.
Title: Details are unprintable : Wayne Lonergan and the sensational café
  society murder / Allan Levine.
Description: Guilford, Connecticut : Lyons Press, [2020] | Includes
  bibliographical references and index. | Summary: "Examines the murder of
  Patricia Burton Lonergan and the subsequent arrest, trial, and
  conviction of her husband, Wayne Lonergan"— Provided by publisher.
Identifiers: LCCN 2020004418 (print) | LCCN 2020004419 (ebook) | ISBN
  9781493050918 (hardback) | ISBN 9781493057870 (epub)
Subjects: LCSH: Lonergan, Wayne. | Lonergan, Patsy Burton, 1921-1943. |
  Murder—New York (State)—New York—Case studies.
Classification: LCC HV6534.N5 L398 2020 (print) | LCC HV6534.N5 (ebook) |
  DDC 364.152/3092 [B] —dc23
LC record available at https://lccn.loc.gov/2020004418
LC ebook record available at https://lccn.loc.gov/2020004419

For Angie, with love

Throughout the pattern of the Lonergan murder case are woven the purple threads of whispered vices whose details are unprintable and whose character in general is unknown to or misunderstood by the average normal person.
— NEW YORK JOURNAL-AMERICAN,
OCTOBER 30, 1943

I hope that (a) people who attend and read about the trial will take a short course in abnormal psychology beforehand; (b) they'll realize that Wayne Lonergan is on trial not because of sexual irregularities, but on a charge of having murdered his young, beautiful wife.
— THYRA SAMTER WINSLOW, NEW YORK DAILY MIRROR,
FEBRUARY 29, 1944

There is a really good book in this incident.
— WAYNE LONERGAN, GLOBE AND MAIL (TORONTO),
FEBRUARY 19, 1972

Contents

Acknowledgments

First and foremost, I would like to thank Rick Rinehart, executive editor at Globe Pequot Press/Rowman & Littlefield for his initial interest in this project and for his diligent comments and editing on the manuscript; and my literary agent, Hilary McMahon of Westwood Creative Artists for her continued support and friendship. At Rowman & Littlefield/Globe Pequot Press/Lyons Press, my thanks also to senior production editor Meredith L. Dias and Bruce Gore for designing the cover and jacket; as well as freelance copyeditor Melissa Hayes for her superb work with the final manuscript.

For their assistance in providing me with a digital copy of the New York District Attorney's files of the Lonergan case, I extend my sincere gratitude to Kenneth R. Cobb, assistant commissioner, New York Department of Records & Information Services and his colleague, Rossy Mendez, the head of Research Services. Other important archival and research support came from: Prof. Ellen Belcher of the Lloyd George Sealy Library, John Jay College of Criminal Justice/City University of New York; Darren Yearsley, senior media librarian, CBC; and librarians and archivists at the New York State Archives in Albany; New York University Medical Archives; Manuscripts and Archives, Yale University Library; Dolph Briscoe Center for American History, University of Texas at Austin; University of California, Los Angeles, Library Special Collections; and Library and Archives Canada in Ottawa.

I am most grateful to Daniel Richman, a former US federal prosecutor and a professor at the Columbia Law School, for his perceptive review and commentary of the various legal issues raised in the case. Thanks, as well, to these legal scholars and writers who took the time to answer my many questions on New York State law and US Supreme Court decisions: Christopher Slobogin and Nancy King of Vanderbilt University Law School; Stephen Gillers, New York University School of Law; Richard Leo, University of San Francisco School of Law; Brandon Garrett, Duke University School of Law; Beth Schwartzapfel, the Marshall Project; New York criminal lawyer Marvin Schechter; and author D. P. Lyle.

For their assistance in arranging interviews and for agreeing to speak with me about Lonergan or matters connected to the case, I thank: agents Ronda Cooper and Penny Noble; actors Gordon Pinsent and Leah Pinsent; journalist Ken Lefolii; Major William March (retired), historian Royal Canadian Air Force; Cynthia Sutherland of the 21 Club; Gerda Ray, the daughter of J. Franklin Ray; Justice Gerald Loehr and his brother John G. Loehr for speaking to me about their late father, John Loehr, and for providing me with a photograph of him; and editor Margaret Happel Perry for information about the work of her late husband, author and journalist Hamilton Darby Perry.

My family, as usual—my wife, Angie, and our children, Alexander, Shannon, Mia, and Geoff—offered their support and encouragement for which I am always most appreciative. I want to especially acknowledge Mia's enormous assistance in organizing the digital version of the case files and for her work as my in-house graphic designer and photographer; Shannon's keen eye and stellar copy editing in polishing the draft manuscript; and Angie, who this book is dedicated to, for her discerning advice and for being my most honest critic during the past thirty-eight years (on occasion, she doesn't think I'm listening, but I always am). Finally, to my three beautiful grandchildren, Ana, Kole, and Mickey, for inspiring me every day and for making me realize what is truly important in life.

Allan Levine
Winnipeg, Canada
June 1, 2020

CHARACTERS

PRINCIPAL CHARACTERS

Patricia Burton Lonergan: The murder victim, who was known to her friends and family as Patsy. Born into a wealthy German-Jewish New York family in 1921, she was killed in New York City at her residence, 313 East 51st Street, on October 24, 1943. She was twenty-two years old and the mother of William "Billy" Wayne Lonergan, who was eighteen months old at the time of her death.

Wayne Lonergan: Patricia's estranged husband, who was accused of murdering her. He was born in Toronto, Canada, in 1918, and moved to New York in 1939. Weeks after he arrived, he met Patricia and her father, William O. Burton.

MAIN CHARACTERS

Elizabeth Black: English-born governess hired by Patricia to care for her son, William "Billy" Wayne Lonergan.

Edward V. Broderick: Wayne Lonergan's bombastic attorney, who represented him at his two murder trials.

William O. Burton: Patricia's father, the son of a successful brewer, Max Bernheimer, and his wife, Stella. He died from a heart attack on October 21, 1940, at the age of forty-four. He and Lonergan may have had an intimate relationship prior to Lonergan's marriage to Patricia.

Lucille Wolfe Burton: Patricia's mother, the descendant of a prominent Southern Jewish family. She and William O. Burton married, divorced, and remarried, though were living separately when William died.

Alex Deans: Toronto police detective who detained Wayne Lonergan on October 25, 1943.

Peter Elser: Patricia's friend, and, in October 1943, a US Marine captain. He discovered Patricia's body at the crime scene.

Thomas ("Tom") Farrell Jr.: A magazine publisher and friend to Mario Gabellini, who dined and danced with Patricia at the Stork Club on Saturday, October 23, 1943.

Judge John J. Freschi: A judge of the Court of General Sessions in New York, who presided over Wayne Lonergan's first murder trial, from January 31 to March 4, 1944.

Mario Enzo Gabellini: A forty-three-year-old Italian decorator who was dating Patricia in the fall of 1943. He accompanied her to the Stork Club on the evening of Saturday, October 23, 1943.

Jean Goodwin: A twenty-year-old model and the girlfriend of Thomas Farrell. She saw Patricia on the last night of her life.

Jacob Grumet: A Manhattan assistant district attorney in charge of the Homicide Branch, who was the lead prosecutor in the case against Wayne Lonergan.

John F. Harjes: The scion of a banking family and a friend to Lonergan. He invited Lonergan to stay at his residence on East 79th Street during his visit to New York City on the weekend of October 22 to 24, 1943.

Arthur Harris: A detective with the Toronto Police Department, who detained Lonergan on October 25, 1943, and subsequently interviewed him.

Dr. Milton Helpern: In 1943, he was the deputy medical examiner of New York City and performed the autopsy on Patricia. He was appointed the chief medical examiner in 1954. He had a reputation as "Sherlock Holmes with a microscope."

Frank Hogan: District attorney of New York City from 1942 to 1974.

Stella Steinam Bernheimer Housman: Patricia's grandmother, whose first husband was Max Bernheimer, a brewery magnate. When she died in 1954, she left an estate valued at about $7 million—approximately $66.6 million today.

Jean Murphy Jaburg: A twenty-eight-year-old blonde former showgirl, and Lonergan's date on the evening of Saturday, October 23, 1943.

John Loehr: A Manhattan deputy assistant district attorney, who traveled to Toronto to interrogate Wayne Lonergan and escort him back to New York. He subsequently was involved in eliciting a confession from Lonergan.

William "Billy" Wayne Lonergan: Patricia and Wayne Lonergan's son, born July 1, 1942. He was only eighteen months old when his mother died. Following the murder, his grandmother, Lucille Wolfe Burton, who raised him, changed his name to William Anthony Burton. He also inherited his mother and great-grandmother Stella Steinam Bernheimer Housman's multimillion-dollar estate. He is now seventy-eight years old and presumed to be living in the United States.

Nicholas Looram: A New York City detective who investigated Patricia's murder and accompanied Wayne Lonergan back to New York City from Toronto.

Emile Peeters: John F. Harjes's butler, who interacted with Wayne Lonergan on the weekend of October 22 to 24, 1943.

Josephine Peeters: The wife of Emile Peeters, who worked as a maid for John F. Harjes, and who interacted with Wayne Lonergan on the weekend of October 22 to 24, 1943.

William Prendergast: A New York City detective who investigated Patricia's murder and accompanied Wayne Lonergan back to New York City from Toronto.

Annaliese Schonberg: The nurse and governess who worked for the family of J. Franklin Ray Jr. and lived in the suite above where Patricia lived, at 313 East 51st Street. Standing in a common hallway, Schonberg heard the murder, though she did not call the police.

Marie Tanzosch: Patricia's maid, who saw Wayne Lonergan when he visited his son on Saturday, October 23, 1943.

Judge Garret Wallace: A judge of the Court of General Sessions in New York, who presided over Wayne Lonergan's second trial, from March 9 to April 17, 1944, and sentenced him.

Prologue

Belle of the El Morocco

New York City, Sunday, October 24, 1943

SHE WAS TWENTY-TWO YEARS OLD, vivacious, fun-loving, and intelligent, with a zest for life. Patricia Burton Lonergan—Patsy to her family and friends—was impeccably dressed, as usual. She was wearing an expensive, short, opulent mink coat, and the rest of her attire was fashionably black and pricey—a silk dress that tastefully hugged her slender figure, silk hat with a small plume of feathers, nylon stockings, evening pumps, and matching gloves. Beneath the gloves, her manicured fingernails were painted with red lacquer polish. With her penetrating brown eyes, slender and small nose, and soft reddish-brown curls, Patricia was attractive and pleasing to the eye. A "classy dame" was how she was described in the vernacular of the 1940s. As the daughter of a wealthy, assimilated German-Jewish family, she was also rich and spoiled.

By 6:30 a.m. she had been out for close to sixteen hours on a date, dancing, dining, and drinking fairly steadily during much of that time; in short, a typical evening for a young socialite of New York's café society. Still tipsy, Patricia gingerly climbed the stairs to the second-floor master bedroom of her renovated Turtle Bay–Beekman Place area brownstone at 313 East 51st Street, half a block from Second Avenue, trying to be as quiet as she could. Asleep in the nursery down the hall was her eighteen-month-old son, William, or "Billy," under the care of his nanny, Miss Elizabeth Black.

Patricia had recently separated from the boy's father, her husband of two years, Wayne Lonergan, a slick and charming Canadian. Less than two months earlier, he had enlisted in the Royal Canadian Air Force (RCAF) and was undergoing training in Toronto. That weekend, he had been granted leave and was visiting New York City. Wayne and Patsy's relationship was rocky and difficult—and that was putting it mildly. As a child of a middle-class family, Lonergan had fully embraced café society, reveling in the outings to the Stork Club and El Morocco and the carefree party atmosphere these homages to wealth and decadence generated. Yet, he also resented Patricia for enjoying it so much, especially since they had split up. He had heard stories about her gallivanting with other men, which deeply wounded his ego. Angry, he sarcastically derided her as the "belle of the El Morocco."

Reaching her bedroom, Patricia dropped her hat and purse on a side table. She undressed, threw her mink jacket, dress, nylon stockings, and shoes on a settee at the foot of her oversized bed, and climbed in. The bronze dolphins on the four posts in ormolu surrounding the bed seemed to be staring at her—but on this morning, she ignored them. The top of the nearby dresser was stocked with all types and shapes of French perfume bottles. And, on a table about seventeen feet to her right, were two green-glass or onyx candleholders with heavy brass square pyramid–shaped bases.

For the rest of the day, Patricia's bedroom door remained tightly shut. Elizabeth Black knew better than to trouble her mistress. Miss Black had risen about half an hour after Patricia had collapsed in her bed. The seasoned governess lovingly tended to Billy, who wanted something to drink and eat. Just before 9:00 a.m., Black had gone downstairs to the ground-floor kitchen to eat her own breakfast and prepare food for Billy. She did not hear any fighting or other unusual sounds coming from inside the bedroom. Nor did she see Wayne Lonergan or any other person enter or exit the apartment. Once the boy had been fed at approximately 10:00 a.m., she took him out for a walk in his carriage, returning by noon.

Annaliese Schonberg did hear a brief argument from the Lonergan apartment, however. She was a twenty-two-year-old German-born governess, a plain-looking young woman with rimless glasses who worked for the family living in the duplex on the third and fourth floors, located above Patricia's apartment. At about 9:00 a.m., she had walked down to a common stairway area shared by the residents of the house on the second floor to fetch the Sunday newspaper. She had just opened the door of the butler's pantry when she heard a woman's bloodcurdling scream emanating from behind Patricia's locked bedroom door. It was "loud and shrill," she later recalled. Startled, she halted and listened for another moment.

"What are you doing? Stop that. Oh my!" she heard the woman shout. Then, silence.

Schonberg took the paper upstairs, glanced at the Sunday "funnies," and immediately returned. She was about to knock on Patricia's bedroom door, but then stopped herself. "It wasn't my place to interfere," she later explained. She heard a "shuffling" sound, yet no other voices, male or female.

Dutifully, Schonberg walked back up the stairs to where J. Franklin Ray Jr., his wife Mary, and their six-year-old son Jeff (or Jefferson) resided. Franklin Ray regularly commuted between New York and Washington, DC, where he worked for the federal government. Schonberg was caring for the boy, who was ill with scarlet fever and quarantined. In 1943, owing to the availability of penicillin within the past year, scarlet fever was no longer as deadly a disease, but her young patient required rest. As she reached the Rays' suite, she heard another scream, and then nothing else.

———

It was a typical Sunday afternoon on East 51st Street. Some neighborhood children played a game of touch football. A few stray cats prowled through the garden at the back of several brownstones. At about two o'clock, Miss Black found a package left inside the vestibule, though she did not open it. Once or twice, she turned the doorknob to Patricia's bedroom, yet it was locked each time. Later in the afternoon, she took Billy to see his grandmother, Lucille Wolfe Burton, at her suite at the Hotel Elysée on East 54th Street and Park Avenue. She arrived back with the child two and half hours later, around 5:30 p.m. Still, there was no sign of Patricia.

Black bathed Billy and then fed the boy his dinner. She was, however, growing increasingly concerned about Patricia, and finally telephoned Lucille Burton, who walked over. Lucille vigorously knocked on Patricia's bedroom door.

"Patsy, are you there?" she called out.

When there was no response, she attempted to open the door, but like Black, was also unable to do so. This was typical behavior for her daughter, she thought, whose antics often aggravated her. Had Patricia traveled to the country for the day without bothering to let Miss Black know, she wondered. This made no sense, she quickly realized, since if Patricia was away, the bedroom door could not possibly be locked. The only other thing that popped into her head was that Patsy must have a nasty hangover and was sleeping it off.

So why, then, did Lucille feel queasy? Call it a mother's intuition, but in her gut she suspected something was amiss. In her heightened state of anxiety, Lucille did not notice large bloodstains on the wall next to the stairway, and neither did Elizabeth Black.

At that moment, the telephone rang, startling both of them. Black answered. It was a call from Patricia's friend, twenty-three-year-old marine captain Peter Elser. Husky and fit, he was a former star football lineman and polo player at Harvard. He was visiting the city and staying at the Savoy Plaza on Fifth Avenue and East 59th Street.

Several nights earlier, when Elser had been at the El Morocco, he had run into Patricia and they had danced together. He wanted to say good-bye to her, as he was leaving New York the next day, returning for duty to Parris Island, South Carolina.

Prior to the evening at the nightclub, Elser had not seen Patricia in two and a half years, since they both had been skiing at Franconia, New Hampshire. He first had been introduced to her in November 1939 at a ritzy Park Avenue cocktail party. They became friends after that. Elser, who later met Wayne Lonergan after Patricia had married him, was unimpressed by her choice in a husband. He believed that Lonergan would cause her no end of grief.

Lucille grabbed the receiver from Black and implored Elser to please come over to Patricia's right away. "Patsy has been in the room all day, and I am worried," Lucille told him, her voice trembling.

Elser arrived at the apartment about 8:00 p.m. At Lucille's urging, he tried opening the door with a key he found in a closet on the lower level. But the key wouldn't turn. Removing his black frame glasses, he attempted to force his way into the bedroom with his shoulder. The door was thick and solid and would not budge. He then noticed that the pins holding the door hinges were sticking up enough so that they could be pried off. Black provided him with a screwdriver and he removed the pins and lifted the door up and to the side.

Elser gingerly peered inside. The room was fairly dark, illuminated only by two low lights, flickering in the far corner of the room. As his eyes gradually adjusted, he looked around more purposefully and then he saw her. He instructed Miss Black to keep Lucille out of the room. He found the telephone and called the police.

Lucille would not listen to the governess. She walked into the bedroom. "Oh, no, no," she cried out in agony.

Lucius Beebe, who, arguably, provided the most intellectual reporting on the machinations of café society, pointed out that to be recognized as one of its glamorous stars, worshipped and envied by other partygoers, a person needed lots of money and a "presentable metropolitan scheme of living." Yet, "the dominant requisite for an elite membership," he added, "is a name that is news, a warrant for existence." Patricia Burton Lonergan's name was about to become prominent in the news for the next six months; sadly, she wasn't able to bask in this tragic explosion of celebrity.

The Making of a Hustler

ON MONDAY, JANUARY 14, 1918, the day Wayne Thomas Lonergan was born in Toronto, Ontario, Canada, the Great War was almost into its fourth bloody year. It was to take another ten long months, until November 11—which Americans mark each year as Veterans Day, and Canadians, as Remembrance Day—before the conflict was finally to cease. The end was hastened by the United States' entry into the war a year earlier. Nonetheless, it was a bittersweet victory; during four years of fighting, 20 million people, soldiers as well as civilians, died, and another 21 million were wounded.

There was more tragedy to come in 1918. Several months before the Armistice, there were widespread outbreaks of influenza in North America and Europe. At a time when there were no antiviral drugs to treat flu viruses, physicians and nurses could do little. As the outbreak spread, it turned into the worst pandemic since the medieval Black Plague—and that lasted for a century. In only six months, during the latter half of 1918 and the early part of 1919, about 500 million people, a third of the world's population, were infected, and more than 50 million died. That included an estimated 675,000 Americans and 50,000 Canadians. In Toronto, during the first year of Lonergan's life, approximately 260,000 people—or more than half the city's population—had become ill; of those, 1,300 died.

On January 14, 1918, Toronto was still digging out from a record snowfall. At Union Station, the trains started moving again after two days without regular service. The poor weather also meant that orders for coal had dramatically increased, so that frigid Torontonians could heat their homes. The city's populist mayor, Tommy Church, having just won his fourth election in a row, presided over a new session of city council. Church expressed concern that the federal government in Ottawa, a coalition union government under Conservative prime minister Robert Borden, was not sufficiently looking after the interests of Toronto, and Canadian soldiers. Too much responsibility for the men's welfare, the mayor stated, was being left to the Canadian Patriotic Fund, a private fund-raising organization, and the Red Cross.

In international news, the British Admiralty announced that it had developed a new system of camouflaging ships, but that did not stop a German destroyer from bombarding Yarmouth in the county of Norfolk on England's east coast. That same day, the first of ten assassination attempts was made on the life of Vladimir Lenin, the Russian revolutionary leader, who had led the Bolsheviks to power at the end of 1917. As Lenin was chauffeured in a car following a speech he had given to a detachment of the First Socialist Army in Petrograd—as St. Petersburg had been renamed—gunmen opened fire. Fritz Platten, a journalist accompanying Lenin, pushed the Russian leader's head down, thereby saving his life.

———

None of this, of course, was then known to young Wayne, who grew up in a middle-class neighborhood near Bathurst and Bloor Streets, west of Toronto's downtown. His father, Thomas, from the village of Norwood, Ontario, a hundred miles east of Toronto, was forty-two years old when Wayne was born. Norwood was a typical rural Ontario town with a gristmill, foundry, a small furniture factory, and lots of churches. He worked as an agent for the Metropolitan Life Insurance Company. By 1918, he and his wife, Clara, thirty-one years of age, and their two other children—June, seven years old, and William, three—resided in a comfortable two-and-a-half-story, semi-detached, Edwardian-style brick house with a gable roof at 599 Markham Street, one block south of Bloor and west of Bathurst.

Before moving to Markham Street, the Lonergans had either rented or owned a home a short distance away on Palmerston Avenue. The house on Markham cost Thomas and Clara approximately $3,500—worth about $60,000 in 2020, but a far cry from the $1.5 million-plus homes in the same neighborhood in Toronto's high-priced real estate market. In the 1980s, the Lonergans' house was owned by the colorful entrepreneur, "Honest" Ed Mirvish, whose bargain emporium dominated the corner of Bloor and Bathurst Streets. He had intended to tear down the house and several more nearby for a parking lot, but instead converted the residence to an artist studio, which was part of "Mirvish Village," for a time, a chic cultural hub with trendy shops and galleries. As of late 2019, 599 Markham Street is home to the Listening Centre, an independent clinic.

Clara was born in 1886 to John and Ellen Stauber, who were both Roman Catholic, in the northern Michigan county of Menominee, about ninety miles north of Green Bay, Wisconsin. When she was a young girl, she and her family moved to Saginaw, closer to Detroit. The most significant fact about Clara was that she suffered from extreme anxiety and manic-depressive psychosis—a bipolar disorder—throughout her life, right up to her death from chronic heart disease in 1942, at the age of fifty-five. The anxiety and psychosis often made her indifferent to her young children, as well as paranoid and delusional. On at least four occasions between 1912 and 1933, she was hospitalized at Ontario Hospital (as it was called from 1919 to 1966), on Queen Street West. (Prior to that it was called the Hospital for the Insane, from 1907 to 1919, and today it is the Centre for Addiction and Mental Health.) One of those times was in July 1918, six months after Wayne was born. When he was seven years old, in June 1925, she was admitted for a three-month stay, and for another five months in April 1933.

Clara met and married Thomas in (about) 1909. His roots were Irish Catholic, like thousands of other immigrant families in Ontario. During the nineteenth century, the Irish, both Protestant and Catholic, were the largest European group in the province. (Before Canadian Confederation in 1867, Ontario was known as Upper Canada, from 1791 to 1841, and Canada West, part of the Province of Canada, from 1841 to 1867.) Many lived in Toronto, or eventually were drawn there to find work, like Thomas Lonergan.

From its incorporation as a city in 1834, Toronto (originally known as York) was predominantly White, Anglo, and Protestant, which in 1921 represented approximately 70 percent of the city's population. For decades, it was nearly impossible to be elected mayor or to city council without the backing of the Orange Order, the extreme Protestant organization. Each year, thousands of loyal Orangemen celebrated the Glorious Twelfth to mark the victory of William of Orange and his Protestant supporters over the Catholic King James II at the Battle of the Boyne in 1690. They were not shy about publicly showing their support for the British Empire or their enmity toward Catholics.

With the arrival in North America of the Famine Irish in 1847—"Black '47"—impoverished refugees altered the character of Toronto (as well as such cities as New York and Boston). In Toronto, like elsewhere in North America, the Irish were the victims of hostile prejudice and discrimination. Suddenly, at least according to the Protestant majority, Toronto was overwhelmed with thousands of needy, troublesome Catholic immigrants. By 1921, 25.2 percent of the city's population, or about 130,500 people, declared their ethnic origin to be Irish—and more than half were Catholic. In the latter part of the nineteenth century, the rise of a distinct Irish Catholic presence had frightened many of Toronto's narrow-minded citizens. "No Irish Need Apply" was a common sign posted in the city's shops and factories. Irish Catholic immigrants "will find out through bitter experience," declared the Toronto-based newspaper, the *Irish Canadian*, in September 1869, "[that] their prospects are damped, their chances are curtailed, and the openings of employment lessened, because of their religion."

In line with his parents' religious beliefs and philosophy, Wayne received an education steeped in Catholicism. For grades one through eight he attended two Catholic schools, St. Peter's School, a block from his home, and De La Salle Collegiate, operated by the Christian Brothers on Bond Street, right next to St. Michael's Cathedral Basilica, close to the corner of Yonge and Dundas Streets in downtown Toronto. (In 1931 the school relocated to a grand property further north on Avenue Road, referred to as the "Oaklands," where it is today as an independent, coeducational, university preparatory school.) Then and now, the school was "centred on a life of faith," as Brother Domenic Viggiani, the president of De La Salle College "Oaklands" explains on the school's website. "In such a school, God's presence is a lived reality. It is a Christian school in the Roman Catholic tradition which proclaims the message of the Gospel to today's youth."

In the fall of 1932, for grade nine, Lonergan attended the main neighborhood school, Harbord Collegiate Institute on Harbord Avenue, west of Bathurst Street, which at the time had a large percentage of Jewish students, the children of East European and Russian immigrants. In 1932, among the members of the graduating class were Frank Shuster and Louis Weingarten, who were to find acclaim as the comedy duo of "Wayne and Shuster."

Lonergan's public school experience lasted only a year. In September 1933, his parents transferred him back into the Catholic system to St. Michael's High School, an all-boys school on St. Joseph Street, which was affiliated with St. Michael's College, now part of the University of Toronto. For some reason, he is listed in the 1933–34 yearbook by his middle name, Thomas, rather than Wayne.

St. Michael's offered an even more rigorous education than De La Salle. The school and college, according to its 1933 yearbook, *The Thurible*, was meant "to prepare the present generation for that earthly happiness they so ardently desire." Emphasized was that "man was not created solely to enjoy earthly happiness, and so true education must prepare the student for what he has to be and do here below in order to attain the sublime end for which he was created. It must aim at securing the Supreme Good, that is, God, for the souls of those who are being educated, and the maximum of well-being possible on this earth for society."

The switch to St. Michael's might have been triggered by Wayne's delinquent behavior. At the end of 1932, Lonergan—who was an average student, but with an IQ of 123, indicating "very superior intelligence"—had gotten into trouble. It was his first run-in with the law, though by no means his last.

Five days before Christmas, Wayne was arrested and detained as a juvenile delinquent for stealing several items from a store, including a microphone, a purse, and a cigarette lighter. (He was already a heavy smoker and would remain so for the rest of his life.) Since it was his first offense, he was placed on probation.

Yet when he ran away to Windsor, Ontario, 225 miles west of Toronto, he was sent for a short stay at the St. John's Industrial School, a protectory operated by the Christian Brothers to help wayward boys. Opened in 1895, the school in 1933 was located on Victoria Avenue, in the eastern part of Greater Toronto, in Scarborough. Lonergan and the other boys were not "inmates," and St. John's was not a prison, or even a reform school; rather, as the Brothers noted, it was a place where Catholic youngsters "are trained to useful citizenship . . . [these children] have shown tendencies which if unchecked would lead them to lives of wrongdoing." A typical day was devoted to academics for several hours, followed by industrial training. There was also time for athletics.

Lonergan did not seem to benefit from his stay at St. John's or to appreciate the important message the Brothers were delivering. In late March 1934, while he was a student at St. Michael's, he was arrested again for shoplifting. This time, he talked his way out of trouble, and the charges were withdrawn.

To be fair, Lonergan's tenth-grade year was difficult for another, more emotional reason. His father was ill. On May 21, 1934, Thomas Lonergan died of coronary thrombosis (a blood clot inside a blood vessel of the heart), at the age of fifty-eight. That same day, Wayne was arrested for stealing bicycles. He was remanded for a week and placed on probation for two years. Within a few months he had violated the probation terms, and as a sixteen-year-old, was sentenced to thirty days at the Langstaff Jail Farm in Richmond Hill, north of Toronto (today, on the northeast corner of Yonge Street and Highway 7). A minimum-security institution for first-time offenders and "petty criminals," "the Jail Farm," as it was commonly referred to, did not have a barbed-wire fence or armed guards.

Thomas's death and Wayne's ongoing legal problems coincided with one of the worst years of the Great Depression—it was also Toronto's centennial year—when 25 percent of Torontonians (160,000 people) were unemployed and on government relief. It got so bad that people advertised their services for $1 a day—which even in the 1930s was a paltry wage. Still, as a life insurance agent, Thomas had wisely provided for his wife and children. Clara and the family were able to remain in the house on Markham. After Clara passed away in 1942, June and William lived in the house for several more years; Wayne had already left Toronto.

Like other teens, Wayne dropped out of school when he turned sixteen years old. He attended the Dominion Business College on Bellevue Avenue and College Street, where he took courses on business arithmetic, salesmanship, and advertising. Lonergan, however, was impatient. He was in search of other adventures and wanted to make some money.

—◆—

For someone like Lonergan who desired excitement, Toronto—particularly during the period from the 1920s to the late 1950s—could be positively dreary. The truth was that Canada's second-largest city, with a population of about 630,000 in 1931, had a well-deserved reputation for being dull. (It was only in 1981 that Greater Toronto surpassed Greater Montreal in population to become the largest city in Canada.) With its puritanical Lord's Day laws—which at the time forbid using city park toboggan slides on Sundays and where the police actually padlocked playground swings—the city could not shake its staid image from the 1880s as "Toronto the Good," a bastion of Victorian morality. "Christ, I hate to leave Paris for Toronto the City of Churches," Ernest Hemingway, then a reporter for the *Toronto Daily Star*, protested to a friend in a 1923 letter.

The brash and bold Hemingway, a personality Lonergan would have no doubt admired, spent part of the period from 1920 to 1923 in Toronto (as well as in Paris as the *Star*'s first European correspondent) when he was in his early twenties. Despite developing a keen interest for hockey and Chinese food restaurants, he found Toronto excessively boring. Ontario's repressive liquor laws, a holdover from World War I, were a particular sore point. Not that it was difficult to obtain a bottle of whiskey; the Ontario Temperance Act did not ban the production of booze—which, as Hemingway noted in a June 1920 article was the reason so much Ontario liquor was "pouring" into the United States during American Prohibition.

Hemingway was by no means the only one to claim that Toronto was stuffy and tedious. Anarchist Emma Goldman on a lecture tour in December 1927 came to the same conclusion and also deemed Toronto "deadly dull." Asked by a *Star* reporter to elaborate, she replied, "Because it's church-ridden. Toronto people are smug and don't think for themselves." The best comment on the city's character, however, belongs to Leopold Infeld, a world-renowned physicist who taught at the University of Toronto from 1939 to 1950. "It must be good to die in Toronto," he wrote in 1941. "The transition between life and death would be continuous, painless and scarcely noticeable in this silent town. I dreaded the Sundays and prayed to God that if He chose for me to die in Toronto He would let it be on a Saturday afternoon, to save me from one more Toronto Sunday."

Free of school, Lonergan sought opportunities anywhere he could find them. For several months in 1934 and 1935, he worked for the International Nickel Company (Inco), the leading supplier of nickel in the world, at its biggest mining operation in Sudbury in Northern Ontario. (Since late 2006, Inco has been owned by Brazilian mining company Vale.) He returned to Toronto more rugged and fit.

According to medical reports later submitted to the New York police department, in 1935 Lonergan was treated for gonorrhea. Today gonorrhea can be easily remedied with antibiotics, yet at the time it was a disease not understood as clearly or consistently dealt with. In a July 1937 article in the African-American journal, the *New York Amsterdam News*, for example, Dr. John B. West asserted that gonorrhea "may be contracted by the use of common toilet seat which has been previously contaminated by an infected person," which we now know is nonsense.

Gonorrhea was not as dangerous as syphilis, which together with tuberculosis and influenza was a leading cause of death in the United States in 1934; that year, only heart disease killed more people, while cancer was third on the list. Starting in 1937, medical studies showed that patients with gonorrhea recovered when given injections of sulfonamide, an antibacterial drug. This was two years before Lonergan contracted the disease. In 1935, many physicians recommended antigonococcus serum and vaccine treatment, as well as "bladder irrigation and massage of the prostate." It is not known precisely how Lonergan was treated, only that he recovered.

In 1937, Lonergan accepted a position as special constable for the Ontario Provincial Police (OPP) to combat alleged Communist influence in labor unions—a job that was courtesy of Mitch Hepburn, the unpredictable and somewhat erratic Ontario premier. To get the job and avoid any questions about his juvenile delinquent record, he used his brother's name on his application form, William Joseph Lonergan. This was a ploy he continued using for several years, especially when he traveled to the United States.

Only the desperate economic times could have propelled someone like Hepburn, an onion farmer from the city of St. Thomas, 122 miles southwest of Toronto, to the leadership of the Ontario Liberal Party in 1930, and the premiership four years later, when he was only thirty-seven years old. Hepburn was a populist and understood the common man more than most political leaders of his day. "People believe he is honest; know he is fearless; and regard him as efficient in administration," Canadian prime minister William Lyon Mackenzie King, who famously feuded with the Ontario premier, wrote begrudgingly after Hepburn had won a second majority government on October 6, 1937. Hepburn was the exact opposite of King. He was impetuous, inconsistent, impulsive, vindictive, reckless, and, worst of all, from King's puritanical perspective, a sinner. Hepburn had a well-deserved and notorious reputation for being a drinker and a womanizer. There was one story about Hepburn being caught with three young girls in his suite at Toronto's downtown King Edward Hotel, and another about the premier bedding one woman in a Kingston, Ontario, hotel and doing the same with another in Ottawa the next night. King had no doubt that Hepburn would "eventually destroy himself."

In the spring of 1937, Hepburn took a ruthless stance against thousands of striking workers at the General Motors plant in Oshawa, thirty miles east of Toronto. Paranoid about the Communist threat and no fan of organized labor, he regarded the strikers as dangerous because they were now members of the United Automobile Workers (UAW), which was affiliated with the Committee for Industrial Organization, or CIO (later, the Congress of Industrial Organization) that had been established by the American labor organizer John L. Lewis in 1935.

To Hepburn and others, the CIO was militant, and the Oshawa workers were seemingly on the verge of instigating another Bolshevik revolution. In fact, they merely wanted an eight-hour day, better working conditions, higher wages, and recognition of their union. Nonetheless, Hepburn was furious that the federal government offered to mediate the dispute, which he incorrectly regarded as an attempt to embarrass him. Then, he became angrier when Prime Minister King refused his request to put the officers of the Royal Canadian Mounted Police at his disposal. Instead, Hepburn created his own force of special police, referred to derisively as "Hepburn's Hussars" and "Sons of Mitches"—to harass the strikers. "We know what these agitators are up to," Hepburn said. "It has to stop, and we are going to stop it. If necessary we will raise an army to do it."

One of the strapping young men hired to do the premier's bidding—among an estimated four hundred that were recruited—was Wayne Lonergan. He was given an OPP uniform, paid $25 a week, and promised future work after the strike was over. Lonergan and his fellow special constables, however, were not given pistols, "just the usual [wooden] batons," as the premier explained. In the end, there was no real violence—unlike other American and Canadian strikes the CIO already had been involved in—and Lonergan and the other "Hussars" did not see real action or stay around for very long after the strike was settled, two weeks after it had started.

Returning to Toronto during the summer of 1937, Lonergan was employed as a lifeguard at the Simcoe Beach Park in the city's east end, on the shores of Lake Ontario. His supervisor, Edward Blair, later recalled that Lonergan frequently neglected his patrol and spent his time socializing or going for rides on a motorboat. Lonergan soon found another job as an administrative assistant for the talented pianist Horace Lapp, who conducted a popular dance band at Toronto's posh Royal York Hotel. Lapp thought highly of him.

As a photograph from the late 1930s shows—of Lonergan, posing in his bathing trunks—he was tall, dark, and Hollywood handsome, with an impressive physique that made women swoon and men envious. He exuded confidence and had a magnetic sexual appeal that was instantly attractive to anyone he crossed paths with. He did not reputedly have a bad temper, and certainly nothing in his character indicated that he had a violent streak. In fact, it was quite the opposite: Wayne was smart, charming, and debonair. He only lacked the cash to make the dream of the good life a reality.

In 1939, he announced to his family and friends that he had landed a job as a bus dispatcher for Greyhound Bus Lines. Admittedly this was not a step toward fame and fortune. Still, it was an enticing offer, as he was to be based at the company's headquarters at the New York World's Fair—one of the largest and most exciting events then being held. Lonergan said he wasn't planning to be back in Toronto anytime soon. His future, he added, was in the United States. He could not have foreseen how prophetic a remark that was to be.

There is one more crucial point to consider about young Wayne Lonergan as he departed for New York, and that is his sexual orientation. It is central to the story of Patricia Burton Lonergan's murder and to understanding the many complexities of Lonergan himself. During Lonergan's trial, the subject also attracted a great deal of newspaper coverage, much of it salacious.

Though Wayne frequently—but not always—publicly denied that he was bisexual or gay, the evidence strongly suggests otherwise. According to a report prepared in January 1944 by Detective Sergeant Arthur Harris of the Toronto Police Department, Lonergan, as a troubled teenager, bragged to his friends that "he made easy money through male perverts [homosexuals]." And in a revealing moment in October 1943, when Lonergan was being questioned by the New York District Attorney's office about his culpability in Patricia's death, his one overriding concern was publicity about his "morals." This was after he had admitted to participating in so-called "acts of perversion" with another man—a claim he later retracted. The New York Police Department and DA's office also learned of "homosexual activity" Lonergan was involved in.

In 1942, Dr. George Henry, then the director of the Payne Whitney Psychiatric Clinic at New York Hospital, examined Lonergan at the request of the US Selective Service System. A year earlier, Henry had published a two-volume study—a second and more widely read edition was published in one volume in 1948—entitled *Sex Variants: A Study of Homosexual Patterns*. Unlike other academics and physicians of the era, Henry had a more dispassionate and levelheaded approach to the issue. His books were praised for presenting the facts in an "unprejudiced manner." He concluded that Lonergan was a "psychopath, and that he had relationships with both men and women." He also told the New York DA's office that Lonergan was a consummate liar—which proved to be an accurate judgment.

There is the assessment, too, of journalist and magazine publisher Hamilton Darby Perry, who passed away in December 2009 at the age of eighty-five. Perry was a onetime Florida crime writer. He interviewed Lonergan in the late 1960s and early '70s for a book he wrote about the case, *A Chair for Wayne Lonergan*, which was published in 1972. At the time, he was not able to fully address Lonergan's sexual identity in a world still overtly hostile to the LGBTQ community, nor would Lonergan have consented to cooperate with him if he had. In any event, the two had a falling-out prior to the book's publication. In 2000, however, when a second edition of Perry's book was included as part of the specialized Notable Trials Library Series, published by Gryphon Editions, Perry added an afterword in which he noted the truth of the matter: Wayne Lonergan was indeed bisexual.

2

The Burtons

LIFE WAS GOOD for twenty-three-year-old William Oliver Burton in the summer of 1920. Seemingly, he did not have a care in the world. On his twenty-first birthday, in October 1917, he had inherited a trust fund of $250,000—the equivalent today of about $6.3 million. That money, and William's privileged upbringing—in 1910, he and his parents, Max and Stella Bernheimer, his older brother George, and his maternal grandparents had five servants to attend to their daily needs—was the result of Max inheriting his father's lucrative brewery business and expanding it.

William, however, short and small in stature, fancied himself an artist. He had no interest in manufacturing beer for the rest of his life—and he didn't have to. His substantial wealth enabled him to explore his creative interests. He studied at the Yale University School of Art, the Art Students League of New York, and the New York School of Fine and Applied Art, and on many trips to Paris worked alongside the noted landscape artist, Marius Avy.

France was, in fact, where he wanted to be to expand his artistic horizons. In this quest, he was no different than a large number of late-nineteenth-century American artists—among them, Julius LeBlanc Stewart, Mary Fairchild, and Impressionist Mary Cassatt—who painted portraits and landscapes in Parisian studios, exhibited their works at annual well-attended salons, and socialized into the wee hours of the night at smoky Left Bank cafés.

Paris also afforded William another freedom: to be completely at ease with himself and who he was at heart. Though William's sexual orientation cannot be absolutely confirmed, there is sufficient evidence to strongly suggest that—like Wayne Lonergan—William Burton was gay, or certainly bisexual—a fact also strongly suggested by Hamilton Darby Perry in 2000.

During much of the twentieth century, France was one of the few places on Earth where homosexuality was more or less tolerated—at least, in comparison to the United States, Canada, and Britain, where it was illegal, morally repugnant, regarded as sexual perversion at its worst, and as one headline from a 1940 Baltimore newspaper put it, a "crime against God."

In the United States, the stories of discrimination, disgrace, and harassment against the LGBTQ community are inexhaustible. In November 1944, the board of regents at the University of Texas in Austin fired Dr. Homer Rainey as president because the board believed he had failed in his duty to weed out "a nest of homosexuals" in the faculty. In Washington, DC, in July 1946, the police blamed the suicide of sixteen-year-old Tommy Alwine on the fact that he was associated with the city's "pervert fringe." According to the *Washington Post*, "known homosexuals, older youths and men . . . led him into the upside-down world and then fought to keep him there." And in May 1948, E. K. Johnson, a fifty-year-old veteran journalism professor at the University of Missouri in Columbia, was arrested on charges of being the head of a "homosexual ring" which threw "mad homosexual parties" at Johnson's apartment.

In France, on the other hand, sodomy laws were repealed in 1791 at the start of the French Revolution. "Fairy nice boys," as the slang of the day had it, could freely socialize at nightclubs in Montmartre, Pigalle, and Montparnasse. When William was in Paris, he could live his life as he saw fit. He did not have to look over his shoulder as he did in New York in order to safeguard his secrets.

William's family made other demands on him, however; they had specific expectations for his future, one of which was for him to find a nice girl and get married, settle down, and have children. In 1920 there was definitely no "closet" to come out of; you kept your private life as private as was possible. Hence, during the first week of August that year, William's engagement to the lovely, Jewish, and pampered Lucille Wolfe was announced in the New York and Chicago newspapers.

Lucille, who was three years older than William, had grown up along with her three younger brothers and a sister surrounded by modest wealth and (a few) servants. Her heritage was in the Deep South. Lucille was the daughter of Hartwig Wolfe from South Carolina. His German immigrant parents, Sailing and Sarah, had thirteen children; Hartwig, who was born in May 1867, was number ten. The Wolfes had owned and operated several plantations in Winnsboro, about seventy miles south of Charlotte, North Carolina. The Wolfe family were proud Southerners and slave owners. They lived in a columned mansion, enjoyed musical evenings around the fire, and had their every whim and desire attended to by their slaves. This mint julep and bourbon-sipping lifestyle ended with the advent of the Civil War in 1861.

In February 1865, as the war was coming to an end, the family's home, property, and cotton, like that of nearly all of their neighbours, were pillaged and then burned and destroyed by the pitiless Union soldiers. Commanded by General William Tecumseh Sherman, the Yankee forces inflicted havoc and a wave of destruction as they marched through the South.

"Indelibly impressed upon my memory," recalled Isabelle ("Belle") Wolfe, Hartwig's older sister, "is the vision of the suffering and agony of dear women, who were left to the mercy of the hostile soldiers, who swarmed over [our] beautiful town." When the smoke cleared, the Wolfes were nearly destitute, forced to start over again in nearby Camden during the Reconstruction era. It was an arduous challenge, one that Sailing Wolfe did not overcome. He died at the age of eighty-four in poverty.

In 1867, Isabelle married Dr. Simon Baruch. He had served in the Confederate Army as a surgeon, and was later a public health advocate and hydrotherapist, who promoted the healing powers of water. (Simon and Isabelle died within seven months of each other, in 1921.) Their son, Bernard, became a noted financier in New York, where many members of the extended Wolfe family relocated in the early 1880s. Bernard Baruch was also an advisor to two US presidents: Woodrow Wilson during World War I, and, more significantly, Franklin Roosevelt, during World War II.

Family connections boosted Hartwig's career. In 1871, another of his sisters, Rose, had married Henry Lytton, who had been born in New York in 1846 as Henry Levi, into a British-Jewish family. Lytton, who lived to be 102, was the founder of the Chicago department store, Lytton's, known more popularly as "The Hub," which became a multimillion-dollar enterprise, with several outlets elsewhere in Illinois and Indiana.

———

Like his bride-to-be, William Burton's family roots were also in Germany. But it was New Yorkers' penchant for light German lager in the latter half of the nineteenth century that was the basis of his personal fortune. Escaping economic hardship and restrictive government regulation, nearly three million German-speaking immigrants arrived in the United States in the period from 1820 to 1880, of which an estimated 150,000 were Jewish. Many

Germans, Jews and non-Jews alike, ended up in New York City; by 1880, one-third of the city's population, or more than 370,000, were German.

Among the multitude was Emanuel Bernheimer, who in 1844, at the age of twenty-seven, bid farewell to his family in the Baden-Württemberg area in central Germany near Stuttgart and journeyed to the new world. He landed in New York City with a bit of money and trained as a brewer. Within six years, he and a partner, August Schmid, founded the Constanz Brewery on East 14th Street. After that Emanuel expanded his business interests with the more well-known Lion Brewery on Columbus Avenue. In 1862, he was also one of the organizers of the United States Brewers Association, America's first trade association.

Two factors contributed to Emanuel's growing success. First was the enormous popularity of German lager that was more carbonated and not as heavy as the English "top-fermented" ales and porters that New Yorkers had been imbibing. And second, Emanuel was a marketing wizard. He was one of the first brewery owners in the city to advertise in the press, and astutely opened boisterous beer gardens and saloons to promote his beer.

By the time of Emanuel's death in March 1890, he and his wife Fannie and their four children—Simon, Max, Flora, and Henry—were members of New York's German-Jewish upper class. This was a Jewish elite that included such luminaries as the Straus family, who owned Macy's department store; garment factory owner William Seligman; and investment bankers Joseph Seligman, Henry Lehman, Marcus Goldman, and his partner, Samuel Sachs. They were assimilated "Israelites" and patriotic Americans, rather than "Hebrews" or Jews. They resided in grand brownstones on Fifth Avenue, or closer to the still-undeveloped area around Central Park. Nonetheless, the bourgeois Gentile elite whose acceptance they sought never quite let them forget they were Jewish immigrants and outsiders. The wealthy socialites who dominated the *Social Register*, the coveted and snooty official list of New York blue bloods, did not disdain the Germans Jews as much as they later did the "pushy" and backward Eastern European Jews—who, starting in the early 1880s, inhabited the Lower East Side in huge numbers—yet the German Jews were bothersome all the same.

Joseph Seligman and his family were reminded of these very real societal barriers in June 1877 once they arrived for their vacation at Saratoga Springs in Upstate New York. When they attempted to check in at the luxurious Grand Union Hotel, where they had stayed before, they were told by the hotel manager that on the order of Judge Henry Hilton, the hotel's administrator (and the executor of the estate of the hotel's owner, department store magnate Alexander T. Stewart, who had died in April 1876), "no Israelites shall be permitted in the future to stop at this hotel." Jewish protests were ignored. Hilton was certain that the hotel was losing money because its Gentile guests objected to the presence of an ever-increasing number of Jews who vacationed at the Grand Union. (Hilton was not related to Conrad Hilton the founder of the Hilton Hotels.) This episode marked only the start of anti-Semitic and discriminatory treatment faced by American Jews. During the next two decades, wealthy and prominent German Jews—who much to their chagrin were lumped in with the uncouth East European Jews—found that social clubs were closed to them, elite private schools refused to admit their children, and they could not purchase property at various summer resorts.

Nothing was written in stone, however, and there was an ebb and flow to the prejudice and discrimination. A case in point: The Bernheimers' brewery sales did not suffer from their Jewish background. Emanuel's son Max (William Burton's father), who joined his older brother Simon in the business in 1889, had attended Grammar School No. 35, a prestigious boys school on West 13th Street near Sixth Avenue. The Bernheimers were generous philanthropists to Jewish and non-Jewish charities. They were members of the Temple Emanu-El, the first true Reform congregation in New York, where German (and then English) was used in prayer services, rather than only Hebrew. In 1868, the Bernheimers, along with other members, helped to raise more than $650,000 (about $11.5 million today) to erect what the Temple's website notes was "the largest and most spectacular synagogue in America, a gorgeous house of worship of Moorish design at Fifth Avenue and East 43rd Street."

At the synagogue on June 8, 1887, Max, who was thirty-two years old, married Stella Steinam, nineteen years old. It was a union of two prominent German-Jewish families. Stella was the daughter of Abraham Steinam, who as a young man in the 1840s had come to the United States from Bavaria and eventually established a successful clothing business. Like the Bernheimers, he was also a generous philanthropist, most notably providing $100,000 in the early 1900s ($2.9 million today) for the establishment of the Hebrew Technical Institute for Boys on East Ninth Street, in honor of his and his wife Mathilda's son Lucas, who had died at a young age. Abraham Steinam passed away in January 1914 at the age of seventy-five.

Max and Stella and their two sons—George, who was born in February 1894, and William, born in October 1896—lived in style in a roomy Upper West Side apartment on 72nd Street, not too far from the Dakota, the elegant residence across from Central Park built by Edward Clark, who made his money as co-owner of the Singer Sewing Machine Company. (The Dakota, most famously, would one day be the home of Beatle John Lennon and Yoko Ono.)

The Bernheimer family's idyllic life was shattered on September 24, 1913.

Max was at a courthouse in Brooklyn testifying in a civil case. A painter by the name of Gustave Kenz was suing his brewery company for $10,000 in damages. In the lawsuit, Kenz claimed that while working at the brewery his eyes had been injured from acid emanating from vats on the premises. As soon as Max had finished giving his testimony, Kenz's lawyer handed him another subpoena to appear again on that day. Max was angered by this ploy and grew visibly agitated. He stumbled for a moment and then collapsed. By the time he arrived at nearby Brooklyn Hospital, he was dead at the age of fifty-eight. He was laid to rest at the Salem Fields Cemetery in Brooklyn. Established by the congregants of Temple Emanu-El in 1851, it is the final resting place for several generations of prominent German-American Jews.

Stella and her sons were devastated, but they didn't need to worry about money. Max left an estate worth more than $4 million (about $89 million today). Apart from a $20,000 charitable bequest, Stella received the bulk of it, while sons George and William were each left $250,000 in trust funds accessible on their twenty-first birthdays.

The very wealthy Stella did not stay a widow for long. In March 1915, she married fifty-year-old Frederick Housman, the head of a Wall Street brokerage firm. Housman was the son of German-Jewish immigrant parents and had been born in New York City. He had the regal bearing of a Prussian duke, and was distinguished by a neatly trimmed Van Dyke beard and handlebar mustache. He was also rich in his own right. The couple lived in a luxurious Midtown Park Avenue suite.

During the hot and humid summer months, they retreated to their magnificent home at Elberon, a resort favored by the rich and famous along the New Jersey coastline. Elberon and nearby locales like Rumson were especially popular among wealthy Jewish families such as the Seligmans, Lehmans, Shiffs, and Warburgs, where they were welcomed rather than shunned. There, amid the European-style villas and beaches, these Jewish families enjoyed sunbathing, golf, tennis, dinner parties, river lunches, horse shows, and "automobiling" down the coast. The New York weekly, the *American Hebrew and Jewish Messenger*, for example, ran a summer column entitled "Society and Its Doings: On the Jersey Shore," to keep its readers apprised of the comings and goings of the Jewish elite. For some years, Housman served as president of the local Society for the Prevention of Cruelty to Animals (SPCA). Elberon was also well-known as the favored vacation spot for several US presidents, including Ulysses Grant, William McKinley, and Woodrow Wilson. President James Garfield died in Elberon in September 1881, eighty days after he had been shot by writer and lawyer Charles J. Guiteau.

Later Stella and Frederick owned property in Palm Beach, Florida, as well. Housman died in late 1945, and Stella lived until early 1954, passing away in Palm Beach when she was eighty-six. By then, she had experienced much tragedy, with the deaths of her two sons and the murder of her granddaughter, Patricia.

In 1917, however, that was far into a future that neither George nor William could have ever predicted. Even before they received their inheritances, the two brothers, like Henry Lytton and many other assimilated New York Jews of the day—wanting to eschew the anti-Semitism that they believed impacted on their lives—changed their last name from the German-Jewish-sounding "Bernheimer" to the more American "Burton." William also rid himself of the middle name "Solomon" for the Christian name "Oliver." William later claimed that he and George had abandoned their father's surname primarily because in the midst of World War I—their name change did coincide with the US entrance into the war in April of 1917—their "Teutonic" family name attracted anti-German sentiments. That was probably true, to a point. Yet what the brothers really wanted was complete acceptance as full-fledged members of the Park Avenue elite, which proved elusive, even if they were the scions of a notable German-Jewish family with roots in the United States going back to the mid-nineteenth century.

— ⁓ —

On a near-perfect warm autumn day, Saturday, September 25, 1920, William Burton married Lucille Wolfe at Stella and Frederick's Elberon home. The newlyweds honeymooned in Paris, and then decided to stay for several more months while William painted. They returned to Elberon in time for Lucille to give birth on September 1, 1921, to a beautiful baby girl, Patricia Hartley Burton—as WASP-y a name as a Jewish couple could come up with. She had her mother's dark eyes and her father's long and slender nose and narrow chin.

By the new year, William, Lucille, and baby Patsy, as she had been dubbed, were back in France. Much of Patricia's early childhood was spent journeying between New York, where the family had an apartment near Park Avenue and 72nd Street, close to where Stella and Frederick lived; Paris, living at a residence and studio at the famed Villa des Arts in Montmartre, on rue Hégésippe, where such luminaries as Paul Cézanne and Auguste Renoir had once painted; and, best of all, at William's opulent villa at Mougins in the south, not far from Cannes. As was the custom of the rich, Patricia—who one day would follow this custom herself, with her own child—was essentially raised by two governesses, Miss Wilmott and Mademoiselle Aimone. When the family was in Mougins, the nanny and Patricia lived together in a guesthouse on the property, so that she did not bother her parents while they partied or disturb them while they slept.

As inspiring as painting at the Villa des Arts must have been, the experience did not transform William into another Cézanne or Renoir. His art career never reached the high level he had anticipated. A few months before he was married, William was commissioned for a $1,000 fee to paint the portrait of a family friend, Miss Claire Cornell, described in the press as a "society girl," and the twenty-four-year-old daughter of business executive Albert Cornell of the brokerage firm E. F. Hutton. As decor and background for the painting, Claire sent William a Chinese jade necklace, Chinese lamp, and a fine Chippendale chair—all worth in total about $700.

The trouble began when William presented the portrait to Claire and her mother. They did not like his work and refused to pay William his fee. He took them to municipal court and won. Unwilling to accept the court's decision—that they had to pay William the $1,000—the Cornells appealed the judgment to a higher court. William made matters worse for himself when he refused to return Claire's property in lieu of not receiving his fee.

As William, Lucille, and Patricia boarded a Cunard ship back to Europe on October 19, 1921, Claire and her mother appeared with a city marshal, who had a civil arrest warrant for William. In order to avoid arrest and detention, William was forced to give Claire a check for $700. He did not fare much better at the appeal trial seven months later. At the proceedings an art dealer, testifying on behalf of the Cornells, denounced the portrait William had painted of Claire—which William had stated was "a good and fair portrait of the subject"—as "amateurish," and not resembling Claire at all. The appellate judge agreed with this assessment, that the portrait was "not a proper likeness," and overturned the lower court's decision. It was all humiliating for William and an insult to his status as an artist, especially since his altercation on the ship, as well as his legal troubles, had received attention in the New York newspapers. (Claire Cornell had other problems: In December 1925, she broke off her engagement to the Marquis de Avilés (a cousin of the queen of Spain, Victoria Eugenie of Battenberg) and married Robert Stevenson, an artist, only to annul the marriage three days later. Then, in July 1926, she was charged with shoplifting two silver vases at a Fifth Avenue shop. During her trial, a neurologist testified that she suffered from a "nervous disorder.")

———

There were still more gossipy and embarrassing headlines for the Burtons. George Burton equally enjoyed the benefits of his trust fund. On the day of his twenty-first birthday in February 1915, when the money became accessible, he threw a party for all of his friends at Delmonico's on Fifth Avenue and 44th Street, one of the finer restaurants in New York, famous for its steaks. He frequently visited Paris, as well, traveling first-class on ocean liners and residing at a lavish apartment on rue Alfred de Vigny, a mile and a half north of the Champs-Élysées. Like his younger brother William, George had no real full-time job, though he did serve in the United States Army Air Service (after 1926, the US Air Force) during 1917–1918. He, too, had artistic pursuits, and attempted—with limited success—to develop a career as a musical comedy performer using the stage name Charles Bernheimer.

In 1922, George—who was twenty-eight years old, and at six feet and more than 230 pounds, a big man—announced his engagement to Charlotte Demarest. She was the nineteen-year-old daughter of Warren Demarest, a well-off automobile broker, and his wife Elizabeth. Charlotte preferred the family's roomy summer residence at Évian-les-Bains in the South of France, rather than their New York residence. She, in fact, had met George in Paris. He was instantly smitten and showered Charlotte with thousands of dollars' worth of gifts. The couple was soon engaged to be married.

She was no wallflower. Charlotte had a vivacious personality, deep, penetrating dark eyes, and an attractive bobbed hairstyle in vogue at the time. She could have been a character in an F. Scott Fitzgerald novel. Her short brown hair symbolized that she was a young woman with a mind of her own—as George was soon to find out.

While she was in Paris, Charlotte had been introduced to twenty-three-year-old Count Edward Zichy, the dashing and handsome son of Hungarian count Béla Zichy and his American wife, Mabel Wright. The Zichy family lived in the British seaside resort of Eastborne in the southeast of England. The meeting was uneventful, yet there were definite sparks between the two. Charlotte soon returned to New York, and George followed her. So did Edward Zichy, a skilled dancer, who relocated to Manhattan.

Zichy's attempts to woo Charlotte away from George were initially unsuccessful. But George was all too aware of his interest in her. This undoubtedly explained why his wedding to Charlotte was moved up to May 22, 1922, at his grandmother Mathilda Steinam's (Stella's mother) home in Elberon. A special train was arranged to transport the guests from New York City.

On the morning of the wedding, Charlotte told her family that she needed some air and was going for a walk. In fact, she met Zichy, who had announced to his friends that he was going to elope. They thought he was joking, but he wasn't. Edward and Charlotte headed to City Hall where they were married; Charlotte became Countess Zichy. The newlyweds then took a train to Philadelphia. Charlotte telephoned her mother, Elizabeth, who was naturally distraught. The family physician immediately called Mathilda's home with news of what had transpired, and that was how poor George learned that he had been left at the altar.

The sensational story of how Charlotte jilted her wealthy fiancé and eloped with Zichy was front-page news across the country. In time, George recuperated from the ordeal, mainly by partying in Paris. Little did he know that his life was to be cut short. On the morning of Friday, April 25, 1924, he suffered a devastating heart attack at the age of thirty. Stella and Frederick, who were vacationing in Deauville on the northwest coast, were summoned to Paris. George died before they arrived.

Meanwhile, William and Lucille's brief marriage was falling apart—in all probability because William was trying to live his life as a heterosexual husband, and his dishonesty frustrated and angered him. Lucille may have had an affair and claimed that William had become violent toward her, in front of Patricia. She later listed his various transgressions in a court proceeding: In April 1922, he had "used profane language in front of their home and caused a crowd to gather"; on a family trip to Biarritz, a popular and pricey seaside town on France's southwestern coast, she claimed William hit her, knocked her head against the wall, and ordered her out of the villa they were staying at; during a vacation at the charming resort town of San Sebastian, Spain—thirty-one miles south of Biarritz—he allegedly threw a suitcase at her and "put her in fear of her life"; and in early April 1924, she said that he had pushed her down the steps in their home in the presence of guests, locked her in a bedroom for two hours, and then took Patricia to an undisclosed location, where the young girl was kept for several days away from her mother.

By mid-March 1925, after less than five years of marriage, Lucille had had enough and sought a separation on the grounds of cruelty. With William residing in Paris at the time, the authorities in New York served him the papers at his residence at the Villa des Arts. He vehemently denied he had hurt his wife, but the courts in New York and Paris did find her version of their troubled marriage credible. William had remained in France for so long that Lucille was legally able to charge him with desertion. In May 1926, a court in Paris granted Lucille a divorce decree. As alimony, William was ordered to pay Lucille $18,000 ($257,000 today) annually. Lucille took little Patsy back to New York, where they stayed for the next four years.

Then, the unexpected happened.

Only the couple can truly know the state of their relationship. Quite inexplicably in August 1930, Lucille agreed to remarry William in a ceremony in Cannes. Lucille later said that she and William mainly did this for their daughter, who they both "worshipped." Given all that had gone on between the two of them, it was, nonetheless, a bizarre turn of events, one applauded by Lucille's mother, Clara, who was then living in Los Angeles.

Patricia's home life got back to a semblance of normalcy—at least, what was normal for the rich. The family remained in Europe during much of the 1930s, journeying back and forth from the Riviera to New York every so often. Patricia's early education proceeded with private tutors and elite schools. Both William and Lucille—according to Lucille, at any rate—were strict parents. When she became a teenager, they did not permit her to accompany them to late-night parties, bob her hair, "varnish" her nails, or wear red lipstick.

But that eventually changed. By the time she was twenty years old, like most young women of her generation, she had gained sufficient independence from her parents to make her own fashion decisions.

3

The Debutante and the Dispatcher

AS THE ONLY CHILD of a couple whose relationship could best be described as awkward, problematic, and occasionally turbulent, it is not at all surprising that Patricia was spoiled rotten by both of her parents as they competed for her affection. By the time she was eighteen years old, she had become a wealthy and cultured debutante—in search of a respectable husband, yet not too busy for late-night socializing. In line with the duty of all debutantes, she was active in a variety of charity projects, especially once World War II broke out in September of 1939.

Needless to say, with her father supplying her with a monthly stipend, the poverty and desperation that impacted the lives of millions of Americans during the Great Depression did not trouble Patricia or her family all that much. To her credit, she did take her philanthropic work seriously.

Patricia had accompanied her father home from Europe a few days before the start of the war. They sailed on the Cunard ocean liner, the RMS *Aquitania*, boarding on a stop at Cherbourg in northwestern France on August 23, 1939, and arriving in New York six days later. They both resided at William's suite at the Ritz Tower on 57th Street and Park Avenue. Lucille stayed in Europe for more than a year, an odd and dangerous decision, considering the Nazis had occupied France by June 1940. But by then, she and William had separated again.

William's large yacht, durable enough for an ocean crossing, was packed with valuable paintings and jewelry and soon followed him to the United States. The story was that by the time the yacht docked in New York Harbor, the crew had stolen half of his precious cache. There was no report of the theft, possibly because William was trying to sneak this treasure of goods into the country without notifying customs officials.

Patricia's social calendar in late 1939 and the first half of 1940 was jammed with teas, fund-raising events, and regular gatherings of the Debutante Club. Usually, Patricia and her mostly non-Jewish friends, all daughters of the New York elite—among them, misses Elise Cavanagh, Florence Wardwell, Constance Mitler, Elizabeth Fuller, Elaine Jacoby, Sally Page Williams, and Suzanne Close—met for afternoon tea in the elegant Corinthian Room of the Pierre Hotel on Fifth Avenue, across from Central Park.

In late December 1939, Patricia attended a benefit dinner and dance called "A Night in Cannes," in which her father was involved. Before William had departed from Europe, he had generously donated his villa in Mougins to the French government for the duration of the war (which also meant that Lucille was living elsewhere in France during 1939 and 1940). It was converted into the American Auxiliary Hospital. The gala was held at the St. Regis Hotel under the auspices of Princess Martha de Bourbon, the wife of Archduke Franz Joseph. Apart from drinking champagne, eating fine food, and mingling, the goal of the ritzy event was to raise money for a new fifty-bed hospital in Mougins.

Less than two weeks later, Patricia attended a tea held at the home of Ellen Adams, the wife of railway executive Frederick B. Adams, on East 69th Street, in honor of Sara Roosevelt, President Franklin Roosevelt's eighty-six-year-old mother. This gathering was hosted by the senior committee members who were planning the president's Birthday Ball and Society Circus that was to take place at the Waldorf Astoria on January 30, the day of FDR's fifty-eighth birthday. Patricia was one of the cochairwomen of the group's junior committee. The women and girls were raising funds to support what was then referred to as "infantile paralysis," or polio, the disease that afflicted Roosevelt and confined him to a wheelchair for much of his life.

FDR's birthday celebration was followed by Patricia working as a volunteer ticket-taker for the American premiere of the French film, *The Baker's Wife*, a 1938 French drama (with English subtitles) directed by Marcel Pagno, held at the World Theatre on West 49th. Money raised at the showing benefited Le Paquet au Front, an organization that sent thousands of kit bags to soldiers at the French front. She also volunteered her time for a debutante ambulance drive to aid the British American Ambulance Corp. And early in 1941, the fateful year when her life was to be altered forever, she was one of five debutante models featured at a supper dance held at the Midtown Le Coq Rouge restaurant. The event was sponsored by the National Women's Division of the Committee to Defend America by Aiding the Allies.

By then, she was seeing Wayne Lonergan.

—◆—

There is no record of Lonergan's reaction the first time he walked through the gates of the New York World's Fair in the spring of 1939. Like the other twenty-six million visitors to the fair in 1939 and 1940, he must have been duly impressed. Financial support totaling a hefty $155 million (about $2.4 billion today) from businesses and government had transformed a massive and remote 1,200-acre landfill in Flushing Meadows in Queens into an extraordinary site that celebrated "Building the World of Tomorrow," with parks, lagoons, greenery, fountains, architecturally eye-pleasing buildings, tree-lined roadways, and ingenious exhibits. The fair highlighted human achievement in transportation, communications, education, medicine, health, and food production—and that included the wonders of frozen food. (The site was later used for the 1964 World's Fair and is today the home of the USTA Billie Jean King National Tennis Center, among other attractions.) Its most iconic symbols were the 610-foot Trylon, which seemingly reached the heavens, and the mammoth Perisphere, 185 feet in diameter. These modernistic structures themselves cost $1.7 million, and were visible from as far away as Midtown Manhattan and the Bronx.

For New Yorkers and other Americans and tourists, who had endured a brutal decade of economic hardship, the fair, above all, offered a liberal view of progress and an optimistic outlook on the future. Such exhibits as General Motors' "Futurama" and the Fair Committee's "Democracity" set inside the Perisphere anticipated a world where everyone would be able to buy a suburban home with a white picket fence and city life that was safe and welcoming. In short, the fair made people feel good, and few who experienced this Disney-like extravaganza ever forgot about it. The fair "is a more nearly honest performance, on a more comprehensive and beautiful scale, than any event of its kind with which comparison in degree of public service and usefulness is possible," wrote journalist Gardner Harding in a June 1939 *Harper's Magazine* feature following his visit. Admission to the fair was initially seventy-five cents, but then dropped to fifty cents. About the only issue that visitors grumbled about was the fact that food at the concessions was pricey; you couldn't buy a proper dinner for less than a dollar (although hot dogs and hamburgers cost just a dime each).

Greyhound Bus Lines ferried visitors in sleek new buses from subway stations and nearby bus terminals to the fair's gates. The company also transported visitors between pavilions in a tram-style shuttle service that featured bench seating for fifty passengers in windowless cars, pulled by a gas-powered engine. Lonergan's job was to ensure that the buses and shuttles kept to a set schedule and that there were an adequate number of vehicles operating to keep up with demand. He worked more than a hundred hours per week and was paid $135 per month, an above-average wage for the time.

The fair's first season of operation ran from April 30 to October 31, 1939, and then shut down for the winter, reopening from May 11 to October 27, 1940. Lonergan was laid off at the end of October 1939. Greyhound management rated him a "fair" employee—the middle grade on their scale. He soon found other employment at Abercrombie & Fitch, which in the 1930s was a sportswear store for men and women located at Madison Avenue and East 45th Street. While the store was considered "exclusive," Lonergan rightly regarded his pay of $30 per week as too low.

One day in late 1939 or early 1940, William Burton, who was forty-three years old, met Wayne Lonergan, who was twenty-two, and was immediately drawn to him. The feelings were apparently mutual. For Lonergan, moreover, who was just getting by as a bus dispatcher, Burton's wealth and lavish lifestyle were immensely appealing. Decades later, Lonergan told Hamilton Darby Perry that a friendly manager at the George Washington Hotel on 23rd Street and Lexington Avenue, where Lonergan was staying, had first introduced him to William and Patricia when they were dining at the hotel one evening.

Newspaper reports, on the other hand, later noted that Lonergan had initially met William when he had worked at the World's Fair as a chair pusher, another of his jobs. Sponsored by the American Express Company, young, strong men were hired to push visitors around the fairgrounds in large, wide comfortable chairs on wheels. Whatever the truth of the inaugural meeting, Lonergan insisted it was Patricia he was immediately interested in, not William. At the same time, Lonergan did not hide the fact from Perry that William was known to be bisexual, although this, he claimed, had nothing to do with him.

The other and arguably more believable version of this story is that William was entranced by the handsome, charming, and physically attractive Lonergan, and for a brief time, they became lovers. As a *New York Journal-American* story later (caustically) put it, Burton had "a penchant for picking up impecunious young men and lending a helpful hand."

William and Wayne's close relationship is given further credence by the statement that Sidney Capel Dixon, a Lonergan family friend from Toronto, told the New York district attorney's office. In 1939, Dixon was forty-nine years old and single, working as a radio program director for the Canadian Broadcasting Corporation (CBC). That October, he visited Lonergan in New York, and the two men went out for dinner and drinks several times, and attended the theater together. Here was how he later recalled Lonergan's lifestyle: "Lonergan's conversation on the occasion of four or five meetings about what he did, the places he went to and the money he spent indicated to me that he had an extraordinary source of income. I concluded from his general behavior, conversation and attitude that this income was being derived from homosexuality."

Lonergan did spend a lot of time with Burton at his apartment at the Ritz Tower. More importantly, as Dixon observed, Burton introduced Lonergan to a life he could have only dreamed about: fancy and expensive dinners at the best restaurants in New York, fine champagne, and an entrance into the nightclubs of the city's café society. It was also Burton who introduced Lonergan to his daughter Patricia.

It is certainly understandable that both Burton and Lonergan would have tried to be discreet about their bisexuality or homosexuality. Not only was there a fear of being publicly humiliated or ostracized, it was also downright dangerous to be gay in New York in 1940. "Although New York was certainly the most progressive, liberal, and heterogeneous metropolis in America," explains former *New York Times* writer Ralph Blumenthal, "the entire society remained color- and caste-divided." Homosexuals and lesbians, who were compelled to lead secret lives, were at the bottom of this hierarchy, routinely shunned as lepers. Plainclothes detectives stalked known gay bars with the intent of entrapping innocent victims. Violent crime and homosexuality were intrinsically linked by the police, press, and physicians, especially in the relatively new field of psychiatry. Gay men were routinely portrayed as "sexual psychopaths" who lacked self-control.

Typical was this assessment by J. Paul de River, a psychiatrist for the Los Angeles Police Department, who wrote in his best-selling 1949 book, *The Sexual Criminal: A Psychoanalytic Study*: "The sex pervert, in his more innocuous form, is too frequently regarded as merely a 'queer' individual who never hurts anyone but himself. All too often we lose sight of the fact that the homosexual is an inveterate seducer of the young of both sexes, and that he presents a social problem because he is not content with being degenerate himself; he must have degenerate companions, and is ever seeking for younger victims."

Similarly, the respected psychiatrist Benjamin Karpman explained in a 1951 journal article that "if one person forces another person under threat into homosexual activity, it is regarded legally as a sexual offense. However, if two persons by mutual consent engage in the privacy of their homes in homosexual relations, such behavior is not commonly regarded as sexually psychopathic." According to his studies, "an absolute homosexual, whose most conspicuous behavior is homosexuality, also suffers from hypochondriasis, syphilophobia [fear of syphilis], anxiety states, suicidal trends, somnambulism [sleepwaking], inferiority feelings, and the like." Such stereotyping and discriminatory attitudes were to haunt Lonergan during his murder trial and for many years thereafter.

Legal authorities—and that included judges—accepted the idea that homosexuals (and to a lesser extent, lesbians) not only suffered from a disease that was probably curable, but also that they were a threat to themselves and society at large. The widely held view was that homosexuality was a "crime against nature," which had to be policed and punished. In New York, it was against the law for two men to be on a dance floor together without women as partners. Bartenders who served a drink to a customer who they knew was gay could be held liable, and their establishments charged with disorderly conduct.

Much more serious was the New York State sodomy law of 1881, which was still in force in the 1940s; if caught committing the act—or allegedly so—the individuals arrested faced a prison sentence of five to twenty years. (It was worse in Illinois, where gay men were incarcerated in a psychiatric ward until they were declared cured, and then upon release were charged with sodomy, which carried a ten-year maximum sentence.) The judges in New York, who were as prejudiced against gay men as anyone else during this era, were tough and unsympathetic. A 1938 study published in *Mental Hygiene*, the journal of the National Association for Mental Health, indicated that the vast majority of New York judges almost always imposed a prison sentence on a gay offender, and it generally made no difference if it was the first time the accused had been charged with a sodomy offense. In the event of a person charged a second or third time, the jail time dramatically increased.

— ⁓

We will never know for certain what the exact relationship was between William Burton and Wayne Lonergan. By all accounts, it only lasted a few months. Lonergan, who liked to be in the company of beautiful women—and according to one unnamed woman Dominick Dunne interviewed twenty years ago, he also took them to bed, though not that enthusiastically—was smooth, yet untrustworthy. Nevertheless, with Burton's approval, Lonergan began escorting Patricia to nightclubs, though he was still seen in the company of Burton as well.

Everything changed on Monday, October 21, 1940. William was alone in his apartment when, like his father and brother, he had a heart attack. He died at the age of forty-four. Lucille, who was still in Europe and did not attend William's funeral, was listed as his spouse on the death certificate. William was buried at the family plot in the Salem Fields Cemetery.

Lonergan's work at the World's Fair, where he had returned when it reopened in May, had ended on October 20, 1940. He had been fired for not working hard enough, in management's estimation. Thereafter, Lonergan took a keener interest in Patricia and she in him. He was undoubtedly aware that she had a $230,000 trust fund ($3.4 million today) from her late father's estate. On September 1, 1942, the day she turned twenty-one years old, the trust was to provide her with $1,219.30 per month, or about $14,632 per year ($216,000 today), a fair amount considering that at the time, the average annual salary for American workers was $1,885. Patricia also had income from interest from bonds and other family investments. Last, but certainly not least, upon her grandmother Stella's death, she stood to inherit close to $7 million. (Worth more than $109 million today.)

Maybe Wayne was after Patricia's money, or perhaps he was simply attracted to her, as he maintained. Or, maybe, it was a bit of both. Either way, Wayne and Patricia began dating more frequently in 1941.

Lucille Burton had arrived safely back in New York on December 9, 1940, traveling aboard the American Export Lines' SS *Exeter*, which had departed from Lisbon on November 29. It was a nerve-wracking voyage in the dangerous wartime waters of the north Atlantic, considering that German submarines and U-boats had already attacked British passenger ships. Among the targets was the SS *Athenia*, torpedoed in early September 1939, in which 117 people had died, including some Americans. Within a short time, Lucille was living in a suite at the Hotel Elysée on East 54th Street, close to Park Avenue.

Lucille, who likely knew about Lonergan's relationship with her estranged husband, did not approve of his relationship with her daughter. In June, in order to remove Patricia from Lonergan's orbit, Lucille took her daughter to stay with friends in picturesque Santa Barbara, on the sunny Southern California coast.

Lonergan, if anything, was persistent. He borrowed money from acquaintances, bought a $350 return airline ticket, and flew to Los Angeles, a flight that in 1941 took three or four stops and about twelve to fifteen hours. It must have been a joyful reunion, because at the end of July, and in clear defiance of her mother's wishes, Patricia drove with Lonergan to Las Vegas.

—◆—

In the summer of 1941, Las Vegas, with a population of 11,000 or so, was years away from becoming the larger-than-life, kitschy "Sin City" it is today. Still, oversized hotels like El Rancho and the Flamingo were starting to be erected on the Strip, featuring swanky restaurants, swimming pools, and casinos.

The city's "newest industry [was] quick and easy marriages," wrote Hugh Scott of the *Philadelphia Inquirer Public Ledger* in a November 1941 feature article. As you drove into Las Vegas along what was called by the locals "Honeymoon Highway," visitors like Wayne and Patricia were greeted by signs for "The Hitching Post," proclaiming: "Weddings. Day or Night; Immediate Arrangements; Including License." In 1940, 26,636 people had been married in Las Vegas, and officials expected more than 40,000 by the end of 1941. Already, by October 31, 1941, the city had issued 16,932 licenses at $2 each.

Hollywood stars were also taking advantage of permissible Nevada state marriage laws. On July 14, 1941, actor William Holden married actress Brenda Marshall (Ardis Ankerson) in a union that was to last thirty years. Two weeks later—three days before Wayne and Patricia arrived in the city—nineteen-year-old Judy Garland married her first of four husbands,

David Rose, the recently divorced orchestra leader who was twelve years her senior. The woman Rose had divorced, singer and actress Martha Raye, had gotten married in Las Vegas at the end of May to Neal Lang, a Miami Beach hotel executive.

On Wednesday, July 30, 1941, Wayne Lonergan and Patricia Burton added to the city of Las Vegas's coffers. They stopped at the Hitching Post, purchased their wedding license, and became husband and wife. Only the *Daily News* in New York ran a story about the nuptials, a brief mention by the paper's society reporter, Nancy Randolph. However, the man who had captured the heart of young Patricia was mistakenly listed as "Wayne Larnagan."

The lies started immediately. Wayne convinced Patricia that he had his own money and a steady income from investments. She was sufficiently gullible to believe him, though nothing could have been further from the truth. Regardless of what she accepted about his finances, her decision to marry Lonergan was impetuous and curious, given that she may well have known about her father's relationship with her new husband. Seemingly, she did not care. Besides, Patricia had always done what was best for her, no matter the consequences. As she later was supposed to have said about Lonergan, according to novelist and *New York Daily Mirror* columnist Thyra Samter Winslow: "If he was good enough for my father, he's good enough for me."

4

Starring in the Most Exciting
Floor Show in the World

A RITE OF PASSAGE for every New York City debutante was an evening spent drinking champagne cocktails and dining on terrine de foie gras, green turtle soup, and broiled, stuffed Maine lobster at the one and only Stork Club. The swanky Stork on East 53rd Street, less than half a block from Fifth Avenue, as well as its chief competitors—the El Morocco ("Elmo's") on East 54th near Third Avenue, and the 21 Club (the only one that still exists), on West 52nd between Fifth and Sixth Avenues—represented the glamour and hedonistic excesses of the city's so-called "café society." This Parisian-style designation was likely coined as early as 1919 by the well-informed *New York Journal-American* society columnist Maury Paul, aka, "Cholly Knickerbocker." (In 1938, Barney Josephson, a Jewish shoe salesman and entrepreneur, opened a club in Greenwich Village that he cleverly called Café Society. It was the first truly integrated nightclub in New York, where Billie Holiday, among other African-American singers, performed.)

Patricia not only wanted to be part of this excitement, she craved it. She was what Walter Winchell, the famed syndicated society gossip columnist who was a regular fixture at table 50 at the Stork, called a wannabe "celebutante"—a term he invented in April 1939 to describe the Canadian-born socialite Brenda Frazier—a beautiful "poor, little rich girl" who was "famous for being famous." She was the Paris Hilton or Kim Kardashian of her day.

Patricia, too, was later described in the press as a "poor, little rich girl" for enduring a strict upbringing surrounded by enormous wealth. On their first date in late 1939, Patricia, who was only eighteen at the time, talked Wayne into escorting her to the Stork Club for her inaugural visit—an outing sanctioned by her father.

All evening, like clockwork, black limousines and yellow-and-red DeSoto Skyview taxis pulled up on East 53rd in front of the Stork's green canopy. Exiting the cars were men in black tuxedos and silk top hats accompanied by women in furs and shiny evening gowns with sequins and beads. The well-heeled patrons were immediately greeted by the club's doormen, wearing distinctive blue uniforms. The guests made their way past the entrance and the bronze doors to come face-to-face with the maître d' standing behind a gold chain, checking for reservations. Like Saint Peter at the gates of Heaven, he decreed who was permitted into the club. On a busy evening, five hundred people might be turned away.

If you were deemed one of the chosen, you passed by a long bar with room for sixty or more clients and a lengthy mirror, where you could stop to glance at yourself. The bar area led through glass doors to the main dining and dancing area, where the fun never stopped, until at least four in the morning. At the Stork and the other clubs, the mark of being a "somebody" meant you were usually greeted by the club owners and seated at a preferred table. On the other hand, being shown to a table at the back of the room was akin to exile in Siberia.

Since their plans that evening were spur of the moment, Patricia and Wayne did not have coveted reservations. In Lonergan's no doubt exaggerated telling of this story, as he and Patricia approached the maître d' by the gold chain, they were warmly welcomed and greeted with "Good evening, Mr. Lonergan," as they were led to a table near the front. The date was a success and seemingly enjoyable for both. There were more nightclub outings in the weeks that followed.

Wealthy and pampered, Patricia expected a lot out of life, and partying at nightclubs several nights a week, rubbing shoulders with the Vanderbilts, Harrimans, and Astors, as well as such Hollywood and Broadway stars as Lana Turner, Gloria Swanson, Joan Blondell, Peter Lorre, Greer Garson, and Frank Sinatra, was a dream come true. The object was to be seen, to be part of the nightly "parade"; to have Jerome Zerbe, the pioneering, but respectful "society photographer," snap your photo. Even better was to rate a mention in a column by Winchell. Or, the more-erudite Lucius Beebe—"Luscious

Lucius," as Winchell called him—who in his syndicated *New York Herald-Tribune* column, "This New York," skillfully and elegantly chronicled café society's comings and goings; hence, his other nickname, the "orchidaceous oracle of café society." During the late 1930s, Zerbe and Beebe, who did not hide their homosexuality as much as most men of the era did, had an intimate relationship. For a few years, Beebe referred to Zerbe so many times in print that Winchell caustically suggested Beebe's column should be renamed "Jerome Never Looked Lovelier."

Beebe was effusive in his musings on café society and, in particular, the Stork Club. "To millions and millions of people all over the world," he wrote in 1946, "the Stork symbolizes and epitomizes the de luxe [*sic*] upholstery of quintessentially urban existence. It means fame; it means wealth; it means an elegant way of life among celebrated folk. . . . The Stork is the dream of suburbia, a shrine of sophistication in the minds of countless thousands who have never seen it, the fabric and pattern of legend." Or, as another café society observer noted, the ultimate show at the Stork "consists of common people looking at celebrities and the celebrities looking at themselves in the mirrors—and they all sit popeyed in admiration."

The Stork's astute owner, the classy former bootlegger Sherman Billingsley, as well as his chief rivals—the affable John Perona at the El Morocco and the immortal duo, cousins Jack Kriendler and Charlie Berns of the 21 Club—encouraged and promoted the press attention and their establishments' perceived exclusivity. What businessman wouldn't want such free advertising? (The nightclub owners would have salivated at the publicity afforded by today's social media.) It was the reason Perona wooed Zerbe away—and paid him $150 a week, plus expenses—from the Rainbow Room, another café society dining institution at the top of the RCA Building (now 30 Rockefeller Plaza). Billingsley cultivated close relationships with Winchell and Beebe (who also covered the scene at the El Morocco). Though the Stork and El Morocco were highly lucrative business ventures—in the early 1940s, the Stork Club was grossing about $3,500 a day, or an estimated $1.25 million a year ($22 million today)—the competition was often severe, and the various owners were always looking for an edge. They also spied on each other, sometimes hiring the same private detectives.

Born in rural Oklahoma in 1896, Sherman Billingsley went from milking cows and gathering eggs and kindling to running one of the hottest nightclubs in Manhattan. Influenced by his older brother Logan, at a young age Sherman became involved in selling bootleg whiskey. He moved around a lot. While he was living in Seattle in 1914, he was arrested for selling liquor illegally. He managed to talk his way out of that charge, but got caught in another sting, for which he spent a few months in Leavenworth Prison in the early 1920s. (The conviction was eventually overturned.) He landed in New York City as Prohibition, the "noble experiment," was inaugurated in 1919 (and officially began in January 1920).

Prohibition was a major failure. In New York and other large cities, millions of Americans regularly broke the law. Reporters from the *New York Telegram* were assigned the task of finding liquor in Manhattan. It was the easiest job they had ever been given, for it was everywhere. They found liquor in "dancing academies, drugstores, delicatessens, cigar stores, confectionaries, soda fountains, behind partitions of shoeshine parlors, back rooms of barbershops, from hotel bellhops . . . in paint stores, malt shops . . . boarding houses, Republican clubs, Democratic clubs, laundries, social clubs, newspapermen's associations." Under Prohibition, prices naturally rose, so that the same bottle of Scotch whisky, which used to cost a few dollars, now could run as high as $16 for a quart. Champagne was even pricier, at anywhere from $25 to $40 a bottle.

After purchasing a pharmacy in the Bronx and dabbling in real estate, Billingsley teamed up with a couple of partners—two gamblers he knew from Oklahoma, Carl Henninger and John Patton, who had married sisters. They entered the speakeasy business in 1926, opening the first version of the Stork Club on West 58th Street. What Billingsley did not know until several years later was that Henninger and Patton were frontmen for a rogues' gallery of gangsters that included Owen "The Killer" Madden, who was part owner of the Cotton Club; William "Big Bill" Dwyer, who made a small fortune smuggling booze during Prohibition; and Madden's close associate, boxing promoter George Jean "Big Frenchy" DeMange ("Le Mange") who up to the day he died in 1939 at the age of forty-seven had been arrested thirteen times, yet somehow never served a day in jail.

Though lucrative, running a speakeasy was risky and dangerous. In December 1931, the Stork Club was raided by federal agents and shut down. Billingsley then reorganized and took advantage of the repeal of Prohibition in late 1933. Selling pricey Scotch and champagne became even more profitable. For the café society set, the end of Prohibition was truly liberating: It meant life inside an "amiably demented whirl" of festive partying; or, as Beebe vividly described it, "living in a white tie till six of a morning before brushing the teeth in a light Moselle and retiring to bed."

Billingsley bought out his mobster investors and in 1934 moved to the location on East 53rd Street. By this time, he had received a big boost from Walter Winchell, who had in his widely read *Daily Mirror* column dubbed the Stork Club "New York's New Yorkiest place." Stars like Irving Berlin, Tallulah Bankhead, and Ethel Merman (with whom the married Billingsley had a torrid affair in the late 1930s) frequented the club, and it acquired a reputation and aura of glamour that Billingsley nurtured for decades.

Much of the club's success was due to Billingsley himself. He was a sharp dresser with a perpetual tan, owing to regular sunlamp use at the New York Athletic Club near his Park Avenue apartment. He was also a dictatorial boss, whose authority with his diligent staff of two hundred was absolute. The term *micromanager* does not quite describe his hands-on approach. Working sixteen hours a day, often seven days a week, he controlled literally every aspect of the Stork Club, right down to the abundant fresh flowers, classic black ashtrays on the table with the club's logo on them, deciding which selective guests were permitted into the exclusive confines of the quieter Cub Room, and, above all, ensuring there were always plenty of pretty young women around. The daily grind took its toll; Billingsley popped tranquilizers or "nerve pills" as necessary, according to Ralph Blumenthal.

Billingsley had his own secret code worked out with the maître d'. If he tugged his left ear, he wanted the customer thrown out; lighting a cigarette meant the guest could have one of the best tables in the house; and blinking rapidly told the maître d' to seat the customer in the bar, but there was to be no access to the Cub Room. Billingsley purposely scanned the society pages on the lookout for the most beautiful debutantes. "I have to bring good-looking girls in here," he said in a May 1939 interview in *Cosmopolitan*, "because beautiful women are the only decoration worth a damn in a nightclub room."

Nothing was too expensive for the Stork's clients: Billingsley had stone crabs flown in daily from Florida, and ensured that Beebe's favorite drink, Southern Comfort, then regarded as an exotic beverage, was stocked in the bar. As a marketing tool, Billingsley frequently presented his guests with expensive gifts. Beebe, for one, was impressed. "He distributes free orchids and other costly corsages, magnums of champagne, Cartier clips and match-boxes, dollar cigars and other glittering largesse to customers who will most appreciate it and will talk about it most afterward," he pointed out in a 1943 book, *Snoot If You Must*. Possessing the smarts of *Mad Men's* Don Draper, the most widely distributed photograph of Billingsley showed him at a Stork Club table in a finely cut suit. In the fingers of his right hand is a lit cigarette, except that Billingsley never smoked. The cigarette was only a prop he used to give him a particular masculine appeal.

Many of Billingsley's patrons were Jewish (Walter Winchell among them), and on occasion, African Americans were admitted, though seated far at the back of the main room and out of sight as much as was possible. It would be fair to say that, like most other club owners—Barney Josephson at Café Society was the notable exception—Billingsley favored a WASP clientele. In 1951, Billingsley (and Walter Winchell) became embroiled in a well-publicized spat with the curvaceous African-American dancer, Josephine Baker, who accused Billingsley and some members of his staff of discriminatory treatment. The fight dragged on for almost a year, with the reputations of both Billingsley and Baker suffering.

Expensive labor problems forced an ailing Billingsley—who died in 1966—to close the Stork Club in 1965 and sell the property to the Columbia Broadcasting System. On part of it, CBS built a cement park dedicated to the company's founder, William S. Paley. Now the Paley Park Café, it has a twenty-foot waterfall for a backdrop. The adjacent property is a friendly restaurant, Burger Heaven; none of the people the author spoke to who work there had any idea the site was once home to one of the most popular nightclubs in the city.

Over at the El Morocco, where Patricia Burton Lonergan drank and danced during the last week of her life, John Perona was in charge. Born in in 1897 as Eriane Giovanni Perona in Chiaverano (part of Metropolitan Turin) in northern Italy, he left his homeland at the age of sixteen, like millions of other Italians in search of better economic opportunities who sought to escape what was called the *miseria*—high taxes, unemployment, subsistence wages, terrible farmland, and few resources. He migrated to England first, and then worked in South America before arriving in New York City.

Perona found a job at the trendy Hotel Knickerbocker's restaurant, the Grill, which in its day, from 1906 to 1920, was a top attraction around Times

Square. Working there, he learned the intricacies of the restaurant and bar business and lessons about catering to the rich. He soon went out on his own, opening a small club and eatery on West 49th Street that served a tasty Italian lunch for $1.25, and the finest (and quite expensive) Prohibition-era liquor—which ultimately attracted attention from federal agents, who made life difficult for him for a while. By 1932, he had moved on, opening up the El Morocco on East 54th Street, and during the summer months, the Westchester Bath Club in the picturesque village of Mamaroneck in Westchester County. The end of Prohibition boosted Perona's business opportunities as it did for Billingsley, his chief rival. In a June 1935 column, Beebe anointed Perona "the night life king of the white tie and monocle scene."

Perona was more laid-back than Billingsley. He was "one of the best hosts in the world," said Jerome Zerbe, "an extraordinary man!" Perona spent years making the El Morocco, with its celebrated decor—palm trees of gold leaf, white-painted cactus, and Moroccan grilles on the walls, and its distinctive blue and white zebra stripes on its chairs and banquette seating—Manhattan's café society nightclub of choice. The El Morocco was "where smart New Yorkers welcome the elite of the world"—as the 1930s advertisement declared.

The *New York Post*'s Broadway columnist, Leonard Lyons, designated it "the capital of café society." Added Beebe in 1935: "One feels that when, if ever, the Morocco is supplanted by a dizzier, costlier or more Babylonish night club, it will be run by John Perona."

Like at other nightclubs, the all-powerful maître d'—Frank Carino at the El Morocco—was the official gatekeeper, deciding who entered the inner sanctum past the velvet rope and who did not. "Oh, it was a ritual," actress Nanette Fabray, who passed away in 2018, remembered. "One entered, and there was a hierarchy of where one sat. The first table on the right was the best; the second was reserved for the owner, John Perona. You didn't dare go unless you were perfectly turned out." In the winter months, it could be chilly waiting for your turn to enter the sanctum. "I was there in the war years," she added. "I was fortunate enough to have silk stockings, but they were freezing. I would wear long underwear, check it, and then put it back on in the ladies' room."

Despite what Billingsley might have boasted about the high number of celebrities who regularly dined and danced at the Stork, as many or more frequented Elmo's. It was a regular hangout for such stars as Errol Flynn, Marlene Dietrich, Gloria Swanson, Clark Gable, Greta Garbo, Cary Grant, Judy Garland, Gary Cooper, and Rita Hayworth—to name only several. One night during the war years, Diana Vreeland, who was then a fashion columnist for *Harper's Bazaar* (and later, the editor in chief of *Vogue* magazine), arrived at the club with Hollywood star Clark Gable. He was then having an affair with her good friend, the socialite and fashion maven Millicent Rogers. "We stood behind the red velvet rope," Vreeland wrote in her memoirs, published in 1984. "By then, word had gone out that Mr. Gable was in the house, and Mr. John Perona, the owner, came to take us to our table. Clark grabbed my hand. 'Don't look left,' he said, 'and don't look right, just keep walking. Hold on to your hat, kid, this place is gonna blow!' As he said it the place went berserk, I mean berserk! The stares! The people leaning out over their tables! These are 'sophisticated' people I'm talking about. . . . It was almost animalique, like a roaring zoo. All I can tell you is that the place did blow."

The ladies took an elevator up one flight to the rose-and-pink powder room, and then, with hundreds of pairs of eyes watching intently, made their grand entrance back into the club's main area via a wide staircase. For those who sought a little more privacy, there was the club's Champagne Room, a good place "to hold hands with your girl," according to Broadway columnist Dorothy Kilgallen.

Dancing until the wee hours of the morning was on a crowded and shrinking floor, as tables were added, to the sounds of a polished orchestra. "I wore red silk; red makes me happy," recalled the late Kitty Carlisle Hart, the Broadway and film star (and panelist on the TV game show *To Tell the Truth*) in a 2004 interview. "I danced with Gershwin, and we had a bet as to whose song would come on next, his or mine? There were two bands, one that played mostly Gershwin and Porter, the other, mambos and rumbas." Yet it was people-watching that made a visit to Elmo's especially entertaining and memorable. As Beebe aptly put it in a 1937 series he wrote about café society for *Cosmopolitan*, the El Morocco "is maintained on the basis that the most exciting floor show in the world is provided by the patrons themselves."

— ⁓ —

Being a part of that daily "floor show" was integral to Patricia and Wayne Lonergan's brief married life. Thanks to her trust fund and investments, they had the money and time for regular indulgent evenings out at the Stork Club, El Morocco, and other nightclubs. Later, the gossip about her was nastier; not only that she dated a lot of men after she and Wayne separated, but that she enjoyed "abnormal" sexual intercourse. (The reference likely meant anal sex.) This subject came up when Lonergan was first interrogated by a Manhattan assistant district attorney, and Lonergan stated that Patricia "did not like" sex this way.

In any event, it is not all that surprising that on the last night of Patricia's life, both she and Wayne, though separately and with other partners, spent that fateful evening at café society hot spots.

———

Like her parents' marriage, Patricia's marriage with Lonergan was doomed from the start—though it took a little while for Patricia to come to that conclusion. For part of the summer of 1942, Patricia and Wayne rented a suite at the historic Red Lion Inn in Stockbridge, Massachusetts, in the scenic Berkshires, where they enjoyed the mountain air, lakes, "sparkling streams," and outdoor activities.

It was not all hikes through the forest and embracing nature, however. While they were there, Lonergan saw a physician, Thurlow Pelton, because he feared that he had had a relapse of the gonorrhea he had contracted in 1935. Dr. Pelton's examination would reveal that this was not the case.

Once the newlyweds returned to New York, they leased for $350 per month a spacious six-room suite at 983 Park Avenue, near 83rd Street. It was (and still is) a stately white sandstone building, typical of the avenue, with a green awning and thirteen stories, including the top-floor penthouse. It was also the most luxurious home Wayne had ever had.

Patricia insisted on hiring a butler, maid, and laundry girl—"servants," as they were referred to by the New York elite in those days. Her monthly stipend from her trust fund ($1,219.30), interest on bonds ($247.50), dividends from the Borden Company National Dairy ($20), and interest on mortgages for an apartment she owned—likely part of her father's estate, at 251 West 96th Street ($60)—totaled $1,546.80 (about $23,000 today). At the beginning of July 1943, she also had $7,940 in her bank account, out of which she withdrew that month an extra $1,853.20—$500 of which was given to Lonergan. From January 1 to July 31, 1943, her income from the trust fund, investment income, and cash was $27,555.67, while she withdrew and spent $11,850 ($175,000 in 2019 dollars). She and Lonergan were definitely living comfortably. But Patricia wasn't worried. She was well aware that in the near future she was to inherit her grandmother Stella's estate; in fact, had Patricia not been murdered, the inheritance would have passed to her in less than decade, following Stella's death in February 1954.

Patricia gave Wayne a monthly allowance of $700 (by check) to cover household and his personal expenses (it is unclear whether or not that included paying their monthly rent). In the short term, this meant that Lonergan did not have to find regular employment. His usual weekday schedule was to get up about 10:30 a.m., have breakfast, and then go back to bed until later in the afternoon, when he roused himself to eat a late lunch. In the evening, he went out to the El Morocco, the Stork, or one of the other clubs, with (or without) Patricia.

Patricia, on the other hand, took a nurse's aide course at Bellevue Hospital, completing it in early March 1942, and volunteering three days a week, there and at St. Clare's Hospital. She was also on twenty-four-hour call at the blood bank.

Lonergan did not have any qualms about being a "kept husband," at the beginning of their marriage, or even after they had separated—though it later contributed to the negative public perceptions about him. The mores of the time frowned upon such an arrangement because "it reversed the order of nature," as the widely read and respected Dorothy Dix (Elizabeth Gilmer) noted in a March 1936 column. For more than twenty-five years, Dix's popular syndicated advice column ran in 273 newspapers around the world. She offered her estimated sixty million readers a mixture of wholesome wisdom, common sense, and a progressive outlook. She believed, for example, that there was no shame in a wealthy wife sharing her inherited money with her husband. Yet, she was forced to concede in an earlier column of November 1931 that "the marriage of a poor man with a rich girl seldom brings either one happiness," adding again some years later that when the woman has money and the man does not, "it is almost sure to cause trouble."

So it was in the case of Patricia and Wayne.

⸺ ⸺

Lonergan was often short of cash, and Patricia usually looked after his ever-expanding bills for clothing—including $90 for silk shirts; more than a dozen suits at $125 each; double-breasted jackets and trousers for $235; $55 for a monogrammed dressing gown; and a closet full of shoes at about $40 a pair, which he especially fancied.

If anything, Lonergan was the consummate champion social climber: He made the most of his new status as the husband of a rich wife. When he was not lounging in bed, he spent much of his free time playing bridge, sometimes for money. He was skilled enough to make a few dollars from the unsuspecting wealthy retirees who invited him to their lazy afternoon games. He was often a fourth at W. Somerset Maugham's bridge gatherings, when the great British novelist and playwright was visiting New York during the war years and holding court at the Carlyle Hotel, where he had a suite. He had been introduced to Maugham by his mother-in-law, Lucille, who was acquainted with the novelist from her time in the South of France. Maugham's well-known bisexuality might have had something to do with his fondness for the much younger Lonergan.

Consider, too, Lonergan's acquaintance with George Lambert, who in 1943 was a twenty-nine-year-old radio actor then starring in the CBS serial, *Amanda of Honeymoon Hill* (he also worked on the successful radio soap opera, *Stella Dallas*). Lambert had met Lonergan in the spring of 1939, soon after Wayne had arrived in New York. Some months later, Lonergan ran into Lambert at a theater performance.

Lambert lived in a suite he rented at the swanky Park Central Hotel, across the street from Carnegie Hall on 7th Avenue, between 54th and 55th Streets. His lifestyle made an impression on Lonergan. He and Lambert went to a film together. Next, Lonergan began using Lambert's swimming pool privileges at the hotel. After Lonergan and Patricia were married, Lonergan invited Lambert to a cocktail party in the fall of 1941, and then later saw him again after Billy was born.

Patricia's decision to elope with Wayne had caused some tension between her and her mother. Yet like any twenty-one-year-old, Patricia still sought out her mother's guidance and love. Her pet name for Lucille was "Doodles," while her mother called her daughter "Mouse." Lucille never approved of Wayne as a husband for Patricia, but she aimed to make the best of it. Helping Lonergan gain entrance into exclusive bridge games seemed like the right approach to take, but Lucille paid the price for that gesture, embarrassed after her friends refused to play cards with Wayne any longer because they accused him of cheating.

Wayne and Patricia did enjoy playing tennis, yet nearly everyone the police later interviewed mentioned that Patricia was usually unhappy. Lonergan often went out on the town without her, something that did not go unnoticed by other café society types. According to Remis Soucy, who worked as a general housekeeper for the Lonergans from October 1942 to May 1943, she was told by Patricia that Wayne often abandoned her after they arrived at a nightclub—for the company of other women and men—and she was forced to find her own way home, usually in tears.

Lonergan frequently skipped dinner with his wife as well. It was Soucy's job to get on the phone and track down Lonergan, who was frequently at the Plaza Hotel steam baths or at the residence of one of his friends. Sometimes he brought women and men Patricia did not know back to their apartment. She objected to this; he ignored her. The housekeeper was instructed to keep a watch on Patricia's expensive perfume and even the curtains in the suite (which went missing, despite her efforts).

Lonergan may or may not have had a brief contract to review Broadway plays for a local radio station. He did meet Lucius Beebe, who, like Maugham, was undoubtedly attracted to a handsome and charming man in his early twenties who reciprocated that interest. The two men went out to dinner on several occasions, to the 21 Club.

Wayne and Patricia were in many ways part of café society's chorus, members of the company just waiting for their big break—to be noticed. That tragically came soon enough. Thyra Samter Winslow later noted in her column that she "never knew Wayne or Patsy well," but she "had always thought of them as pleasant and jolly people who like parties, a gay time—and had the money for it."

Their relationship, however, was more complicated than that.

5

A Marriage Mistake

THE NIGHTCLUB PARTYING ASIDE, Patricia and Wayne's married life was wracked by tension due to Lonergan having limited control over their finances, and more than likely because of his inner conflicts about his own sexuality—exactly like the marriage of Lucille and William Burton. Patricia, too, who had gotten her way on most everything for much of her life, was at the age of twenty-one emotionally immature.

That combustible combination produced a lot of heated arguments and screaming matches, according to their friend Reginald Wright, the British-born dance teacher whose family owned a château in Biarritz, France, where he had met the Burtons many years earlier. (In November 1943, the *Daily News* gossip columnist Danton Walker described Wright, who had a messy divorce in late 1942 from his wife of eighteen years, Cornelia Brady Harris, as a part of the so-called "Lonergan café society.") "They fought like cats and dogs," Wright told New York TV columnist Mel Heimer, who wrote about the Lonergan case in 1955. "There was never any peace between them. Once, when they got into an argument, I heard her say to Wayne, 'I suppose that's to be expected when a girl marries a man who is beneath her.'"

They did stop fighting long enough for Patricia to become pregnant in mid-October 1941. Their son, William Wayne Lonergan, was born on July 1, 1942. He was named for his late grandfather and father. The boy was also Jewish, since Jewish law follows matrilineal descent. This was true, despite the fact that Patricia, like other members of her family, was by no means an observant Jew and had married a Gentile.

Patricia loved little Billy, as the infant was affectionately called. After she died, when Lonergan was asked by a New York assistant district attorney if Patricia "exhibited the usual motherly attitude," he caustically replied "No." But he did not offer any specific examples of what he meant by this accusation. He also conceded that he was not a "normal father." Whatever the truth, becoming a parent did not put a cramp in Patricia's social life. Her datebook was full, and she often danced the night away at clubs or at private parties with her wide assortment of friends. From her perspective, life was to be enjoyed to the fullest extent possible—and she did. Still, she was not completely selfish or without compassion, as her volunteer work with the Red Cross and hospitals demonstrated.

If either of them was truly indifferent to the infant, it was arguably Lonergan. He came and went from their apartment without any concern for what the child was doing or how he was. Remis Soucy later told the police that at a stag party held at their suite, which Lonergan organized for a friend, he and his guests were drunk. In Patricia's absence, that did not stop Lonergan from displaying Billy to everyone at the gathering.

Lonergan was rarely alone with his son. Almost always present when he did interact with Billy (though not at the stag party) was the full-time live-in nanny Patricia had hired in early January, Miss Elizabeth Black, a sixty-three-year-old English-born governess. Black was slight of stature and hard of hearing, as the police later noted. Cared for by a nanny more than he was by his own parents, Billy's early years were no different than Patricia's had been, or those of other children of the affluent. (Katherine Graham, the publisher of the *Washington Post*, recalled in her memoirs that when she was less than a year old, in 1917, her well-to-do parents left her and her three older siblings, ages two, four, and six, in the capable care of a nanny at the family's home in Manhattan while they resided more or less full-time in Washington, DC. This continued for several years while her father served on federal government boards, and he and her mother enjoyed the city's high society.)

The children of the wealthy "were likely to be sequestered in a children's wing or on the top floor of a townhouse," writes Mary Cable in her 1984 book about the American rich, *Top Drawer*, "and they saw their mother only as she paused to admire them on her way to a party." Patricia was not quite as indifferent a mother as Cable describes, but she also had no qualms about the fact that Billy's day-to-day needs were lovingly attended to by the devoted Miss Black. A maid, Marie Tanzosch, who had been hired in November 1942, also worked long hours at the Park Avenue apartment.

World War II also put stress on Patricia and Wayne's faltering relationship. As a Canadian living in the United States, Lonergan was eligible for the US draft, not something he relished. If he had to fight in the conflict, then he wanted to do it for Canada—or so he later told Hamilton Darby Perry.

Months before he married Patricia, Wayne had received a questionnaire from the Selective Service Board. It was addressed to "William Joseph Lonergan," because (as noted) when Wayne had crossed the US border in 1939, he had used his brother William's name, as he had to obtain jobs in Toronto and elsewhere starting in 1936. William was four years older, so Wayne thought it made sense at the time. By 1942, and likely earlier, he was using his own name in legal documents, as he had on a trip back to Toronto in late October 1942, after his mother had died. As Lonergan had anticipated, a draft notice to report for a medical examination arrived one day in the mail, in late December of 1941.

Lonergan's sexual orientation may have played a role in his interaction with American military officials, as well. Even before the Japanese attack on Pearl Harbor on December 7, 1941, bringing the United States into the war, the military establishment had tremendous fear and paranoia about homosexuals enlisting in the US Armed Forces. Working initially with several psychiatrists, a screening protocol was devised and implemented to ensure that any recruit thought to have homosexual "proclivities" would be immediately weeded out. The regulations identified homosexuality as a "personality disorder," which incorporated: "psychopaths who were sexual perverts, paranoid personalities who suffered from homosexual panic and schizoid personalities who displayed homosexual symptoms."

Medical exams and interviews with potential soldiers were brief, so the military devised a variety of tests and questions, which from today's perspective were absurd. In one suggested scenario, the selectee was compelled to be naked so that the medical examiner could study whether the individual was "self-conscious," thereby detecting "slight signs" of homosexuality. There were also intrusive questions about masturbation that were supposed to provide clues about a man's choice for a sexual partner.

In the months following the US declaration of war, the generals had less patience, and the anti-homosexual regulations became stricter. Stopping "sexual perverts" was the overall objective, and officials and physicians were proud of their work. "We question [the selectee] about his sexual habits, and, in general, about his relationship with the opposite sex," explained psychiatrist Carl Binger, who consulted for the US Army, in a *Saturday Evening Post* article in January 1944. "If there is reason to suspect it, we try to find out whether the selectee is homosexual, a common enough aberration, but one which the Army has found it necessary to exclude from its ranks." Dr. Binger conceded that the screening process they used was not perfect. "Entirely too many neurotics and potential neurotics slip through," he added. Or, as a headline in the Washington, DC, edition of the weekly *Afro-American* put it in September 1943, "Sissies Get into Army Despite Many Precautions."

By March 1942, the War Department had ordered examiners to be on the lookout for these allegedly telling signs of homosexuality: "feminine bodily characteristics," "effeminacy in dress and manner," and a "patulous [expanded or spreading] rectum." To this end, thousands of young men were asked "if they liked or dated girls, if they were homosexual or had homosexual experiences or feelings, or if they masturbated with or had sex with other men or boys."

When word got out that it was possible to avoid the draft by pretending to be gay, many men for a variety of reasons lied and faked their way through the official interview. According to the *Afro-American*, the elaborate ploy of selling yourself as a "she-man" included showing up to the recruitment office with manicured nails, well-coiffed hair, open-toe shoes, and a "colorful costume." If that still did not do the trick, then draft dodgers when asked about sex declared their "aversion to women" and their preference for their "own sex."

More fuel was added to the armed forces' paranoia about homosexuals infiltrating their ranks in mid-March 1942, following a police raid in Brooklyn on a "house of assignation"—or a "house of degradation," as the *New York Post* called it—where rich men paid for time alone with gay soldiers and sailors. The owner of the house was Gustave Beekman, a Swedish immigrant, who later got caught up in further scandal when it was alleged his male brothel was being used by German spies to obtain information from unsuspecting American servicemen. A US senator from Boston, David Walsh, was embroiled in this case, as well, after it was alleged—mistakenly, as it turned out—that he was a frequent visitor to Beekman's establishment.

At his initial induction meeting, Lonergan did not wear open-toe shoes or a brightly colored jacket, but he did show up intoxicated, according to the army official in charge. He was rejected for alcoholism, though this was merely a temporary reprieve. The board sent him a second induction notice and ordered him to report on January 10, 1942. This time, Lonergan was sober, but he admitted to the army physician that he was a homosexual.

The draft board classified him as "4-F," or unacceptable, rejecting him on "immoral tendencies."

Nearly three decades later, Lonergan insisted that the whole exercise had been a ruse—that he had told the doctor and draft board that he was gay in order to avoid being conscripted. In a CBC Television interview on December 12, 1965, he repeated the same thing: He had made up the story to evade the draft. Still, this was the first, yet not the last, time that Lonergan would use homosexuality as an excuse to avoid something he did not want to do, or to explain his actions.

Military officials regarded Lonergan as a "malingerer," and suspected that his "sexual perversion" was indeed a deception. Psychiatrist Dr. George Henry, who examined Lonergan for the Selective Service, agreed that "there is no doubt that [he] is probably doing his fair share of malingering," but he recommended rejecting him on the "grounds of moral fitness." He concluded that Lonergan was "probably quite truthful when he says he has had sex with both men and women," and his "personality is distinctly undesirable in every respect." In Henry's learned opinion, Lonergan clearly demonstrated "a psychopathic personality with pathological sexuality."

By the summer of 1943, Patricia had told her mother that her marriage to Wayne "was a mistake," as Lucille's close friend, Rozsika "Rosie" Netcher, the Hungarian-born former vaudeville star—known on the stage as Rosie Dolly—later stated. In the months following the birth of their son, Patricia and Wayne's incessant bickering had increased. He claimed that she was angry with him because he was weary of their café society outings, which was blatantly untrue. Lonergan was as much a "nightclubber" as Patricia; more so, perhaps. It was more likely that Patricia was tired of the all-too-true gossip that Lonergan was after her money and that he preferred the company of men over her. Whatever the reasons, near the end of June 1943, she ordered him out of their Park Avenue suite. There was no formal legal separation agreement—and never would be.

Lonergan relocated for a brief time to the Hotel Van Dorn on West 58th Street, near Seventh Avenue. On several occasions, he entertained a young woman named Connie Kelly at the hotel. She was a hatcheck girl he had met at the Vogue Club and Restaurant on East 50th Street. He registered her at the hotel as "Mrs. Lonergan" and bought her earrings and stockings with money Patricia had given him.

During the summer of 1943, Lonergan spent a few weeks at Fire Island, the skinny landmass off the coast of Long Island. The hamlet on Fire Island known as Cherry Grove had been a popular vacation spot for gay men since the early 1930s. Upon his return to the city, he rented an apartment on East 58th Street, near Park Avenue, about a mile away from Patricia's residence, and was given fairly regular visitation access to Billy.

Lonergan did not have a job, so how did he pay for his vacation and apartment rent that must have run close to $300 a month? When a New York City ADA later asked him about this, he said he used money he had saved. But when pressed, he conceded that Patricia had given him lump-sum payments of cash every so often.

Lonergan also enrolled at the School of Modern Photography at 136 East 57th Street. His tuition was generously paid for by Patricia, who had also transferred $500 to Lonergan's bank account on July 14, 1943. Established by Henry Sidel in 1939, the school promised its graduates successful careers working for magazines and the theater, which would have appealed to Lonergan. It was true that some of Sidel's students found decent jobs in journalism and show business, though most probably did not. Sidel was an astute marketer and regularly ran hundreds of advertisements in photography journals and other publications. The ads often featured the work of one of his instructors, John Hutchins, who went from "rank novice to a salon exhibitor in a little over a year," as the *New York Times* noted in a profile of him in March 1939.

At the photography school Lonergan became friends with another student, George Herascu, a Romanian-Jewish salesman who had been visiting New York on behalf of his employer when the war broke out and was advised by his family to remain where he was. He and Lonergan, whose company he enjoyed, double-dated sisters with the last name of Larkin and lunched together occasionally.

The one positive result from Lonergan's training with Sidel was that in 1943, he was hired as an assistant (at a monthly pay of $30) by noted German-born magazine photographer Anton Bruhel at his studio at the Grand Central Palace Building on Lexington Avenue. This was quite a coup for Wayne. Raised in South Australia, Bruhel arrived in New York at the age of nineteen in 1919 and eventually established a reputation as one of the most creative photographers—he pioneered color photography—in the fashion business. His work appeared in *Vanity Fair* and *Vogue* magazines, among other publications.

Alas, Lonergan's apprenticeship with him lasted only two weeks (according to what he later told officials at Sing Sing Prison). He then landed a job with a commercial photographer at Devon Studio, located on West 33rd, between Fifth and Sixth Avenues. During this period, he saw Billy once or twice a week.

About a month and a half before they separated, Patricia had made plans to leave 983 Park Avenue at the beginning of September. This was a decision Wayne likely did not have a say in. She found a three-floor furnished apartment—which included the ground floor and the first two floors—in a fashionable refurbished four-story brownstone at 313 East 51st Street, off of Second Avenue. The rent was $250 a month, $100 less than she had been paying on Park Avenue (several newspaper stories incorrectly reported the rent as $385 per month). The one-year lease was negotiated in June, and thus, she and Wayne were listed on the agreement as the lessees, since they were still married and living together at the time. (During this era, if a married woman rented an apartment, her husband's name would have been noted on any contract or legal document.) Yet by the time she and Billy moved in, Wayne had already left the Park Avenue apartment. Elizabeth Black relocated with Patricia and Billy into the new residence, and Marie Tanzosch stayed on as the maid.

All through August, Wayne had convinced himself that reconciliation with Patricia was still possible. One day they had another whopper of a fight. Wayne soon apologized via a telegram. "Frightfully sorry about inexcusable behavior," he wrote. "Our Irish temperament is too much. I adore you, and I always will. I am sorry I left you in a bad mood. Hope the next time I see you, you shall be happier. The only sane thing to do is to forget everything. I won't like it, but I am sure you will. My tired old heart beats for you. Love, Wayne."

Patricia, however, was not forgetting anything; in fact, quite the opposite. Less than a week after Lonergan had sent this telegram, she distanced herself from Wayne even further. She altered the terms of her will: He was removed as the sole beneficiary, and their son was designated instead—which meant that Stella Bernheimer Housman's expected $7 million fortune would pass first to Patricia, and upon her death, to Billy. Stella was about to turn seventy-five years of age and was still in satisfactory health, and Patricia was a young woman. Billy would be an old man before he inherited the millions—or so anyone would have thought at the time.

When Lonergan found out about the change in the will, he was angry. In light of their separation and anticipated divorce (at least, from Patricia's point of view), and their animosity toward each other, Patricia's decision made sense.

In hindsight, it also might have determined her fate.

———

Built in 1939, the nearly seven-thousand-square-foot brownstone on 51st Street was owned by Chester Burt Fentress, a retired and wealthy concert singer. In 1937, he sold his fifty-eight-acre estate and ten-room colonial house in affluent Fairfield County, Connecticut, to acclaimed violinist Jascha Heifetz and his wife, Florence, for a considerable sum. Patricia's suite in this brownstone came furnished, though she enhanced it with some expensive furnishings from the B. Altman department store on 34th Street, as well as from W. & J. Sloane on 19th and Broadway.

With the main windows facing 51st Street, the kitchen, dining room, and servants' quarters were on the lower (ground) floor. On the first floor, there was a vestibule entrance reached by climbing a dozen steps that led inside to a sitting room that faced the front of the house and a large living room toward the back. Patricia's master bedroom was on the second floor at the rear of the house, overlooking a small backyard with a few flowerpots. Outside her bedroom windows was a fire escape. Down the hall from her bedroom were Billy's nursery and an adjoining room for the governess, Miss Black. Patricia had access to a private staircase from the basement kitchen to the third floor.

A second set of stairs was located in a common hallway accessible from the master bedroom that led from the first floor near the vestibule to the third- and fourth-floor duplex apartment, where J. Franklin Ray Jr. lived with his wife Mary and their six-year-old son, Franklin. Ray was a government administrator for the war agency's Office of Lend-Lease Administration. In later years, he was involved at a high diplomatic level in US–China relations and the United Nations Relief and Rehabilitation Administration. Most of the time, Mary and her son were alone, since her husband lived five days a week in Washington, DC, and commuted home on the weekends, if possible. The young boy was recuperating from scarlet fever under the care of Anna-liese Schonberg, a twenty-two-year-old German-born nurse.

Schonberg would emerge as a key witness at Lonergan's trial because she almost certainly heard the murder taking place.

———

In another ominous sign, Patricia's new residence was a short walk to Beekman Place, a small and charming, almost hidden street (about six blocks from the United Nations), which was in 1943 home to the rich, snooty, and influential—and still is. Today, it remains a quiet refuge from the 24/7 frantic hustle and bustle of Midtown Manhattan.

In 1924, as the brownstones on the street were being renovated and elegant apartments were erected, the asking price for a seven-room penthouse apartment near the corner of Beekman Place and East 51st was $20,500 (about $300,000 today); by 2000, the same suite was worth $2 million. Patricia likely was aware—as most New Yorkers were—that between 1935 and 1937, three grisly murders had occurred either on Beekman Place or in the nearby neighborhood.

The area is more accurately called Turtle Bay, but "Beekman Place" (or "Beekman Hill") was often used by its residents and the press to describe it as well. The name is derived from the eighteenth-century merchant James Beekman—a descendant of Dutch merchant Wilhelmus Beekman, who arrived in New Amsterdam in 1647—who built a mansion he called "Mount Pleasant," located on what is today East 51st Street and First Avenue, on high ground overlooking Turtle Bay. The area was home for such luminaries as globetrotting journalist John Gunther, the author of the "Inside" series based on his travels; gossip columnist and socialite Elsa Maxwell; and Broadway producer Billy Rose and his second wife, Eleanor Holm, the Olympic swimmer, who was unceremoniously banned—unjustly, she long maintained—from competing in the 1936 Summer Olympics in Berlin when she was caught intoxicated on the ship journey to Europe. Yet, Beekman Hill was not immune to murder and mayhem.

In November 1935, twenty-nine-year-old Vera Stretz, the daughter of musician Frank Stretz (who lived in Beekman Towers at 49th Street and First Avenue), shot and killed her married lover Dr. Fritz Gebhardt, who resided in the same apartment building. The two had a falling-out because Vera assumed from what Gebhardt had repeatedly said to her that he was going to leave his wife—who was back in Germany—and marry her. But on that fateful day, he told Vera that he wanted to keep their relationship as it was. Incensed, she shot him. Dubbed the "icy blonde" by the New York tabloid press, she claimed Gebhardt, who was an old friend of Nazi leader Hermann Goering, had raped her and then forced her to perform sodomy (in some accounts, it is oral sex). The all-male jury believed her—owing in part to the dramatics of her lawyer, Samuel Leibowitz, who portrayed her as "a poor girl trying to get away from a lecherous beast"—and acquitted her.

Several months later, on Good Friday, April 10, 1936, at 22 Beekman Place, Nancy Titterton, a talented fiction writer and the wife of scriptwriter Lewis Titterton, who worked for NBC, was discovered raped and murdered in her bathtub. The killer turned out to be John Fiorenza, a twenty-five-year-old upholsterer. As he attacked his victim, he had unknowingly dropped a small piece of rope. In a brilliant bit of forensics work for the era, a criminologist with the chief medical examiner's office traced the rope back to the shop where Fiorenza worked. Under intense police questioning, he eventually confessed to the crime, was found guilty, and was executed by the electric chair in January 1937.

The third case was the grisliest. Robert Irwin was a twenty-nine-year-old troubled artist and sculptor who had been in and out of mental institutions (once, in order to stop masturbating, he unsuccessfully tried to cut off his penis with a razor). He was obsessed with a young woman named Ethel Gedeon Kudner, who had recently gotten married. During 1933 and part of 1934, Irwin had boarded with Ethel and her parents, Mary and Joseph, and younger sister Veronica (Ronnie), at their home at 240 East 53rd Street, a less than impressive brownstone. Ethel had been kind to Irwin, but had no romantic interest in him. When he learned that she had become engaged to lawyer Joe Kudner, he went "crazy," as he put it in his diary.

Ethel moved out after her marriage to Kudner, and Joseph and Mary, whose life together was rocky, separated. Mary soon sold the house on East 53rd and bought a slightly more upscale brownstone at 316 East 50th Street, less than two blocks from Beekman Place, and around the corner from Patricia's suite. To pay the bills, Mary took in boarders, including Frank Byrnes, an English waiter. Meanwhile, the shapely Veronica, who was twenty years old in 1937, embarked on a semi-successful career as a model for lurid photos—at least, for the time—in *True Detective* and other pulp magazines.

On Saturday night, March 27, 1937, the day before Easter Sunday, Irwin, in a severe depressive and delusional state, arrived at the Gedeons' new home carrying an ice pick to confront and kill Ethel, as he later confessed to the police. He had been inspired by the German philosopher Arthur

Schopenhauer and believed that he was entitled to act on his "free will"—and that included his sexual impulses.

Ethel, who lived in Astoria, Queens, was not there, although she and her husband were invited for Easter Sunday dinner. Mary reluctantly invited Irwin in and they chatted. In the interim, Frank Byrnes arrived, introduced himself to Irwin, and retired to his bedroom. It was past ten o'clock when Mary finally requested that Irwin leave. He refused, and declared that he was waiting for Ethel. When Mary raised her voice, Irwin became angry and attacked her. She fought valiantly as he strangled her. Byrnes had fallen asleep and did not hear the violent struggle.

Next, Irwin took Mary's dead body into a bedroom and sat and waited. He realized that Veronica, who he liked and did not want to hurt, might come home before Ethel did. He wrapped a bar of soap in a dishrag with the intention of stunning Veronica with it. At three o'clock in the morning, Veronica walked into the house. Irwin listened as she went into the bathroom. An hour passed before Veronica entered the bedroom where Irwin was waiting. Before she could utter a word, he struck her hard with his makeshift blackjack. He grabbed her by the throat as she pleaded with him. About two hours passed and he still held on to her. She was weak and repeated his name. At that he tightened his grip around her throat and killed her. As the sun was coming up, he knew he needed to deal with Byrnes, who could place him at the scene of the murders. He went to the bedroom where Byrnes was sleeping and repeatedly stabbed him with the ice pick.

After a prolonged investigation, the police, owing mainly to unsettling references to Irwin in Veronica's diary, determined that he was the perpetrator of the horrific murders. Called the "Mad Sculptor" by the press, Irwin evaded capture until late June, when he finally turned himself in while in Chicago. At his trial he was defended by lawyer Samuel Leibowitz. With the prosecution having Irwin's full confession, Leibowitz was not going to win an acquittal, as he had for Vera Stretz, yet he managed to save Irwin from the electric chair by obtaining a deal for his client, who pled guilty to second-degree murder. Irwin was sentenced to life in prison and was eventually transferred to the Matteawan State Hospital for the Criminally Insane in Fishkill, New York, where he remained until he died from cancer in 1975, at the age of sixty-seven.

Never in her wildest dreams could Patricia have imagined that within a few months of moving into 313 East 51st Street, she was to be the chic neighborhood's next murder victim.

—◦—

Lonergan's marriage had seemingly collapsed, his employment prospects were dim, and he was dependent on financial handouts from his estranged wife. He was still dating, however. Twenty-two-year-old Helen Wing, who had met Patricia and Wayne at a cocktail party, accepted Lonergan's invitation to have a drink together at the Weylin Hotel on East 54th Street. While she found him a "dull" companion, they did discuss the possibility of Lonergan joining the Royal Canadian Air Force (RCAF). And soon after, that's exactly what he did.

All things considered, it isn't entirely surprising that Lonergan decided to return to Canada and enlist in the RCAF. Even if he had wanted to join the US Armed Forces, it would have been impossible given his 4-F designation by the draft board. He later claimed that he had opted for the RCAF primarily "to make some money."

Thus, on the morning of September 6, 1943, he was in Toronto at the Manning Depot—the Coliseum Building at the Canadian National Exhibition grounds, close to the shores of Lake Ontario—where he enlisted in the RCAF following two days of orientation. As he wrote to Patricia, he found the Canadian military authorities polite and honest as compared to those he had dealt with in the United States. (He signed this letter—which was later provided to the Manhattan district attorney's office by Lucille Burton—"all my love to you and Billy.") The RCAF medical board gave him a clean bill of health.

Lonergan became a second-class aircraftman and was sent for mandated training in a program held at the University of Toronto. The university and the RCAF had devised what was called the Pre-Aircrew Education Detachment (PAED) course for recruits like Lonergan, who did not have sufficient academic education. He was assigned to #23 PAED. In addition to the classes held at the university, the recruits also received instruction in mathematics at the Manning Depot and were introduced to rigorous military discipline—which could not have been easy for Wayne.

On the recommendation of his friend Sidney Capel Dixon, program director at the CBC, Lonergan, upon his return to Toronto, had rented a room for a few weeks at the Belvidere Manor, a large, stylish old house at 342 Bloor Street West, west of Spadina Road, and on the edge of the university. It was close to the Markham Street house where he had grown up. The Belvidere, run by a Miss Miller, was tastefully decorated and popular with artists, radio performers, and musicians. Meals were also included. During the two weeks following his enlistment, he had to reside at the Manning Depot and gave up the room at the Belvidere. After that, it is not clear whether he rented another room at the Bloor Street boardinghouse or stayed with Dixon—which is where the police found him the day after Patricia had been murdered.

It is possible that Dixon was misidentified by Syd Boehm of the *New York Journal-American*, who, following Lonergan's arrest, wrote that he had had an intimate relationship with "a wealthy and prominent 32-year-old Toronto man." Dixon, who was not prominent or wealthy, had known Lonergan's mother Clara, and had met Wayne nearly a decade earlier. They were not close friends, but did go out for drinks occasionally, as they had when Dixon had visited New York in the fall of 1939. Dixon later told the Toronto police that he did not know about Lonergan's bisexuality until he read about it in the newspapers.

Lonergan had scrounged whatever cash he could find and pawned some of his jewelry. He planned to return to New York as soon as he was granted a forty-eight-hour leave so that he could see Billy. Other visits were sure to be possible in the weeks and months ahead.

6

Weekend Furlough

IT WAS CLOSE TO MIDNIGHT on Friday, October 22, 1943, when the Trans-Canada flight to New York City departed from Malton Field (now Toronto Pearson International Airport), seventeen miles northwest of downtown Toronto. One of the fourteen passengers on board the Lockheed Lodestar—the return ticket price was $25—was RCAF Aircraftman Second Class Wayne Lonergan. He was smartly dressed in his dark blue uniform, with a belted jacket, white shirt, black tie, and a side cap resting uneasily on his head.

He was happy to serve—it gave him a much-needed focus for his life—and even happier that his enlistment in the RCAF training program permitted him to travel to the United States. The war had all but stifled leisure travel from Canada to the United States. In the summer of 1940, the Canadian federal government, fearful of a drain on the supply of Canada's "hard currency" (convertible to US dollars), felt it had no choice but to curb nonessential tourist spending. As a member of the air force who possessed the requisite papers, however, Lonergan was allowed to spend his weekend furlough in New York City.

As the propeller-powered Lodestar bumped on the choppy air, barely rising above the clouds over the farm fields below, Lonergan was unusually fidgety. He was anxious to get to New York and looked forward to seeing Billy, who he missed. The apparent failure of his marriage and the separation severely depressed him. He hoped beyond hope that Patricia would take him back. Being cut off from his wife's sizable inheritance also must have consumed his thoughts. According to his later testimony to the district attorney's office—and again, the veracity of this statement is open to question—he had contemplated suicide twice in the past few months.

A few days before his trip, he had telephoned Patricia—like everyone else, he called her Patsy—and told her that he would be in New York on the weekend. The brief conversation was polite enough. She informed him that he was welcome to stop by on Saturday afternoon to see Billy, who would be with Miss Black. But Patricia was planning to be out, and then had a date with her latest beau, Mario Gabellini, who Lonergan had met during his last visit to New York City three weeks earlier.

Lonergan later claimed that during the first week of October, he had received a telegram indicating that Patricia was in the hospital with appendicitis and required surgery. After he explained the situation to his commanding officer, he was granted a leave. Yet once he arrived in New York, he learned that he had been a victim of a supposed prank; Patricia was neither ill nor in the hospital. Asked later by a New York ADA to show him the cable, Lonergan said he had thrown it out. The DA's investigators were never able to find a trace of it for the simple reason that it did not exist, and was surely another of Lonergan's lies.

While he had been in New York from October 5 to 8, he had been loaned $550 from the Provident Loan Society on East 25th Street, near Fourth Avenue. For collateral, he put up diamond and gold cuff links, a gold cigarette case, a gold tie clasp, two pearl studs, and two rings. One evening during this trip, Lonergan had accompanied Patricia and Gabellini, a smooth-talking Italian decorator who was twenty years older than she was, to dinner at the El Morocco. Even if this outing was rather unusual—"abnormal" was the term the New York DA's office used to describe it—Lonergan had thoroughly enjoyed himself. True, Gabellini might have been interested more in Patricia's bank account than forging a meaningful relationship—which did not appeal to her under any circumstances—but the lively Italian was a fun person to spend an evening with at a nightclub. Enthused by the music provided by Chiquito's rumba band, Lonergan had shared a few dances with his estranged wife. Later, Gabellini remarked that Lonergan displayed no signs of jealously toward him and conceded that Lonergan was a better rumba dancer than he was.

Lonergan later told John Loehr, the New York City deputy ADA who initially questioned him, that he and Patricia had had sex during this first furlough. Given her antipathy toward him—despite the entertaining night out at the El Morocco—this seems highly improbable, and likely yet another of Lonergan's calculated falsehoods. Or, perhaps, she was intoxicated from all of the drinking at the club and succumbed to Lonergan's advances? Even so, a few minutes in bed did not mean she wanted him permanently back in her life.

Once Lonergan knew he could spend the weekend of October 22 in New York, he had also telephoned Helen Wing, a young woman he had dated, and invited her out to dinner on Saturday night. She told him that she would be busy with her family and had to decline. He suggested they meet up for drinks on Sunday before he had to fly back to Toronto.

Right on schedule, at 2:30 a.m. the plane touched down at LaGuardia Field (or the New York Municipal Airport, as it was also known). Lonergan grabbed his duffel bag and hailed a taxi to take him to 140 East 79th Street, at the corner of Lexington Avenue, the address of the luxurious apartment of his friend, John F. Harjes.

John Frederick Harjes, tall and broad-shouldered, was everything Wayne Lonergan ached to be: He was well-connected, a respected member of the city's upper crust, an heir to old money, and rich, very rich. His grandfather, John H. Harjes, a Philadelphia businessman, was one of the founders—along with noted banker Anthony Drexel and Eugene Winthrop of New York—of Drexel, Harjes & Company, an investment bank established in Paris in 1868. In a restructuring that took place a few years later, New York financier J. Pierpont Morgan, whose empire soon extended across North America and Europe, joined the partnership, and eventually assumed a controlling interest. The company's stock grew considerably when it became a major lender to the cash-strapped French government at the conclusion of the Franco-Prussian War of 1870–71. Drexel died in 1893, and the Paris branch—part of the burgeoning House of Morgan—became known as Morgan, Harjes & Company. Harjes retired in 1908 as the senior partner in the Paris office. He was celebrated in 1906 for donating a statue of Benjamin Franklin to France, which sits in the southwest corner of the Place du Trocadéro. When he died in 1914 at the age of eighty-five, he left his family an estate worth $10 million (about $256 million today).

John's son, H. (Henry) Herman Harjes, who turned forty years old in 1912, had been involved in the business since 1898 and eventually replaced his father as the senior partner. During World War I, Herman, who was a close friend of Theodore Roosevelt, played a key role in arranging loans for the Allies. Later, he was the chief representative of the American Red Cross.

When the United States entered the war in 1917, he enlisted and eventually was given the rank of lieutenant colonel, as the chief liaison officer of the American Expeditionary Force. For his service, the French government awarded him the prestigious Croix de Guerre military decoration. At the conclusion of the war, Morgan, Harjes & Co. continued to prosper, granting credit to French and American businesses based in France.

Tragedy struck the family in 1923 when Herman's twenty-four-year-old daughter Hope—from his first marriage to Marie Graves, who had died in 1899—was killed when she was thrown from her horse during a stag hunt at Château d'Abondant, the family's country home outside of Paris. Then, three years later, another terrible accident. This time, Herman was playing polo, a sport he loved and excelled at. His horse stumbled and rolled over him, breaking his spine and fracturing his skull. Doctors were brought in from London, but he never regained consciousness and died. He was fifty-four years old. He left his second wife, Frederica, who he had married in 1905, and their three sons, Herman Jr., Charles, and John, all under twenty-five years old.

John, the youngest, was only twelve. None of the boys were interested in joining the family business at this time, and given the size of the estate, none of them ever had to work another day in their lives if they chose not to. The family remained in France, though frequently visited New York City. They joined the ranks of the wealthy listed in the esteemed *Social Register*—summering in Newport, Rhode Island, in a mansion along the Atlantic shore, and staying with Frederica's family, who had a suite at the Pierre Hotel. Their various social and philanthropic activities were usually noted in the New York newspapers' society pages. In August 1936 in Paris, Frederica married Seton Porter, who had done well in the liquor business as head of the National Distillers Products Corporation, especially once US Prohibition was repealed.

John attended Cambridge University, graduating in 1936. He then followed in his father's footsteps and joined Morgan, Harjes in Paris. When World War II broke out, he served with the American Field Service as an ambulance driver until the Nazis occupied France. At that point, he returned to New York City and began working as a volunteer field representative for the Office of Civilian Defense, headquartered at 80 Centre Street in Lower Manhattan.

Harjes's path crossed that of Lonergan in May 1941 at a posh cocktail party to raise funds for homeless children. Wayne's connection to Patricia and the Burton family was the main (actually, the only) reason for him being on the invitation list. The two men were seated at the same table and enjoyed the sumptuous hors d'oeuvres and live entertainment. Their friendship grew after that, so much so that in late January 1943, when Harjes's engagement to Alice Whitehouse—her mother, Vira Boarman Whitehouse, had been a prominent suffragist—was announced, Lonergan was named as one of two ushers, along with Harjes's brother Herman, who was to be the best man. As reported in the *New York Times*, the wedding took place on Monday, February 1, in the chapel of St. Bartholomew's Episcopal Church on Park Avenue. The newlyweds immediately headed to California for a honeymoon before settling down at Harjes's apartment on East 79th Street.

This bliss, however, was short-lived, and John and Wayne soon shared something in common: They were both separated from their wives. By the spring of 1944, in the midst of Lonergan's trial, Alice declared her intention to divorce Harjes. On May 12, she filed legal papers in Reno, Nevada, on grounds of cruelty.

Lonergan arrived at Harjes's apartment about 3:00 a.m. He slept for several hours, and then he and Harjes had breakfast together, prepared by Josephine Peeters, the wife of Harjes's butler (or "manservant"), Emile Peeters (incorrectly spelled in newspaper reports as "Emil Petters"). Emile, who was sixty-one years of age, and Josephine, who was fifty-six years old, had immigrated to the United States from Belgium in 1932, working for many years for Harjes's aunt in Connecticut. Harjes was leaving for a weekend at East Williston on Long Island to attend a friend's wedding, taking his three dogs with him so Wayne would have the place to himself. Harjes, however, had instructed Peeters that Lonergan—and he had told Lonergan this as well—could sleep at his apartment and have breakfast there during his stay, but he was to eat lunch and dinner elsewhere.

Lonergan informed Harjes that he had acquired two tickets to a new Broadway musical, *One Touch of Venus*, starring the incomparable Mary Martin, and asked him if he could assist him to find a date for Saturday evening. Harjes said he did know a real "stunner," a young woman he knew as Miss Jean Murphy, a twenty-eight-year-old blonde former showgirl and would-be Broadway and movie star. She lived close by at 132 East 79th Street. (Both 140 and 132 East 79th Street had—and still do—private entrances for their residents. Between them is 136 East 79th Street, built in 1928. Today the corporation that owns 136 also owns the entire complex, incorporating 132 and 140, which since 1949 has been a cooperative.)

Harjes assured Lonergan that she was fun and as beautiful as movie star Betty Grable, with an "upswept hairdo" (as the *New York Journal-American* was later to describe it) and the same long legs and captivating smile. With her colorful dresses, jackets, stylish hats, and fine soft skin, Miss Murphy usually looked as if she had just stepped off the stage of a Broadway musical.

In truth, her résumé was thin. She was born in 1914 near Seattle to George and Mamie Murphy; her father was a Canadian. They had five children, and Jean was the eldest. By 1943, she had performed once or twice in Broadway musical productions as a showgirl and appeared in the film *George White's 1935 Scandals*, a sequel to the 1934 film *George White's Scandals*, which itself was based on White's popular Ziegfeld Follies–like Broadway revue that was a hit from 1919 to 1939. In the 1935 film—which starred James Dunn and Alice Faye and is best remembered for the on-screen debut of Broadway dancer Eleanor Powell—Murphy was featured as one of the "Scandals Beauties."

Around 1935, she married Hugo Jaburg, who was fourteen years older than her and the president of Jaburg Bros., a profitable grocery wholesale business. In 1936, she gave birth to their son, Gregory. The couple had their differences, and in early 1942 they separated, sharing custody of their son. Two years later, she was granted a divorce on the grounds of cruelty and awarded an annual alimony payment of $6,000 (nearly $87,000 today). By the fall of 1943, she had gone back to using her own name, Murphy, though her legal name remained "Jean Murphy Jaburg."

The plan was for Harjes to introduce Lonergan to Murphy Jaburg at her apartment late in the afternoon, before he left the city. Wayne already had a luncheon engagement arranged, plus another curious errand to look after.

Dr. Isidore Michel had been Patricia and Wayne's physician. Dressed in his RCAF uniform, Lonergan had come by the doctor's office at about eleven o'clock on Saturday morning and asked if he could purchase arsenic for an acquaintance. Later, Lonergan stated that prior to his trip he had attempted to obtain arsenic at two Toronto pharmacies, but was unsuccessful. Michel was not especially pleased to see Lonergan, who had not settled his last invoice with him. Nonetheless, the doctor told him to return at

5:00 p.m. Wayne did so, and told Michel that he could give him $100 for a gram of arsenic. That amount was sufficient, the doctor pointed out, to kill fifty people. Wayne also asked about buying strychnine. Michel said he had neither arsenic nor strychnine for him. Lonergan's interaction with Dr. Michel was to be considered at his trial.

Leaving the doctor's office, Lonergan made his way to 780 Madison Avenue, near East 66th Street, where his friend Marcella D'Arnoux resided. Once he arrived, she introduced him to a friend of hers who was already there, Sylvia French. D'Arnoux had a spirited personality. She used the title "Comtesse" (Countess), even though she was not one. The thirty-five-year-old "petite brunette," who had known Wayne and Patricia (her name was listed in Patricia's address book) for several years, was employed as a salesperson at the Hattie Carnegie Salon fashion business on East 49th. The store was owned by Hattie Carnegie Zanft (born Henretta Kanengeiser of Vienna), acclaimed as the "high priestess of fashion."

French was a charming and lovely thirty-year-old real estate broker who worked at the office of William D. May Company on East 52nd Street, near Fifth Avenue. She lived in an apartment three blocks away that was decorated in Regency style, with elegant furniture and a lot of mirrors. She had only met Lonergan one other time before that day.

Lonergan suggested the three of them have lunch at the Marguery Hotel on Park Avenue, near 48th Street, a twenty-minute walk from D'Arnoux's place. D'Arnoux had to remain behind for a few minutes, so Lonergan accompanied French to the hotel, where they were seated at about 1:30 p.m. D'Arnoux arrived a short time later.

Following a pleasant lunch of good food and conversation, Lonergan went for a walk despite the cool and windy weather. He stopped by a shop and bought three small bottles of brandy, then headed for the FAO Schwarz toy store, where he spent $14 on a two-and-a-half-foot-high stuffed elephant for young Billy. He met up with Sylvia French again for a quick drink at her apartment and mistakenly left the toy elephant there.

Shortly before five o'clock he returned to Harjes's apartment so that Harjes could formally introduce him to Jean Murphy Jaburg. Lonergan invited her to accompany him to the play, but she told him that she was intending to visit her sister. Harjes asked her if she could do him a favor and change her plans so that she could go on a date with his friend, a "soldier" from Canada. After more discussion and prodding from both Harjes and Lonergan, she said she would call her sister and then telephone Lonergan at

Harjes's residence to let him know. She was, in fact, keen to see the play; her friend, actress Ruth Bond, had a supporting role.

After Harjes and Lonergan had left, she telephoned her sister and canceled their engagement. She then called Harjes's to speak with Lonergan to confirm their date. Peeters the butler, who answered the phone, told her that Lonergan was out, but said he would relay the message.

＊＊＊

After Lonergan had returned to Harjes's apartment, he had telephoned Patricia's. He spoke with the maid, Marie Tanzosch, who was about to go off duty until Monday morning. (She lived about two miles away, on East 83rd Street, near First Avenue.) He told her to tell Miss Black to keep Billy up and he would be there shortly to visit with him.

Bidding farewell to Harjes (and his dogs)—Harjes drove away in his car with his friend, Harold Le Mon, a fellow banker—Lonergan walked the mile and a half to Patricia's apartment on East 51st Street, arriving there about 6:00 p.m.

Patricia was already out. Marie Tanzosch—who only departed at 8:00 p.m.—answered the door and invited him in. She took him up to the nursery, where Elizabeth Black was with Billy. Lonergan spent about forty-five minutes playing with his son. The boy was happy to see his father. Lonergan promised him that he would return the next morning to deliver the toy elephant.

During the time Lonergan was at Patricia's, he had called Peeters, who told him that Murphy Jaburg had telephoned for him. He then called her and learned that she had changed her plans. He told her how delighted he was that she would be joining him for the evening.

By 7:15 p.m. Lonergan, who was wearing his air force uniform, was at Murphy Jaburg's apartment to escort her to the Imperial Theatre on West 45th Street. As usual, she was impeccably dressed for a Saturday-night outing and looked as gorgeous as ever. Lonergan said he had to pick something up at Harjes's, so they walked back to his suite, where Lonergan made them each a Scotch and soda. She had no idea that he was separated and did not discover that fact until much later in the evening. She later told the district attorney's office that had she known he was married, she would not have gone out with him.

Prior to leaving, they saw Emile and Josephine Peeters, who had returned from shopping. After Wayne and Jean finished their drinks, they left Harjes's and hailed a taxi to take them to the theater. They arrived with a few minutes to spare before the curtain rose at 8:30 p.m.

The musical performance they saw, *One Touch of Venus*, was based on British journalist Thomas A. Guthrie's 1885 novel, *The Tinted Venus*, which incorporated the Pygmalion legend. The story—which included a good dose of racy dialogue, at least for the 1940s—revolves around a statue of Venus, played by Mary Martin (who was about to celebrate her thirtieth birthday), which comes to life when a barber who regards himself as an art connoisseur inadvertently places a ring on her finger. Besides Martin, the musical play featured Kenny Baker, a star from the *Jack Benny Program* radio show, and Paula Laurence, who decades later was to be a fan favorite on the soap opera, *Dark Shadows*. Though *One Touch of Venus* got favorable reviews and ran until February 1945, Lonergan was not enthralled by the production.

After the show ended, Murphy Jaburg went backstage to see her friend, Ruth Bond, while Lonergan remained in the hallway (because Bond was half undressed). Then, Murphy Jaburg and Lonergan walked over to the Waldorf Astoria Hotel on Park Avenue. They were hoping to have a late dinner at the hotel's famed Wedgwood Room, but it was packed. Not wishing to wait, they took a taxi to the Stork Club, yet getting into the Stork on a Saturday night without reservations proved to be even more impossible. Had they done so, however, they might have run into Patricia, who arrived there with Gabellini and a few friends later that evening.

Next they took a taxi to the 21 Club, which arguably served the best cuisine of the various nightclubs, and had more luck. They walked past the restaurant's most distinctive feature, the colorful metal jockeys that guard its entrance. Then, they were personally greeted by Jack Kriendler, who was wearing one of his many elegant custom-tailored suits (made by Spitz Clothier). He was the more outgoing owner of the club; his partner and cousin, Charlie Berns, tended to remain in the background. (Although somewhat quiet and reserved, Charlie was known to be a man of his word.)

With its dark oak panels, the club—which has changed little in the past eight decades—exudes old-school elegance. It was buzzing as usual for a Saturday night in 1943, with an assortment of Hollywood celebrities and elite café society regulars, drinking, dancing, and thoroughly enjoying themselves. Lonergan ordered the chicken à la king and had three shots of Scotch whisky. Murphy Jaburg recalled that he was friendly and knew many of the people in the club. The two of them chatted about various subjects—the war, his training in the RCAF, and her son—but Lonergan barely mentioned anything to her about Patricia or Billy. (Later on, Kriendler and Berns hated that the 21 Club became part of the Lonergan saga.)

Wayne and Jean finished dining at 11:45 p.m. and caught a taxi for the ten-minute ride to the newly opened Blue Angel Café. Operated by Herbert Jacoby and his partner Max Gordon, the Blue Angel was located on East 55th Street, not far from Third Avenue, in the old Kit Kat Club, which had once offered a Harlem-style show and dinner, all for $1.50 in 1939. (This is not to be confused with a second Kit Kat Club that opened in 1998 on West 43rd Street, where model Melania Knauss met Donald Trump.) *Variety* magazine had already raved about the Blue Angel's classy room and an entertaining floor show that featured comedians like Benny Rubin, a talented impersonator; dancer and singer Winifred (or Wini) Shaw; and singer Mildred Bailey. Dooley Wilson, the piano player who had starred opposite Humphrey Bogart in the 1942 film *Casablanca*, had also recently performed at the Blue Angel.

Lonergan and Murphy Jaburg each downed several more Scotches before departing the nightclub at about 2:45 a.m. They took a taxi back to East 79th Street. He invited her into Harjes's apartment for one final nightcap, but she said she wanted to go home. So he walked her to her place. Lonergan later said he kissed her good night several times and she apparently enjoyed it. He also claimed that he "thinks" he fondled her breasts. Murphy Jaburg, however, said he did not kiss or touch her. Lonergan added that he made "no other advances towards her," which she corroborated.

───────

It was now after four in the morning on Sunday, October 24. While Jean Murphy Jaburg went to bed alone, Wayne Lonergan's evening was not quite over yet—at least, that is what he initially told Toronto and New York City detectives and deputy ADA John Loehr about eighteen hours later.

Lonergan decided to go for a walk—the distance between the entrances of 132 and 140 East 79th is about twelve feet. While doing so, he claimed to have encountered—the press later used the term "befriended" to describe it—an American soldier in uniform, a first-class private, whose name he offered as Murray Wooster, which later was changed to Maurice Worcester. They struck up a conversation, and Worcester told Lonergan that he was waiting for a taxi to take him downtown so that he could find a room for the night. Lonergan kindly offered him an empty bed in Harjes's apartment instead, though he apparently had other things in mind.

"Did you contemplate an act of perversion?" Loehr later asked him.

"I vaguely thought about it," Lonergan replied.

Lonergan led Worcester up to Harjes's suite and offered him a drink. They chatted for a little while. Lonergan showed the soldier the guest bedroom and then returned to the bedroom he was using. As Lonergan later told it to the detectives and Loehr, the two men did not stay separate for long.

"After a while I climbed into the other bed with him," related Lonergan.

"What did you do?" asked one of the New York detectives.

"Nothing much—a few things," said Lonergan.

"Acts of perversion?" asked one of the detectives.

"Yes," said Lonergan.

"Was the soldier willing?" the detective asked.

"Not too willing," replied Lonergan.

Lonergan allegedly performed oral sex on Worcester and wanted it reciprocated. But the soldier hesitated. He started to do it, then stopped. The two men argued and a fight broke out, during which, according to Lonergan, Worcester scratched his face. The situation calmed down and Lonergan returned to his own bedroom.

Lonergan fell asleep, and awoke a few hours later to find Worcester grabbing Lonergan's watch and uniform. Lonergan confronted him. Another physical altercation ensued, but Worcester managed to run off with the watch and uniform. Why an American soldier would want an RCAF uniform was not clear to legal authorities and journalists when Lonergan first related this tale, or ever.

Exhausted, and seemingly not troubled by losing his uniform—which would have merited a disciplinary hearing from Canadian air force officials and likely an administrative punishment—Lonergan fell back to sleep.

⁓

Lonergan crawled out of bed on Sunday morning at about ten o'clock. Harjes's butler, Peeters, served him a breakfast of orange juice, two slices of bacon, scrambled eggs, toast, and coffee. Peeters later recalled that Lonergan was irritable and demanded a refill of coffee rather than asking him politely to serve it.

Lonergan tried to put the events of the past evening with the US soldier behind him. He telephoned Jean Murphy Jaburg and invited her to have lunch with him at the Plaza Hotel. She said she was busy with another engagement, which did not please him. With no uniform to wear, he took a pair of herringbone gray tweed trousers and a somewhat matching tweed jacket from Harjes's closet; Harjes was much stouter than Lonergan, and the pants and jacket did not him fit very well.

He left Harjes's place and at noon retrieved the toy elephant at Sylvia French's apartment. She later remembered that she was surprised to see him wearing civilian clothes rather than his uniform and inquired about it. He told her that he had gotten into a "brawl" with a soldier he had met, and this soldier had stolen his uniform. She thought it was a "strange thing." She also did not recall seeing any scratches on his face. After a minute or so, he took the toy, and once outside on the street, hailed a taxi.

At approximately 12:30 p.m. Lonergan was standing in front of Patricia's main entrance and knocked. No one answered. The main door was open, as it usually was, and he walked into the foyer and left the elephant with a note that read, "To Billy, from Dad," by the door to Patricia's suite. That he did not want to hand the toy to his son himself so he could see his expression of joy at receiving it was curious, to say the least.

Returning to Harjes's, he telephoned Murphy Jaburg a second time. She told him she was looking after her eight-year-old son, Gregory, because her maid was off that afternoon. He persisted and invited the boy to come along as well, and she reluctantly agreed. He showed up at her apartment at one o'clock. Taking one look at him, she regretted that decision. Lonergan looked tired, and he was wearing ill-fitting clothes. "He certainly wasn't what you would call personable," she later testified. She quizzed him about his mismatching attire. He told her the story of how he was robbed by the American serviceman and that he had borrowed the clothes from Harjes. The story piqued her curiosity and she started asking him more probing questions. Which camp was the soldier from? Didn't he hear the soldier leaving the apartment? Why hadn't he called the police? He provided her with vague answers to all of her queries.

Murphy Jaburg and her son, along with Lonergan, left her apartment and took a taxi to the Plaza Hotel, where they ate lunch for about an hour and a half. When Murphy Jaburg was later asked by John Loehr, who first questioned her, about whether she had noticed any scratches on Lonergan's face on Sunday morning, she said no. She was also angry that she had become embroiled "in such a scandal."

Back at Harjes's at about 3:30 p.m., Lonergan left a note with the butler for his friend. "John: Thank you so much for the use of your flat. Due to a slight case of mistaken trust, I lost my uniform, and so have borrowed a jacket and trousers from you. I shall return them on my arrival in Toronto. . . . Yours, Wayne. I'll call and tell you all about it."

A short time later, he took a taxi to LaGuardia for the 7:10 p.m. Trans-Canada flight to Toronto, arriving early, at 9:15 p.m. His weekend furlough was over, but his ordeal was only beginning.

7

Out for a Good Time

PATRICIA WAS TRULY GLAD that Wayne planned to see their son—even if it was only for a brief visit. A boy needed his father, after all. At least until Billy was sixteen or seventeen years old, Wayne was to be a part of his life, and hers; that, she accepted. Yet, unlike her mother, who had remarried her father when she was a young girl, there was to be no reunion with Wayne. And on that Saturday, she had no desire to see him. Besides, she was busy most of the day and evening, and in truth, all that needed to be said between them had already been said.

She rose on Saturday morning around 11:30 a.m. Her maid Marie Tanzosch brought her breakfast to her bedroom. Patricia asked Marie to iron her yellow blouse because she intended to wear it on a trip to the country on Sunday.

Around two o'clock, she kissed Billy good-bye and left the capable Miss Black in charge. Her standing instruction with both Black and Tanzosch was that when Wayne was in New York, he was permitted to see Billy whenever he wished. Carrying a clothes bag with her evening outfit, she walked the few blocks to her close friend Mrs. Frederica "Rita" Patterson's apartment at the Carlton House on East 47th Street and Madison Avenue. The two women spent part of Saturday afternoon gossiping and playing gin rummy.

Her date that evening was with a man she had been out on the town with on several occasions, Mario Enzo Gabellini. She had no illusions about him; she knew of his reputation as a playful scoundrel and understood what he wanted from her. Still, he was entertaining to be with and a skilled dance partner for a night out at the Stork or El Morocco.

Gabellini was a debonair forty-three-year-old Italian interior decorator with slicked black hair, a man about town who preferred double-breasted tan suits with wide-cut pants and peak lapels on the jacket, accented by brown suede shoes. He had arrived in New York from Rome in 1929 and had been married and divorced twice.

His first wife, Helen Kearns McCarthey, was the daughter of Jennie Judge and the late Thomas Kearns, a Republican senator from Utah from 1901 to 1905, with lucrative interests in silver mines and railways. He was also an owner of the *Salt Lake Tribune*. Helen was a widow at the age of twenty-seven; in 1926, her first husband, Glen Elroy McCarthey, had died. She had met Gabellini on a trip to Rome. They were married in Paris in July 1928, and he returned with her to the United States. A year later, Helen gave birth to their son, Giancarlo. Owing to Gabellini's infidelity, the marriage ended six years later. He quickly married a second time, eloping in Las Vegas with a young and beautiful woman, Drusilla Dunn—whose mother was married to Birch Hunt Alsop, a member of Los Angeles's social elite—only to divorce her in 1936. (Dunn then married James Todd of New York in 1938, and divorced him on grounds of cruelty in September 1943.)

Patricia had first encountered Gabellini at a British War Relief charity function. She soon learned that he was hardly as rich or successful as he liked to pretend. He had no studio, nor was he listed as a member of the decorators' association. Gabellini's image was all a facade. He had little money and for the past month had been staying with a friend, George Granata, a forty-three-year-old divorced New York–born general exporter, who rented an apartment at 793 Lexington Avenue, near 62nd Street. He had met Gabellini on a trip to Italy in the summer of 1939. Gabellini also had a penchant for dating wealthy divorced women who he liked to impress with his culinary skills—and the younger the better, which explained his fervent interest in Patricia.

———

Gabellini arrived at Rita Patterson's apartment at 7:30 p.m. He was late, and Patricia was not impressed; "she was cross," Gabellini later recalled. Patricia was wearing the outfit she had brought with her to Rita's: a mink jacket, black silk dress, black hat, nylon hose, and black shoes. She looked lovely.

She quickly forgave Gabellini for his tardiness and the two of them headed to the bar at the Peter Cooper Hotel on East 39th Street, where they met up with Gabellini's friend, Thomas ("Tom") Farrell Jr., a forty-year-old magazine publisher of the popular digest, *The Woman,* and his girlfriend, model Jean Goodwin, aged twenty. (A year earlier, Goodwin had been married for two months to an Australian merchant marine sailor before the marriage was annulled; he had told her he was a rich navy officer, and she accused him of fraud.)

For the past eight weeks, Farrell had lived in a suite in the Peter Cooper Hotel. He was personable, though arrogant, and could be a cad. He had begun an affair with Goodwin (who he had met in late October 1940) several weeks after marrying Mary Bland Reynolds, on New Year's Eve, 1941. Reynolds was the daughter of Senator Robert Reynolds of North Carolina, an ultranationalist. She had attempted suicide when she learned of Farrell's indiscretions. Farrell and Reynolds were divorced in March 1943, freeing him to pursue Goodwin.

The foursome sipped cocktails, and they were joined by Farrell's friend, Robert ("Bob") Dasey, a successful real estate broker. Leaving the Peter Cooper, Farrell drove everyone in his car to Luisa's, a family restaurant on 58th Street, near Second Avenue. Gabellini was friends with Luisa, who also owned a farm in Yorktown in Westchester County, forty miles north of the city. Patricia had visited the farm a week earlier with Gabellini. That Saturday evening at Luisa's, Patricia enjoyed what turned out to be her last supper: hors d'oeuvres, broiled lamb chops, and a cup of black coffee.

During the dinner, and later in the evening in Luisa's bar, where they had more to drink, Patricia spoke about her marriage and relationship with Lonergan, telling Goodwin that they got on well enough, and she had no wish to be his enemy. She also remarked that she thought Wayne was handsome and asked Gabellini for his opinion. He agreed with her assessment.

At about 12:30 a.m., Farrell drove everyone (except Dasey, who went home) to the Stork Club, where Patricia might have run into Wayne and Jean Murphy Jaburg, had they not been turned away at the door. Patricia and Gabellini and Farrell and Goodwin had more luck and were shown to a table. Needless to say, Patricia could not have conceived that this was her final café society appearance. Like always, she was a delight, chatting with the many people she knew there, reveling in the music of Russ Smith's orchestra, and especially, the exhilarating rhythm of Noro Morales's rumba band.

"She was out for a good time," Farrell later recalled. "She talked and laughed and danced as if she didn't have a care in the world. She even discussed her husband without bitterness or sorrow. . . . She certainly wasn't worrying about anything." She danced with both Gabellini and Farrell and had a lot of fun.

Gabellini covered his and Patricia's dinner and drink expenses for the evening—somewhat unusual, because as Farrell later remarked, Gabellini was frequently short of cash. The group, joined by a navy lieutenant and his girlfriend who they had met, left the Stork Club at about 4:30 a.m. They stopped for a nightcap and an early breakfast at Farrell's suite at the Peter Cooper Hotel, staying there until just after 6:00 a.m.

It had been another long evening of revelry, of drinking Scotch-and-soda highballs and beer, so that by the time Gabellini saw her home, Patricia was feeling happy yet exhausted. Too exhausted for a bout of lovemaking with the more-energetic Gabellini—though that's what he was in the mood for, and presumably expected.

The sun was beginning to rise on Sunday morning when the taxi pulled up in front of 313 East 51st Street. It was cool and breezy, and the street was still eerily quiet. As the taxi idled, Gabellini got the hint that, alas, his date had finally come to its conclusion. He asked the driver, Felix (Fellipo) Guiffre, a forty-eight-year-old Italian immigrant, to wait for him so that he could guide Patricia up the steps and into her apartment and retrieve a camel hair coat he had left at her place a few days earlier. They climbed the steps to the main entrance and stepped into the vestibule. At that moment, Patricia told Gabellini that he could pick up his coat another time and he had to leave. Unsure then (or later) why Patricia had become agitated, he returned to the taxi and then stopped for coffee with Guiffre, who chatted with him about the Italian homeland. Gabellini was back at his own apartment no more than thirty minutes later.

On Sunday at about 1:00 p.m., George Granata, on Gabellini's behalf, telephoned Patricia's residence and Elizabeth Black answered. He asked to speak with Patricia, and Black told him she was sleeping. Gabellini then took the phone and told the nanny that he hoped Patsy would come to the country with him to visit his friend Luisa at her farm in Yorktown Heights. Black also told Gabellini that "Miss Patsy" was still sleeping. Gabellini insisted she knock on the bedroom door. Black reluctantly did so, but there was no response. She informed Gabellini that Mrs. Lonergan did not like to be bothered and he should call again later. He did so about twenty minutes later, yet was unable to speak to Patricia.

—•—

At about 8:30 p.m. on Sunday night, less than ten minutes after a distraught Peter Elser had called the 17th Precinct Police Station on East 51st with the terrible news of Patricia Burton Lonergan's death, the first patrolman to arrive at the residence was John Casey. He confirmed that Patricia indeed had been killed. Other patrolmen and detectives soon pulled up in front of the brownstone, causing a commotion on the quiet street. They were followed by the high-ranking "brass": Detective-Lieutenant Peter Brennan, the commander of the East Side Manhattan precinct detective squad; Deputy Chief Inspector Patrick Kenny, who supervised the detectives at the 17th Precinct; and Captain Daniel Mahoney, who was in charge of the homicide squad. He assigned detectives William Prendergast and Nicholas Looram to take the lead on the investigation.

Joining the police a short time later was the New York City deputy medical examiner, Dr. Milton Helpern, a forty-five-year-old forensic pathologist, who had been summoned at 9:00 p.m. Helpern, who had graduated from Cornell University Medical College in 1926, had joined the medical examiner's staff in 1931. He would be appointed its chief in 1954, in a career that was to span more than four decades, earning him a reputation as "Sherlock Holmes with a microscope."

The scene the police and Helpern found was shocking: Patricia was naked on top of the large double bed, wearing around her waist a white sanitary belt and napkin. Beneath the napkin, the string of a tampon protruded. The body was cold and rigid. Her arms were raised as if she had been attempting to thwart someone from hitting her. Her head, which lay toward the foot of the bed, was cut open with three deep gashes, and her reddish-brown hair was matted to her face by dried blood that had also seeped through the sheets and mattress onto the floor below. There was bruising on her neck, and her legs were bent at the knees. There was dried blood, as well, underneath the vanity table and chair up against the windows.

Two green-glass or onyx candleholders with heavy brass square pyramid–shaped bases, which normally stood on a table not far from the bed, were soon discovered broken, fragments of which were scattered about the room. Half of one of the candleholders was on the bed to the right of her, and its base, which was bent on three sides, was found on the floor. The second candleholder, which had also snapped in half, was on the floor as well, but its base, not as dented, was on top of the bed. Upon closer examination of the broken candleholder on the floor, Helpern found a "rather thick blood-stain near the upper rim," as he later noted in his autopsy report. One of the detectives also found a fingerprint on the base that was on the bed, but as was later determined, these prints were not sufficient to match to any of the subsequent suspects. The Venetian blinds in the bedroom were drawn, and one of the windows was partly open.

Looking through his Benjamin Franklin–style spectacles, Helpern carefully studied the contours of the broken candleholders. "The [pyramid]-shaped base of the holders could have produced those deep scalp lacerations," he told Prendergast, who was standing closest to him. "She would have died from the skull fracture, but the killer left little to chance. He also strangled her." There was no doubt in the doctor's mind that the killer was male.

"She bled a great deal and put up a desperate struggle for her life," continued Helpern. "Several of her fingernails are broken, and I found the pieces scattered on the floor on both sides of the bed. I also picked up an artificial toe-nail [covered in light red nail polish] which probably came loose when she kicked her attacker." He said he would look at the scrapings under a microscope and report back.

Today, those scrapings, if they were human flesh, as the police believed, could have been for used for DNA testing and analysis, and the perpetrator may well have been identified—but that was not available to Helpern and other medical examiners in 1943, and would not be for four more decades. Helpern's best guess, he told Detective-Lieutenant Brennan, was that Patricia had been dead anywhere from eight to sixteen hours—as early as 4:00 a.m., or as late as noon.

No money or jewelry was missing, and the police quickly concluded that this was not a robbery gone wrong. In fact, the detectives later calculated that Patricia's jewelry in her apartment was worth nearly $23,000 (approximately $340,000 today); the most expensive pieces were a pearl necklace and bracelet with rubies and diamonds, both valued at $2,500 each ($37,000 today). The mink coat she had worn on her last date was worth $1,580 ($21,750 today).

Helpern had asked his associate and old friend from the Cornell Medical College, Dr. Alexander Wiener—an expert on blood groupings (as blood type was then commonly referred to)—to survey the murder site and gather samples. Wiener, thirty-seven years old in 1943, was a member of the department of forensic medicine at the New York University Medical School. He was well-known for his 1937 groundbreaking research (along with doctors Karl Landsteiner and Philip Levine) in identifying the Rh factor in blood—named for the rhesus monkey used in the experimental research. The discovery was enormous for physicians and patients in solving adverse reactions from blood transfusions. He consulted often with Helpern, and frequently was called as an expert witness in murder trials.

Wiener would analyze cigarette stubs found in the living room and bedroom over the next month and a half. In addition to the bloodstain found on the rim of one of the candlesticks, there were other bloodstains found at the scene, as Wiener listed: "on the molding in the doorway of the bedroom, on the plate from the electric light switch in the bathroom, and on plaster from the hall." (He also later found a human bloodstain on a towel the police took from the washroom Lonergan used in Harjes's apartment.) But in the end, the various stains discovered—including the one on the candlestick—proved inadequate to identify the blood grouping (or type).

Also moving carefully around the bedroom were homicide photographers, snapping pictures of the victim and everything else in the vicinity, and technicians dusting for fingerprints. A bloody fingerprint was discovered in the bathroom, as noted in the *New York Times*'s October 28 story on the murder, though it was not referenced again in the investigation or trial because it could not be properly identified according to 1943 fingerprint analysis.

Meanwhile, Detective Prendergast, husky, square-jawed, but baby-faced, gathered all the relevant information from Peter Elser about Elizabeth Black, young Billy, and Lucille Burton, as well as the fact that Patricia was separated from her husband, Wayne Lonergan, an RCAF aircraftman who was in Toronto. Billy was taken to his grandmother's apartment at the Hotel Elysée, where he was cared for by a woman who worked for Lucille; while she, Black, and Elser were escorted to the 17th Precinct to give their statements.

The detectives also sought to interview the family members in the suite above Patricia's, yet were unable to do so because of the scarlet fever quarantine. This questioning took place a few days later. The police finally did speak with the Ray family's nurse, Annaliese Schonberg, about what she had heard. Her testimony soon allowed them to establish the time of the murder at about 9:00 a.m. Sunday morning.

At nine o'clock that evening, Prendergast had telephoned New York deputy assistant district attorney John Loehr at his home in Yonkers, twenty miles north, requesting his presence at Patricia's residence. Loehr, who was about to become heavily involved in Patricia's murder case for the next six months, was about to turn thirty-one years old. He had deep roots in Yonkers; his father, Joseph, had been mayor of the city from 1932 to 1939 and brought a degree of economic order to the city's dwindling finances during the worst years of the Great Depression.

John Loehr, who passed away in 1981—he left the DA's office in 1948 and spent the rest of his career in private practice in New York and then in Farmington, New Mexico (180 miles northwest of Albuquerque), where he also served as an ADA and federal administrative law judge—was bright, scholarly, and "Jesuitical in his approach to the law," says his son, Justice Gerald E. Loehr of the Westchester Supreme and County Court. (Justice Loehr followed in the footsteps of his father and grandfather. During his distinguished career, he also served as assistant district attorney of New York County and was mayor of Yonkers from 1980 to 1981). "My father," he adds, "loved the law, and he was also an excellent athlete and baseball player. He played third base for Fordham University and semi-pro ball after that." His other son, John G. Loehr, who is twenty months older than Gerald and lived with his father for many years in New Mexico after his parents divorced, notes, too, that his father was a humble man, not given to bragging about his accomplishments—which included the fact that he had as a young man won every merit badge that was possible as an Eagle Scout. According to John G. Loehr, his father was in excellent physical shape his entire life. But one day in 1981, he was hiking alone on a trail that reached ten thousand feet and collapsed and died from a cardiovascular event.

On this case, Loehr answered to Jacob Grumet (pronounced *Groo-met*), the Manhattan ADA in charge of the Homicide Branch, who was to be the lead prosecutor in this case. He was then forty-four years old, tall and slender, with oversized ears, a long nose, and a black pencil mustache. In court, he was described by Louis Sobel, a Broadway columnist for the *New York Journal-American*, as having a "coldly aloof" demeanor.

Grumet had previously worked with Thomas Dewey when he was the US attorney for the Southern District of New York. (Dewey was the governor of New York from 1943 to 1954 and, as the Republican Party nominee, lost two presidential elections—the first, to Franklin Roosevelt in 1944, and the second, more famously in 1948, to Harry Truman.) Under Dewey's tutelage, Grumet had shown his mettle in prosecutions of such gangsters as Waxey Gordon (Irving Wexler) and Louis "Lepke" Buchalter, the notorious brains behind Murder, Inc., an organized mob hit squad. After Grumet left the district attorney's office in 1948, he became chairman of the State Commission of Investigation, leading an inquiry into New York government corruption—where he investigated, among others, real estate developer Fred Trump—and became a New York State Supreme Court judge in 1968.

Grumet, in turn, in 1943 answered to New York district attorney Frank Hogan, who had assumed his position a year earlier and soon earned a reputation for his investigations into racketeering and corruption. He was to remain the DA in New York until 1973; only Robert Morgenthau, the DA from 1975 to 2009, served in the position longer. One thing Hogan insisted on was that his lawyers in the homicide division, who were prosecuting cases which could lead to a death sentence, had to observe an electric chair execution so that they could appreciate the gravity of the punishment and to ensure that no errors were made. Hogan's creed among his staff was that you would never be fired for an acquittal at trial. But if you were ever found to have convicted someone because you overlooked or ignored evidence that proved their innocence, that was grounds for dismissal. Today, the Manhattan district attorney's office in Lower Manhattan is located at 1 Hogan Place, named in Frank Hogan's honor. In dealing with Patricia Burton Lonergan's murder, Hogan allowed Grumet to take the lead, as was his custom with all of the ADAs.

When Loehr arrived at the residence, he had to wade through a gaggle of reporters who had heard about the crime and were demanding answers. It was the beginning of weeks of intense interest by newspapers in the city and beyond for every detail, tidbit, and morsel of gossip about Patricia's murder plus her social life, drinking habits, mothering practices, family, and last, though certainly not least, her husband from whom she was separated—Wayne Lonergan.

After visiting the suite on East 51st Street, Loehr made his way to the 17th Precinct where he joined in the questioning of Peter Elser, Elizabeth Black, and Lucille Burton. Apart from hearing the story again about how Elser had broken down the bedroom door to discover Patricia's limp body, Loehr and the detectives learned two other significant facts that would drive the initial part of the investigation. First, that Patricia's estranged husband had been in New York all weekend and had visited his son in Black's presence on Saturday, before he returned to Toronto on Sunday evening; and second, that the last person known to have seen Patricia alive was her Saturday-evening date, Mario Gabellini.

The order was given to find Gabellini. Detectives located him at his Lexington Avenue apartment around 11:30 p.m. He was bewildered and frightened when they brought him in and was stunned when he was informed that Patricia was dead. While rummaging through his apartment, the police believed they discovered a white shirt with blood on it, yet closer analysis showed that it was instead tomato-based meat sauce. Gabellini was questioned for nearly twelve hours, and then for the next week he was detained at the Tombs—the newly constructed Manhattan House of Detention in Lower Manhattan, the third "Tombs" prison since 1838—as a material witness and held on $10,000 bail. The bail was later reduced to $5,000, an amount that he posted, allowing his release early on Sunday, October 31. The interrogation of Gabellini led to intense police conversations with Thomas Farrell and Jean Goodwin, who had been out with Gabellini and Patricia, as well as several of his other friends and associates.

It was, however, Wayne Lonergan, who Loehr and the detectives quickly zeroed in on. It only made sense from their point of view that he was the perpetrator of this ghastly killing, despite—at first, at any rate—the absence of any real evidence directly linking him to the crime.

A Likely Suspect

THE PERCEPTION THAT Wayne Lonergan was involved in his wife's death was quickly reinforced. The detectives in New York had found Patricia's address book in her bedroom, and in it was information on where Lonergan was staying in Toronto, along with his phone number.

Before the sun came up on the morning of Monday, October 25, Inspector Patrick Kenny, having apprised ADA Jacob Grumet—who had been out of the city until about ten o'clock on Sunday evening—of the details of the case, wired the police in Toronto with a request that Lonergan be detained. The telegram from the NYPD indicated that he could be located at the Belvidere Manor at 342 Bloor Street West, in the room rented by Sidney Capel Dixon.

Meanwhile, the reporters, who had been standing in front of Patricia's brownstone Sunday night, had been busy. Murder and crime were always big news stories, and the competition in New York between such tabloids as the *Daily News* and the *New York Journal-American* and the more-serious *New York Times* and *New York Herald-Tribune* was relentless and severe. The *Daily News*, famed for its racy photographs, was arguably the most dogged of the group; anything and everything to gain the upper hand was deemed acceptable and appropriate.

In January, 1928, for example, the newspaper gave Tom Howard, a *Chicago Tribune* photographer not known to authorities at Sing Sing Prison, the assignment of obtaining a picture of Ruth Snyder's execution in the electric chair.

Convicted, along with her lover, the dull Judd Gray—at her insistence, he called her "Mommie"—of killing her husband, magazine editor Albert Snyder, she was to be the first woman put to death in this manner. Showing a lot of guile, Howard attached a miniature camera to his ankle with a long shutter release that went up his pant leg into his pocket. He gained access to the prison execution site—Sing Sing's infamous Death House—and then, just as the executioner pulled the switch, he snapped a photograph. The next day, to an outcry of horror mixed with fascination, the grisly shot ran on the front page of the *Daily News* with the large boldfaced headline: "DEAD!" The paper could not keep up with demand, and its rivals learned a lesson about the power of a picture.

There were no photographs of a deceased Patricia Burton Lonergan on the front pages of the New York papers on October 25. But the story, still in its infancy, was meticulously documented with as much detail as the reporters were able to pry out of their police sources. The *Daily News* offered a fairly accurate portrait of the bedroom crime scene, while Patricia, "the wife of a cadet in the Royal Canadian Air Force, and a member of a wealthy family," was described as "an attractive woman" by the *Herald-Tribune*—along with the fact that she was heir to a multimillion-dollar estate. (Until the RCAF officially corrected journalists in early November, reporters repeatedly referred to Lonergan as a "cadet," when, in fact, he was officially an "aircraftman, second class.") The *Times*, which ran a similar story, added that detectives were seeking "to learn the whereabouts" of Wayne Lonergan. By late afternoon, the Associated Press wire service, carried by newspapers from Texas to Minnesota, reported that Lonergan had been "detained by Toronto police . . . for New York police questioning in connection with the bludgeon slaying of his pretty estranged wife, Patricia Burton Lonergan, 22."

Prompted by what he read in the morning papers about Patricia's death and Lonergan's suspected involvement, John Harjes showed up early at the office of Jacob Grumet to relate his knowledge of Lonergan's weekend. Grumet was especially interested in what Harjes told him about Lonergan's uniform: that it had curiously gone missing, and that he had had to borrow pants and a jacket from Harjes—as was outlined in Lonergan's note, which Harjes provided to Grumet. Harjes also informed Grumet about Lonergan's date with Jean Murphy Jaburg. She and Emile Peeters, Harjes's butler, were added to the growing list of individuals the district attorney's office wanted to interview.

———

Shortly after eight o'clock in the morning there was a loud thump on the door of the boardinghouse on Bloor Street West in Toronto, where Lonergan was staying. The proprietor, Mrs. Miller, who immediately responded to the noise, ushered in two officers of the Toronto Police Department, Detective Sergeant Arthur Harris and Detective Alex Deans. They inquired whether Wayne Lonergan was staying in the room rented by Sidney Capel Dixon. Miller hesitated for a moment and then told them that Lonergan had arrived late the preceding evening. She escorted them to Dixon's room and they knocked. Seconds later, Lonergan opened the door. He was dressed in a dark blue suit.

Harris asked him if his name was Wayne Lonergan and he said it was. Harris then formally identified himself and told Lonergan that they were making inquiries about a homicide that had occurred in New York City. Lonergan said that he had just returned from there last night. Harris confirmed that Lonergan was in the RCAF and asked him why he was not dressed in his uniform. Lonergan explained that it had been stolen while he had been visiting New York. The detective then showed Lonergan the telegram they had received from the NYPD and verified that he was the person the telegram referred to. He nodded that he was. Harris asked him if he had anything to say about it; Lonergan said he did not. Harris noticed the scratches on Lonergan's chin and neck and asked him if he had been in a fight recently. Lonergan offered a vague explanation that he had received the scratches after he had returned to Toronto last night.

Harris explained that he had an extradition warrant issued by the State of New York and said Lonergan was required to come with them to police headquarters on College Street for questioning about a New York murder investigation. Lonergan was not surprised by this order; he had already seen a brief story on page two of that morning's Toronto *Globe and Mail*, "Guest Finds Hostess Murdered," with the news that "the nude body of Mrs. Patricia Burton Lonergan, the 22-year-old wife of member of the R.C.A.F., was found tonight in an East 51st Street triplex apartment."

The detectives first drove Lonergan to the nearby office for the RCAF #23 PAED at the University of Toronto. Harris informed the commanding officer about the homicide, Lonergan's connection to the victim, and that Lonergan was to be detained for questioning. The CO had no objection, though asked that Harris keep him informed of any developments. Harris promised that he would. In later reports, it was alleged that the Toronto police had failed to communicate with the RCAF about Lonergan. Yet, according to Harris's memorandum of October 25, 1943, this was not the case. From the beginning, however, RCAF officials took a rather laissez-faire attitude to

Lonergan's legal troubles; perhaps it was owed to the fact that with the war on, they had more serious matters to deal with. Whatever the reason, they eventually dispatched Philip A. Wait, a squadron leader who worked at the Canadian Legation in Washington, DC, to check on him, though this was not until Lonergan was arraigned in early November.

Back in the car, Harris asked Lonergan—who was curiously permitted to bring with him a paper bag containing three small bottles of brandy that he had purchased in New York—once more about what had happened to his uniform. This time, Lonergan offered a version of his encounter with the US soldier, Maurice Worcester, but without any mention—for the moment, at least—of sexual intimacy. It was, Lonergan said, simply a robbery in which his uniform and watch had been taken and he had been attacked. To Harris this immediately sounded suspicious. The New York police and DA's office had the same reaction after Harris notified them about it. "We want that uniform," Jacob Grumet was quoted as saying in the next day's newspapers. "It might tell an interesting story."

Lonergan, as cool and carefree as could be, asked to stop for breakfast before going to the station, and Harris consented. No doubt Harris believed that if Lonergan was relaxed and fed, he would be more cooperative and tell the police what they wanted to know. At Bassel's, a popular diner on the corner of Yonge and Gerrard Streets, Lonergan ate bacon and eggs, toast, and coffee. With breakfast over, Lonergan was taken to police headquarters.

Harris and every other Toronto detective, constable, and physician who inter-acted with Lonergan during the next twenty-four hours found him obliging, though it was also true that the police in Toronto did not officially interro-gate him, opting to wait until deputy ADA John Loehr had arrived to take charge. For most of the day, Lonergan was left alone in a room where he slept off and on. He had been provided with a pack of cigarettes and smoked those. The bag with the brandy bottles was not allowed in the room and was stored away for him.

Earlier that afternoon, Grumet had instructed Loehr to take the 3:45 p.m. Trans-Canada flight from LaGuardia to Toronto. His plane was sched-uled to arrive at 6:00 p.m. but was delayed for several hours. Meanwhile, detectives Prendergast and Looram had boarded New York Central Rail-way's Empire Express passenger train—the round-trip fare was $19.95 in coach and $32.00 for a more-comfortable Pullman or sleeper car—for the twelve-hour trip north to Ontario. It was close to 10:00 p.m. before Loehr finally made it to Toronto police headquarters. Prendergast and Looram did not arrive until 8:00 a.m. the next morning, October 26, and they did not see Lonergan until later that day.

There were questions raised about the Toronto police's treatment of Lonergan and the alleged violation of his legal rights. Michael Doyle, a Toronto lawyer and a childhood friend of Lonergan, testified many years later that he had been asked by Lonergan's uncle, Joseph Lonergan, to represent Wayne. Doyle stated that he had telephoned Police Chief John Chisholm and informed him of this. Yet when Doyle showed up at the station, the constables at the desk claimed they did not know who he was and inexplicably had no information about Lonergan. Doyle contacted Chisholm again, who apologized and told the lawyer to come back the next day. When he returned on Tuesday, October 26, the chief advised him that he could not see Lonergan because the New York police were officially in charge of the case and of Lonergan. Twenty years later, Doyle argued that if he had been allowed to speak with Lonergan, he might have prevented him from signing an extradition waiver permitting the New York authorities to bring him back to Manhattan.

Another Toronto lawyer, Lionel Davis, wrote a scathing letter about Lonergan's treatment to the *Globe and Mail,* which was referenced in the *New York Times* on October 26. Davis was equally outraged by how Lonergan's rights had been ostensibly trampled. He said the procedure followed by the Toronto police was "most astonishing." It was alleged that Lonergan was questioned nearly nonstop for two days—which was not quite accurate—by Toronto and New York detectives, yet was never brought before a magistrate. As Davis asserted, the police "are not allowed to hold someone for 'the inquisitorial' process euphemistically called 'questioning.' It seems to me the procedure adopted by the police with the acquiescence of the local Crown [provincial government] officials required the attention of the Attorney General."

Frederick Malone, an assistant Ontario Crown attorney, refuted Davis's criticisms and stated that owing to the extradition warrant, Toronto police could have detained Lonergan "indefinitely." Davis disagreed with that assertion as well. "How can anyone pretend that [Lonergan's treatment] is a legal or proper procedure in Canada, or that it was otherwise than disgraceful?" he asked. The *Globe and Mail*'s editors, too, found the actions of the city's police in this matter troubling, arguing that "there is no basis in law or justice, when a man is involved in a violation of the Criminal Code, for his being subjected to all sorts of examination before appearing in court."

〜〜

John Loehr did not address the legalities of the Toronto police's conduct or the extradition warrant, yet he later denied that Lonergan had asked to consult with a lawyer. By 10:00 p.m. on Monday night, Lonergan was tired and hungry, though he had been given sandwiches and had water to drink. Chain-smoking cigarettes, he was fairly calm as Loehr began interrogating him. In the room, too, was Detective Harris.

"I suppose you want to know why you're being held," said Loehr as he sat down at a table opposite Lonergan. "Is there anything you want to tell us?"

"I cannot think of anything to say," stated Lonergan, who decades later described Loehr as "a pretty convincing guy [with a] real honest face."

"Do you want to answer my questions?" Loehr asked.

"I don't know," replied Lonergan.

"Are you willing to tell me the truth about this murder of your wife Patricia?"

"Yes, but I don't know whether I should or not. I have been sitting around all day."

Loehr asked Lonergan if he had been treated fairly by the Toronto police, and he said he had been. Lonergan wanted to know if Loehr planned to charge him with Patricia's murder.

"Is that the idea?" he asked.

"That is about it," said Loehr. "You are going to have a chance to make a clean breast of it."

For a few more minutes, the two men went back and forth as Lonergan contemplated whether or not it would be smart for him to cooperate. He feared that he might "say something stupid." Loehr assured him, as any prosecutor would have, that he did not believe he was a "stupid young man," and was certain Lonergan would be able to avoid "stupid answers." He did, however, warn Lonergan that anything he did tell him could be used against him in a future legal proceeding. Lonergan said he understood this and would answer his questions.

Loehr began with questions about Lonergan's life in Toronto—how he came to move to New York and marry Patricia and why the couple had separated. Lonergan denied that he and Patricia had had "violent quarrels." He described their arguments as "just the ordinary differences between man and wife."

"Nothing unusual?" asked Loehr.

"No," replied Lonergan.

"Did anything happen in the summer of 1943 between you and Patricia— that is, this last summer?" Loehr asked.

"Yes, we were separated," said Lonergan.

"When were you separated?"

"About the end of June or beginning of July."

"Was there any single incident which caused this?"

"Nothing in particular; it was a combination of things."

"Will you tell us what they were?"

"Nothing at all. I became tired of going out during this summer and I introduced her to this fellow I met who took her out all the time."

"Who is this man?"

"A man named Krusi."

This was Tim Krusi, who was attached to the American Field Service. He was an ambulance driver, who had been wounded. Krusi later served in North Africa and the Middle East. Whether Krusi was simply Patricia's platonic friend who enjoyed escorting her to clubs or whether he and Patricia had an intimate relationship is unknown. Yet, considering the conservative attitudes and customs of the day, it was highly unusual for a 1940s husband to set up his wife with another man who would take her out on the town. Later Krusi's name came up at Lonergan's trial, but because he was in India, he was never interviewed by either the DA's office or Lonergan's defense attorney.

After a series of questions about Lonergan enlisting in the RCAF, Loehr asked him if he was subject to the draft by the US Armed Services.

"Yes, I was classified as 4-F," said Lonergan.

"For what reasons?" Loehr asked.

"Moral reasons," replied Lonergan.

"Was it for perversion—homosexual acts?" asked Loehr.

"Yes," said Lonergan.

"Did you ever have convictions?" asked Loehr.

"No."

"Then why were you classed as 4-F?"

"I volunteered the information."

"When was that classification—a recent date?"

"The summer of 1941 or 1942. Fall of 1941, I think." [In fact, it was January 1942.]

"In spite of that you were able to have marital relations with Patricia?"

"Yes."

Lonergan then made the dubious claim that he and Patricia had had sex during his first visit to New York as a member of the RCAF, in early October.

<hr />

The interrogation session continued for about two hours. Lonergan related the story of his New York City weekend and the assortment of people he saw—among them, Sylvia French and Marcella D'Arnoux, John Harjes, Elizabeth Black, and his son, Billy—and the details of his date with Jean Murphy Jaburg. Loehr probed Lonergan's sexuality further. He wanted to know if when he stayed at Harjes's the night of October 22, when Harjes was also there, whether the two of them slept in the same bed.

"No. Another bedroom," said Lonergan, not wincing at the question or the implied accusation.

Lonergan then volunteered information about picking up a US service-man, who he identified initially as "Murray Wooster," after he had said good night to Murphy Jaburg (who he said he kissed "several times").

"Then what happened?" Loehr asked.

"I just kept talking to him," replied Lonergan.

"What did you say to him?"

Lonergan explained that he had offered this soldier a place to stay for the night.

"Did you contemplate an act of perversion—a homosexual act?" Loehr asked.

"I vaguely thought about it," said Lonergan.

"Did he go with you?"

"Yes."

Lonergan told how he and "this so-called Murray," as Loehr described him, had drinks in Harjes's apartment, talked, and then went upstairs to the bedrooms.

"Did you each have a bed?" Loehr asked.

"Yes."

"Did you stay in your bed?"

"No, after a while I climbed into the other bed with him," said Lonergan.

"What did you do?"

"Nothing much. A few things."

"Acts of perversion?"

"Yes."

"Was the soldier willing?"

"Not too willing."

Lonergan added that when he awoke, he found the soldier had left and discovered that his watch and uniform had been stolen—but not his money or plane ticket.

"Do you expect us to believe that?" Loehr asked.

"I wouldn't."

"You are serious?"

"I certainly am."

"Why would anyone want your uniform?" Loehr asked, posing a question that Lonergan never properly answered, then or for the rest of his days.

"I don't know," he said. "The only thing I could think of was that I would have to stay inside until I got some clothes."

———

As Loehr digested the improbable—and astonishing—details of Lonergan's alleged "acts of perversion," Detective Harris briefly took over the questioning. Like a surgeon methodically searching to find the source of a patient's bleeding, Harris pressed Lonergan for more information about his relationship with Patricia and the false statements he was sure Lonergan had made.

"Is it not a fact that both you and your wife had been living abnormal lives and that you had violent disagreements?" Harris asked.

"We never had a violent disagreement," insisted Lonergan.

"Did you always take everything in a cold manner?" Harris asked.

"I suppose so," said Lonergan.

"You thought badly about your wife telling you to get out?" asked Harris.

"I don't know about that," said Lonergan.

"But she had told you something that hurt you?" the detective asked.

"Yes," Lonergan replied.

"It is natural to assume that ever since this happened it has been smoldering in your mind. It became an obsession, and you wanted to get back on good terms with your wife?" Harris asked.

"I was on good terms with her," insisted Lonergan.

"But you wanted to get back there, not only on friendly terms, but the full status of man and wife?" Harris asked.

"I had no intention of doing that after I was in the Air Force and found I could not live a normal life," said Lonergan.

"Did you have natural relationships with your wife?" Harris asked.

Lonergan said they did.

"Did you ever sicken your wife of it?"

Lonergan shook his head.

"Did she ever refuse you?"

"Yes, a couple of times," replied Lonergan.

"Is it a fact that she refused you last Sunday morning and this is what led to trouble?" Harris continued.

Lonergan shook his head. "No."

"Is it a fact that she would not have anything to do with you and that led to the disagreement? That is known to the police and the District Attorney now," said Harris.

"I don't know that," declared Lonergan.

"This is what led to the disagreement?"

"I don't know that."

"You know that when you went to the apartment, your wife would likely be in bed, sleeping, and it was not a reasonable time to be calling there?"

"I don't get it."

"You were out with some other woman Saturday night and not your wife?"

"She was busy somewhere else. I was talking to her. The housekeeper told me she was out for the evening. I did not go to the apartment until Sunday morning, with the package."

"Where did you take the Air Force uniform when you left Harjes's apartment?"

"I did not take any uniform away. My uniform was stolen."

"Suppose I say you were seen carrying it away in a bundle?"

"I don't know anything about that."

"Your wife was in a fortunate position to make life easy for you?"

Lonergan said nothing.

"You were jealous of her affections and you went to New York to try and effect a reconciliation," said Harris.

"No, I realized there was not much point in that."

Harris then got to the crux of the matter.

"It is a fact that your wife was murdered on the day you were in New York?" the detective asked.

"It is very strange," Lonergan agreed.

"The very day you were in New York and she is murdered, and nobody had a better reason for doing it than you?" said Harris.

"What is the motive?" Lonergan snapped back.

"When you went to New York on the previous occasion, you said it was because of a telegram you received saying your wife was ill. Who do you think sent the telegram?"

"I don't know."

"There would be a record of who sent it?"

"If there is a record of who sent it?" Lonergan asked.

"No telegram is taken without the name and address of the sender," explained Harris.

"I don't know anything about that."

"Where did you get the money at that time to fly here?"

"I had the money here."

Harris stepped aside and Loehr resumed the questioning.

"Do you know you were seen going into Patricia's residence on Sunday morning?" said Loehr.

This was not true, but lying to a suspect in an attempt to trap him is a well-tested interrogation technique. Loehr had not yet confirmed that Patricia had been killed between 9:00 and 9:30 a.m. on Sunday. Up to this point, Lonergan had only admitted that he had dropped off the toy elephant for Billy at approximately 12:30 p.m. Loehr's questions suggested wrongly that Patricia had been murdered when Lonergan had stopped by with the toy. His timeline was incorrect, but he was trying to place Lonergan at the scene.

"I don't know that," said Lonergan, not taking the bait.

"You rode there in a taxi?"

"Yes," said Lonergan, referring to when he stopped by with the toy.

"In uniform?" asked Loehr.

"No," said Lonergan; again, he meant when he had stopped by at 12:30 p.m.

"How long were you there?"

"Just a few minutes."

"Suppose I say you were to stay much longer," said Loehr.

"I would say no."

Here Lonergan was telling the truth about the second time he was at the residence that Sunday—at least, according to his later confession to the murder, which placed him there the first time at 9:00 a.m.

"Why won't you tell us the truth?" Loehr implored him.

"That is the truth." And technically, it was.

"You know it isn't?"

"I know it is," Lonergan said more firmly.

Next, Loehr inquired further about Lonergan's interactions with Dr. Isidore Michel.

"Is he your personal physician?" Loehr asked.

"No," replied Lonergan.

"Were you ever treated by him?"

"Yes, for an infection."

"Venereal disease?"

"He said it was gonorrhea, but I went to another doctor, and he said it was an infection that resembled gonorrhea."

Though he never elaborated, he likely was referring to non-specific urethritis, though it was not understood as clearly as it is at the present time.

Loehr also asked him about his attempt to secure arsenic from Dr. Michel, with the intent of selling the poison to someone he knew for $100.

"This is a pretty far-fetched story," remarked Loehr, "and you know it is not the truth."

"No, I don't know that," said Lonergan.

"You really want us to believe this story?" asked Loehr.

Lonergan said he did.

"Who else do you think could have murdered your wife?" asked Loehr.

"I cannot think of anyone," replied Lonergan.

"You were thwarted in your efforts of reconciliation with your wife?" asked Loehr.

"I wouldn't say this," said Lonergan.

"She had provided you with money?" asked Loehr.

"No," said Lonergan.

"She had been paying your bills?" Loehr asked again.

Lonergan shook his head again.

"How about that bill of ninety dollars for silk shirts?" asked Loehr.

"She might have paid that," said Lonergan.

Loehr finally delved further into Lonergan's sexual identity.

"Did you get any income from your acts of perversion?" asked Loehr.

"No, it usually cost me money," replied Lonergan.

After a few more queries about the arsenic, Loehr circled back to Lonergan's story of his encounter with Murray Wooster, the US serviceman. By the time this story was released to the press on October 27, the mysterious American soldier's name had been changed to Maurice Worcester, which was the name used in news articles on October 28.

"This man had a uniform," said Loehr. "Why did he want yours?"

"This is what I could not figure out," admitted Lonergan.

"What particular acts of perversion did you commit with this man?"

"There are only two—both of them."

"You did that before you were married?"

"Yes."

"Did you get satisfaction out of living with your wife or any other women?"

"Well, a certain amount."

"Did you ever make love to your wife in any other manner but by natural intercourse?" (In other words, anal intercourse.)

"Yes."

"What was her reaction to this?"

"She did not like it and told me to do it somewhere else."

"Is there anything else you would like to tell us about this murder of your wife, Patricia?" Loehr asked.

"Nothing that I can think of," said Lonergan.

In the days, months, and years to come, Lonergan insisted that he had made up the story of meeting and being intimate with Maurice Worcester, the US soldier—that it was a "fabrication"—and perhaps it was. Yet, his decision to offer the authorities an alibi that centered around a homosexual liaison—as he had done a year earlier, to evade the US Army draft—was telling. It is not an exaggeration to say that it colored everything else that happened to Lonergan. It led to lurid headlines, which widely portrayed him as a twisted pervert, and unquestionably prejudiced the members of the jury against him—even after he vehemently denied the veracity of the story.

Loehr and Harris, who heard the tale first, were taken aback. No one knew what to make of it.

"The story was so revolting that even hardened police officers at Toronto headquarters were shocked," the *Journal-American* later reported. "A guilty man, I imagine, would not have offered us an alibi as degrading as this one," commented Harris in a press interview he gave two days later.

Informed via a telephone call about the missing uniform, the scratches on Lonergan's face, and the story about Maurice Worcester—which was not released to the press until late on October 27—Grumet and the police officials were convinced of Lonergan's involvement. They were so certain that they decided, impulsively in hindsight, not to wait until Lonergan was back in New York to rush to judgment.

"He is a very likely suspect," Deputy Chief Inspector Patrick Kenny told reporters on Monday night, as they milled around Grumet's office, located at 155 Leonard Street, around the corner from the Manhattan Criminal Courthouse on Center Street.

Grumet later told Lonergan that he thought the episode with Worcester was "fantastic," and, more significantly, that it was unlikely a male soldier would have scratched him in a fight. "A man would [have] punch[ed] him," he said. The implication was, of course, that a woman—namely, his wife Patricia—had scratched him in the course of a deadly struggle.

The Sex-Twisted Playboy with a Crew Cut and a Sneer

ON MONDAY EVENING, October 25, 1943, while John Loehr and Toronto and New York police officers continued to spar with Lonergan, detectives back in Manhattan had tracked down Jean Murphy Jaburg, who was brought in for questioning. She related the details of her weekend dates with Lonergan, adding that he had been wearing his air force uniform on Saturday night, but not on Sunday afternoon.

"When I asked him what happened to it," she continued, "he told me some American soldier stole it. I told him he should report it to the police." What about any scratches on Lonergan's face, she was asked. She said that she had not seen any, yet conceded that she might have missed them.

Murphy Jaburg was not happy then, or later, to be caught up in a murder investigation. "It's such a sordid thing," she remarked to reporters, "I don't want to be mixed up in it." She also told law officials that "Mr. Lonergan acted the perfect gentleman all the time." One thing was clear: A "sordid thing" or not, from the photograph that was published in the newspapers—of her leaving the DA's office on Monday night, smiling, waving, and looking radiant—she definitely reveled in the attention she was subjected to.

On his way to Toronto Police Department Station Number 3 on Claremont Street, west of downtown Toronto—a ten-minute drive from police head-quarters—in the early hours of Tuesday morning, Lonergan reiterated to a reporter who was waiting for him when he stepped out of the car that he was not involved in Patricia's murder. There were as yet no formal charges against him in New York. Detective Harris, however, got creative: To ensure that the

Toronto authorities could legally detain Lonergan overnight, they booked him on a charge of vagrancy. If the Toronto authorities crossed the line in their treatment of Lonergan, it was with this bogus act. Nor was it relevant, as Harris reported, that Lonergan did not question the charge. Given what he found himself in the middle of, it was doubtful that he would have challenged the police.

At about 9:00 a.m. the police provided Lonergan with more cigarettes and a hotel-style breakfast of half a grapefruit, cereal, bacon, eggs, and potatoes, and coffee. He ate much of the food, though did not finish the bacon and eggs, because he said he was not that hungry.

For the remainder of the morning, Lonergan dozed on and off. He asked Patrol Constable Ronald Harrison, who was watching him, for a newspaper, but the officer informed him that he could not give him one, as it had been declared by his superiors to be censored material.

"I guess I'm in a helluva spot," remarked Lonergan.

Constable Harrison did not respond to that comment, yet offered to provide him with a copy of *Life* magazine, which Lonergan happily accepted from him. At 12:30 p.m. Harrison brought Lonergan his lunch—soup, meat and vegetables, and dessert and coffee. Lonergan ate about half of each item.

In short, the accusations made later—that Lonergan was kept in a room and not fed for the thirty hours or so he was detained by the Toronto police—were false. Constable Harrison noted, too, that at no time during this period did Lonergan ever ask to speak with a lawyer. "Lonergan appeared to be rational," added Harrison in his official statement, "but I thought he was a 'pansy' [homosexual] from the way he spoke and acted."

Two hours later, Detective Harris arrived to speak with Lonergan. He was followed over the next sixty minutes by New York detectives Prendergast and Looram and deputy ADA Loehr. Lonergan was told about the revealing stories published in the New York newspapers that day: the extensive coverage of the murder of an "heiress," and that he had been identified as the prime suspect. More discussion followed, until Lonergan finally consented to Loehr's request to sign an extradition waiver—dictated over the telephone by a Crown attorney to Harris, which he typed out—and return to New York accompanied by Loehr, Prendergast, and Looram. It was the only way, Lonergan believed, that he could clear his name, attend Patricia's funeral, and see his son.

What Lonergan did not know was that Patricia's funeral was taking place that afternoon on a rainy, windy, and cold day in Manhattan. Lucille Burton, still in shock, had arranged for Patricia's body to be sent to the Frank E. Campbell Funeral Home at Madison and East 91st Street. At two o'clock, pallbearers (who were unidentified) carried the casket to a waiting hearse that transported Patricia the short distance to Temple Emanu-El. The service was conducted by Rabbi Nathan Perilman, who had known the Bernheimer and Burton families for several years. It was a small gathering at the synagogue. Patricia did have a lot of friends, but for a variety of reasons—possibly because of the way she died, and the fact that her husband was the prime suspect—many did not show up at her funeral. Following the service, the hearse and a few cars—"a pitiful procession," in the words of *Globe and Mail* columnist Jim Coleman, who was there—took her to her final resting place at the family's plot at the Salem Fields Cemetery in Brooklyn, where she was interred beside her grandfather Max Bernheimer, father William Burton, and uncle George Burton.

At the graveside, Rabbi Perilman, who had a reputation as an "eloquent speaker," recited the 91st Psalm, which begins with the words: "He who dwells in the shelter of the Most High will lodge in the shadow of the Almighty. I shall say of the Lord [that He is] my shelter and my fortress, my God in Whom I trust. . . . You will not fear the fright of night, the arrow that flies by day; Pestilence that prowls in darkness, destruction that ravages at noon." His words were comforting, although nonetheless ironic, since in the early hours of October 24, Patricia had experienced "the fright of night" and the "pestilence that prowls in darkness."

The mystery of why Jean Murphy Jaburg did not see the scratches on Lonergan's face was answered that same day. John Harjes returned to Grumet's office with more incriminating evidence against his friend. While tidying up at his residence, he had found a Max Factor Suntan No. 2 compact; it contained thick theatrical makeup. Harjes's first thought was that the compact must have belonged to his maid, Josephine Peeters, but she assured him that it was not her compact. Detectives next checked with Jean Murphy Jaburg; she told them that the compact was not hers either.

The police fanned out over the neighborhood and adjacent area and stopped at every pharmacy and store that sold makeup, asking druggists and clerks whether anyone had purchased this type of makeup recently. They finally got lucky when they entered Max Levinson's pharmacy at 1440 First Avenue, close to 75th Street. The fifty-five-year-old pharmacist told them that he did sell the Max Factor compact they showed him. More significantly, he remembered selling one on Sunday morning, October 24, to a man, for $1.50. He later testified that the person in question was indeed Wayne Lonergan, though as Perry rightly points out, Levinson also admitted that he had seen Lonergan's photograph in the newspaper. When Grumet was informed of the detectives' conversation with Levinson, he was fairly certain that Lonergan had purchased the makeup to cover up the scratches on his face before he had lunch with Murphy Jaburg.

———

Deputy ADA Loehr and detectives Prendergast and Looram took charge of Lonergan. Before he left the police station with them, he was permitted to speak to his uncle and aunt, Joseph and Gertrude Lonergan, and his sister, June Cummins, who worked as a secretary for the distiller Gooderham and Worts. After the family farewells, the four men boarded a train at Sunnyside Railroad Station on King Street West on Tuesday evening, for the overnight trip to New York.

Though Lonergan did not bring a suitcase with him, he did have the three bottles of brandy that he had purchased in New York. It's admittedly strange that when they first picked up Lonergan, the Toronto detectives would have allowed him to bring a bag with liquor in it, later returning it to him when they all drove to the railway station. Nonetheless, soon after the train pulled out, the detectives—it is unknown if Loehr partook of any drinking—were happy to share a few glasses of the brandy with him—a clear violation of NYPD procedure. Despite later suggestions to the contrary—that Lonergan was force-fed brandy in a devious plot to take advantage of him—this was the only liquor he or the detectives drank for the duration of the trip. And by all accounts, none of them became intoxicated.

The journey was not without its challenges. Nearly three hours into the trip, the train stopped at Fort Erie, Ontario, across the border from Buffalo. Canadian customs officers told Loehr, Prendergast, and Looram that Lonergan required a monetary declaration form. That took about an hour and a half to process. Then, once they arrived in Buffalo, there were further bureaucratic hurdles: American immigration officials informed them that Lonergan was classified as a "non-desirable immigrant." He was brought before a three-person panel, whose members permitted the detectives to take charge of him with the caveat that he was assisting "in the solution of a crime." The New York Police were to turn Lonergan over to the border authorities once they were done with him. The detectives agreed with the stipulation, but that never happened.

By the time the immigration panel had ended, the train to New York had already departed the Buffalo station. Loehr and the detectives had no choice but to spend the night in Buffalo and take an American Airlines flight to New York early in the afternoon on Wednesday (the one-way airfare was $16.35). They checked into the Statler Hotel (at $4.51 for the night), registering Lonergan under the name "William Maloney" to avoid any pesky reporters or anyone else seeking him out. Since the detectives, who roomed with Lonergan, feared he might flee, they handcuffed him to a bed. This was undeniably rough treatment for someone still not charged with any crime other than vagrancy. Loehr and the detectives denied later accusations made by Lonergan that they had promised him he would be able to attend Patricia's funeral (which was long over by then), physically abused him, or referred to him in a derogatory manner as a "homosexual."

Lonergan finally fell asleep at about 5:30 a.m., and woke up close to 11:00 a.m. The detectives provided him with a substantial breakfast—eggs, bacon, oatmeal, toast, and coffee—and at 2:20 p.m. they departed on the American Airlines flight from the Buffalo Airport, arriving at LaGuardia later that afternoon. A pack of news photographers greeted Lonergan as he was whisked away to Grumet's Lower Manhattan office.

In the hours before Lonergan first met Grumet face-to-face, Grumet and the police had confirmed what Lonergan had told Loehr in Toronto: that the Selective Service Board had designated Lonergan 4-F after he had declared himself to be a homosexual. This information, along with the encounter with Murray Wooster/Maurice Worcester—even if Grumet, Loehr, and the police suspected that this story was false—undoubtedly contributed to their negative bias against him, even if it was not overt. More damaging for Lonergan was the fact that Grumet revealed these particulars to the press, as was his right to do. But he did so with a disdainful attitude that hardly concealed his revulsion at Lonergan's perceived immorality.

Sure enough, by the next morning, Thursday, October 28, the portrait of Lonergan was solidified in the public eye as a dangerous "homosexual" and "pervert," with "indications" that he had "an abnormal psychological nature." While Meyer "Mike" Berger of the *New York Times* (who would win the Pulitzer Prize in 1950) was restrained in his references to homosexuality, the *Daily News* was decidedly not. Its front page had a large photograph of Lonergan arriving at LaGuardia with the scratches on his chin noticeable. The headline above the photo in large font declared: "Lonergan Alibi: Twisted Sex."

(The *New York Times* and several other newspapers initially got Lonergan's age wrong. In October 1943, he was twenty-five years old and would not be twenty-six until January 14, 1944. Yet at the time of the murder, many members of the press had decided he was already twenty-six, and then compounded this error by declaring him twenty-seven years old after his birthday.)

The unrelenting commentary zeroed in on the facts as the journalists and editors understood them: Within the "pattern" of the Lonergan case was "woven the purple threads of whispered vices whose details are unprintable," as the *Journal-American* editorialized two days later. This contributed to a wicked image of Lonergan as a sexual "degenerate" that he could never shake.

Citing research by psychiatrists, the *Journal-American* also pointed out that while Lonergan was married, he was not "physically abnormal"—even though in the view of "medical experts" his marital status did not make him any less objectionable. He was the worst "type" of "pervert": a "bisexual" who was "a degenerate in the moral sense," adding that "while he can be helped at times by psychoanalytical treatment, his real cure depends upon his own desire to behave normally. Such persons—both men and women—have nothing distinctive about their physical appearance or public behavior to set them apart. They are frequently very attractive to persons of the opposite sex. Included in this type are often married persons, of the so-called sophisticate set."

As Charles Kaiser notes in his 1997 study, *The Gay Metropolis*, within the approximate 650 words of this *Journal-American* article were the terms and phrases linking homosexuality with "vice," "damage," "social cancer," "monster," "unnatural," "moral leper," "pervert," "degenerate," "evil," "unscrupulous," "contemptuous of decent people," and "sinister." Before the last week of October was done, the *Journal-American* had labeled Lonergan "a degenerate killer"— "the sex-twisted . . . playboy with the crew cut hair and the easy sneer."

More-levelheaded journalists found this commentary over the top and were incredulous that the Lonergan case had pushed World War II into the background. "Murder has driven the war from the front pages of New York's newspapers," wrote the *Globe and Mail*'s Jim Coleman, who had traveled from Toronto to New York to cover the story. "Thirty thousand die in the bloodstained mud of Krivoi Rog; Americans, Britons, Canadians lie dying in the olive groves and on the dusty roads of Italy; thousands of Chinese starve to death, their crops razed by the invaders—but, in New York the newspapers are emblazoned with the story of a woman who was slain in her Beekman Hill apartment."

Wolcott Gibbs, the *New Yorker*'s drama critic—who also followed the machinations of newspaper coverage in his erstwhile "Wayward Press" column—offered the sharpest criticism in an opinion piece that appeared in the November 6 issue of the magazine. As it turned out, Gibbs lived with his wife, Elinor, and their two children, on East 51st Street, two doors down from where Patricia had resided, so he had a front-row seat to watch the chaos of the police investigation unfold in real time. He castigated the various newspapers for their descriptions of the murder scene based on what their police sources had told them, and in general, for seemingly exaggerating every aspect of Patricia and Wayne's lives. He did add, with some wit, that Jean Murphy Jaburg's remark about Lonergan's alleged intimacy with Maurice Worcester was a "fairy story" that was "to be regarded as double-entendre."

Arriving at the district attorney's office on Wednesday, October 27, at five o'clock in the afternoon, Lonergan was taken to room 608, where the next phase of his interrogation was to continue for twelve more hours. He was given food during this period, yet was unable to rest or sleep. Lonergan was later to declare that he was physically abused by New York detectives, who also threatened him with their pistols. But in court and under oath, the detectives, as well as Grumet and Loehr, vehemently denied that any member of the police department or DA's office had touched Lonergan or waved a gun in his face. Grumet maintained that he never showed Lonergan a photograph of Patricia after she was murdered or referred to Lonergan as a "son-of-a-bitch," as Lonergan charged (though Captain William Mahoney admitted that he had used this offensive term when he questioned Lonergan). Nor did Grumet refuse Lonergan's request to speak to a lawyer—for the simple reason that he didn't ask to do so, according to Grumet and Loehr. Yet it was equally true, as Loehr's official report of the interrogation makes clear, that Grumet believed Lonergan was "the lowest type of human being," a "degenerate," and "100% rotten."

In the confines of the room, Loehr explained to Lonergan several times that his alibi about meeting the US soldier would not hold up in court and urged him, as he later testified, "to do at least one thing to save the situation and tell the truth and eliminate the story about Maurice Worcester and the homosexuality—because it was degrading." He told Lonergan about the intense public interest and warned him that by insisting his alibi was the truth, "he would proclaim to the world his own perverted and moral character." The press, Loehr said, "would have a field day, painting and embellishing the indecent story in lurid language for everyone in the country to read." To add to Lonergan's discomfort, he showed him the various news reports and feature articles already published that referred to his bisexuality, homosexuality, and perverted lifestyle. Still, Lonergan refused to alter his story or admit that he had killed Patricia.

Later that morning, Loehr spoke to Lonergan about the fact that they both had young sons, and said that he could not understand how Lonergan could permit Billy "to be disgraced by telling the world this shameful story." He also tried to appeal to Lonergan as a fellow Catholic, suggesting that Lonergan could not have attended Catholic School in Toronto "without absorbing some sense of what is decent and right."

The tale about Maurice Worcester took another turn when at one o'clock Thursday afternoon, "a tall, bespectacled man" (as the *New York Times* described him) named Maurice Worcester showed up at the DA's office. He was forty-four, had been discharged honorably from the army in South Carolina, and now lived with his wife and three children in New York City. He was employed in Bridgeport, Connecticut, across the Long Island Sound at a plant, one of several in the city which had been awarded lucrative contracts by the federal department of defense. When his name had been noted in newspaper stories that morning about the Lonergan case, his fellow employees had razzed him about being a homosexual.

"I want to clear my name," he told reporters. "I have an unusual name. I don't know whether this man picked it out of thin air, but I want the thing cleared up. I don't associate with Lonergan's type and never did."

Lonergan was present in the room where Worcester was speaking. He did not look up or show any sign that he recognized Worcester.

"Do you know this man?" Grumet asked Lonergan, pointing at Worcester. Lonergan said nothing.

"Have you seen this man before?" Grumet asked again.

After a long pause, Lonergan said, "No."

Worcester was then led from the room.

Of course, the possibility existed that there were other former soldiers named "Maurice Worcester" or the soldier Lonergan claimed he encountered had given him a fake name—at least, that's what Lonergan's argument was for the moment.

— —

The end of this part of Lonergan's ordeal was near. Grumet, Loehr, the detectives, and other police officials continued to pressure him to tell them the truth; to tell them that he had murdered his wife. For another three hours or so, he resisted, offering denial after denial of any involvement or culpability. At long last, exhausted and worn out from the past three days, he agreed to their demands.

Two decades later, Lonergan was adamant that in a private moment, Loehr had offered him a plea deal: If Lonergan confessed to murdering Patricia, providing the authorities with the specific and unvarnished details of what had transpired that Sunday morning, then he would be found guilty of manslaughter, with a maximum ten-year jail sentence. The trouble was, this arrangement was a figment of Lonergan's vivid imagination and reflected his desperate state of mind and his penchant for lying (this alleged plea deal was later advanced by his defense attorney as well during Lonergan's trial). Time and time again, Loehr unequivocally stated—and was supported by Grumet—that he made no such deal with Lonergan, nor was there a document, scribbled or typed, to back up this claim. Besides, if any deal had been made, it would have come from Grumet, the senior lawyer, not Loehr. Justice Gerald Loehr, John Loehr's son, does not believe his father ever would have made Lonergan such an offer.

Lonergan and Loehr did share a private moment together just before the confession was made. Grumet and the other police officials had all left the room. Loehr took notes as the two of them talked.

"What do you want to say, Wayne?" Loehr asked him.

"Suppose I just say I'm guilty and have it over with? Can I do that?" asked Lonergan.

"Why do you want to do it that way?" asked Loehr.

"I don't want the thing to go to court," said Lonergan.

"Well, if you plead guilty, that would have to be in court. That's the only way it can be done; you have to plead guilty before a judge."

"You mean I can't just say I did it and let that be the end of it, here, in this office?"

"No. A judge would have to sentence you for the crime. Sentencing is done only in court. The district attorney's office has no power to do that, to sentence anyone."

"I don't care what happens to me."

"Even the electric chair? You must care about that?"

"Anything, I don't care, as long as I don't have to tell all about how I did it and what I've been."

"For your own good, you should tell me exactly how you did it. Possibly it might be something less than first-degree murder, and then you wouldn't have to go to the chair."

Loehr then explained that he would call in a stenographer who would take down Lonergan's statement, and the legal process—a grand jury, official indictment, an appearance in court to plead guilty, and sentencing—would follow. However, Loehr also told him that if he should be indicted for first-degree murder, a guilty plea was not permitted under New York state law, and he would have to stand trial.

"You know better than I do what kind of act you committed," Loehr said. "Your wife and you were the only ones in the room. As far as I know, from the physical evidence at the scene, it could have been murder, either degree, or manslaughter in the first degree. Your story is the only one thing which can clear that up because there was no one else present."

Lonergan contemplated that for a moment and then got to what was truly troubling him. "Well, suppose I have to go to trial, will you bring out all this about what I am, about my morals?"

"Listen, Wayne," said Loehr, "all the People would prove is this: We prove the death of your wife by the testimony of the medical examiner, by the testimony of the first ones on the scene, and then we get your statement into evidence to show how the death was accomplished. We wouldn't have to introduce any evidence of your bad character. It wouldn't be admissible anyway on the People's case."

Loehr added, however, that if Lonergan himself testified, then his moral character might well become an issue in the cross-examination.

"I don't think I'd take the stand," said Lonergan.

Loehr was being honest, but it was impossible for Lonergan's moral character not to be part of the trial—and the press made sure of that, in any event. At the same time, assuming Loehr's handwritten notes of this conversation are accurate—and there is no reason to suspect that they were not—the question thus became whether the confession Lonergan ultimately made on October 28, 1943, was coerced. That issue was to be addressed at his subsequent trial, and at an appeal that was launched on his behalf in 1965.

Notwithstanding these legalities, his confession was to emerge as the one piece of hard evidence the prosecution possessed to convince the jury of his guilt. Yes, on October 28, Lonergan was tired and had been interrogated almost nonstop for more than fifty hours (though he had slept on the stop in Buffalo). But the transcript of his discussion with Loehr reveals Lonergan's calm demeanor, and that of a man who had something to get off his chest. Thus, it would be difficult to conclude, as his defense lawyer tried so hard to prove, that Lonergan was coerced into telling what happened in his wife's bedroom on Sunday morning, October 24.

At approximately 2:00 p.m., Grumet summoned his young stenographer, Henry Edward Vaccaro, into the interrogation room. Besides Grumet, present, too, were Loehr and detectives Prendergast and Looram. Loehr then explained to Lonergan that he, Lonergan, could decide who would be in the room when he offered his admission. Loehr said that he understood Lonergan did not care much for Grumet, yet he urged him to permit Grumet to remain, because as the ADA in charge of homicide, it would be up to Grumet to determine the charges against Lonergan. Without much hesitation, Lonergan consented to Grumet, Loehr, and the detectives being present.

Lonergan had one more request: that nothing about perversion be included in the confession. Loehr quickly agreed that perversion would not be mentioned, nor, he stated, was the DA's office interested in publicizing this aspect of the case. (This was not quite true, since the subject would come up later during the trial, leading to another round of sensational press headlines.)

A tray of sandwiches and pie was brought in, and Lonergan and Loehr both had some food. As they ate, they also chatted, and Loehr asked Lonergan again about the Maurice Worcester story. Lonergan dismissed it as a lot of "crap."

His appetite satisfied, Lonergan lit a cigarette, while the detectives, Loehr, and Grumet left the room. As Vaccaro waited for them to return, he and Lonergan chatted about the RCAF and the war. Fifteen minutes later, the two attorneys and Looram entered, but Prendergast did not. Grumet said the detective had been delayed, but that another detective by the last name of Shields could take his place until he got there. Lonergan was fine with that.

Finally, at 2:45 p.m., Vaccaro ready with his steno machine, Loehr began the questioning of Wayne Lonergan.

Nothing But the Truth

JOHN LOEHR CLEARED his throat and looked directly at Lonergan. "Are you prepared to tell me the truth, the whole truth, and nothing but the truth about [the death of Patricia Burton Lonergan]?" he asked.

"Yes," Lonergan replied. His voice was calm. He showed no outward signs of distress or intimidation.

Loehr reminded him that anything he said could be used against him in future legal proceedings. Lonergan said he understood.

"Notwithstanding that, your understanding about it, my warning to you, you are still willing to tell us the truth?" Loehr asked.

"Yes," said Lonergan.

"As you told me a short while ago?"

"Yes. Can I put in the provision about no publicity?"

"Yes, you can," replied Loehr. "How would you state that? I will state it for you. Do I understand you, wait a minute, then it will be on the written record; you wouldn't want that, the fact that you had to get a provision about it. Off the record."

"Nothing off the record," interjected Grumet.

"Do you want any provision or not?" asked Loehr a second time.

"Well, I will take your word for it."

In light of later accusations that he was berated, beaten, and coerced into confessing his crime, the official transcript consistently shows that Lonergan was at ease and seemingly comfortable with what was taking place. He was not confused, misled, being told what to say, or fearful of either Loehr or Grumet; in fact, it was just the opposite. He trusted Loehr to protect his interests. In retrospect, this was a questionable, even foolish, way to act for anyone suspected of committing a felony, yet nevertheless indicative of Lonergan's demeanor and frame of mind. He was not a suspect deprived of food and water, who was being unduly pressured to offer a false confession. As the interrogation proceeded, and as is recorded in the transcript, Loehr offered him water on several occasions, which he politely refused.

The question-and-answer session first covered the details of his enlistment in the RCAF, marriage to Patricia, and their recent separation, and then turned to the events of October 24, 1943.

This is what transpired according to Lonergan: Wearing his uniform, which had not been stolen Saturday night by Maurice Worcester or anyone else, Lonergan left Harjes's apartment on East 79th Street around 8:30 a.m. on Sunday morning and walked to Patricia's apartment on East 51st Street, arriving about thirty minutes later. Emile Peeters, Harjes's butler, was not yet on duty, and thus did not see him leave or later return to the apartment.

The main entrance to Patricia's brownstone was open. He walked in through the vestibule and then knocked on the locked door to Patricia's bedroom. A moment passed before she opened it. According to Lonergan, she was nearly naked. She invited him in and then lay down on her bed, half covering herself with a sheet. He removed his hat and gloves and placed them on the side table beside the candlesticks. He took a cigarette out and lit it; she did the same.

Their conversation immediately became acrimonious, and the tension between them was palpable. He chided her for her excessive nightclubbing.

Someone had told him, he said, that she was the "belle of the El Morocco," adding scornfully that she was "behaving like a drunken sailor" and a "tart."

Still lying on her bed, she told him sharply that "it's none of your business," called him a "son-of-a bitch" and "dirty bastard," and castigated him that his own behavior was hardly exemplary.

"What are you doing here?" she demanded to know, putting her cigarette in the ashtray beside her bed.

"I understand you're going to the country and I wanted to talk to you before you left, to tell you to take it easy for a while," he replied.

She asked him what he was doing that day, and he told her that he was going to have lunch with a "very pretty girl"—this, despite the fact that Jean Murphy Jaburg had not yet confirmed the Plaza Hotel luncheon date. Patricia became angry, and from Lonergan's less-than-objective perspective, she acted needy and jealous.

"Why don't you come to lunch with me?" she purportedly asked him. When he said he could not break a (tentative) date, she allegedly became "furious." She said that it "annoyed" her if "she didn't have control of every man."

Given that Patricia had no desire to see Lonergan that weekend, or by all accounts, wanted nothing much to do with him, there is a high probability that this part of their conversation was a lie. Lonergan only included this in his story to make her appear more volatile than he was.

They argued for another minute or two before Patricia ordered him to leave. When he did not move quickly enough, she sat up on the bed and pushed him.

"Get the hell out of here," she said.

He walked over and picked up his gloves and hat on the small table.

"Stay out of here," she screamed at him. "Don't ever come back again, you bastard, and you're not going to see the baby again either!"

That threat was too much for Lonergan and pushed him over the edge. Something snapped inside of him. He grabbed one of the candlesticks with his right hand, rushed toward her, and struck her on the side of her head with it. The blow was hard enough to break her skin and leave a deep gash in her head, but not sufficient to knock her unconscious.

"Good God, what have you done?" she exclaimed in disbelief.

Patricia might have cried out for help from Elizabeth Black, who she knew was in the apartment, yet she did not (a relevant point raised by Hamilton Darby Perry). Perhaps she was disoriented, or, more likely, trying desperately to stop Lonergan from attacking her. And if she had stopped to ask herself at the moment whether she believed Wayne would kill her, she would have answered "no." He had many character flaws, but she never would have believed that he was deranged enough to murder her.

Except he was.

Neither Patricia nor Wayne, who was now in an uncontrolled rage, knew that on the other side of the bedroom door, listening to this screaming and tragic confrontation, was Annaliese Schonberg, the governess for the Ray family who lived in the upstairs duplex suite. The time frame for the heated exchange and the murder, as she later testified—although not exactly as Lonergan described it—was correct.

The candlestick had broken into pieces. His anger exponentially increased. He reached for the second one on the table and hit her again in the head, this time harder. Bleeding, she jumped out of the bed, swearing at him. He ran toward her and, facing her, grabbed her from behind, tightly around her neck. She desperately struggled to get free of him, kicking him and scratching his face (causing the scratches that were still on his chin and neck as he spoke to Loehr). He was too strong for Patricia to fight him off. He choked her with both of his hands for what he estimated was three minutes. She finally stopped moving; he released his grip and stepped back.

Patricia Burton Lonergan, the twenty-two-year-old mother of his son, was dead.

"I was horrified at this mess of blood all over the place," Lonergan told Loehr. He realized that there was blood on his gloves and the front of his uniform. He went into her bathroom and wet a towel, first wiping the blood oozing from where she had scratched him, and then trying to wipe Patricia's blood off of his air force tunic. But nothing he did removed it.

He left her lying on the bed naked and fled the apartment, stuffing the wet and blood-soaked towel in his pocket. In a panic and fearing that he might be seen, he took a circuitous route back to Harjes's residence. He recalled passing "many people," but none seemed to notice the streaks of blood on his uniform.

No doubt Lonergan had an adrenaline rush from what he had done. Walking briskly on East 51st Street, he headed in the opposite direction, toward First Avenue. He turned north and continued four blocks until he reached 55th Street, and then backtracked to Second Avenue. At 57th Street, he walked west to Third Avenue, all the way to 67th Street, and then reached Lexington Avenue. At 71st Street, he walked back to Third Avenue up to 78th Street and then back to Lexington and 79th Street, close to Harjes's apartment building. It was about 10:00 a.m. (Periodically stopping for red lights and traffic—which early on a Sunday morning, Lonergan likely did not do—the author walked this route in thirty-six minutes.)

Once Lonergan was in Harjes's suite, he took a sedative and removed his uniform. He tried again to clean it off, but the stains were too deep and it was impossible. He took out his blue duffel bag and attempted to put the uniform inside of it; the bag was too small. He ran to Harjes's bedroom, found a pair of scissors, and cut up the uniform into small strips. He placed those in his bag together with the towels, his shirt, tie, hat, gloves, trousers, socks, and wristwatch; the leather strap of the watch also had some blood on it. In order to add weight, he took an iron dumbbell that Harjes had, one of four in the apartment, and placed it inside the bag, too, with $100 of cash he had in his pocket. Either he forgot that the money was in the bag, or he needed to get rid of it in order to make his concocted story about the soldier—which presumably he had already worked out in his head—robbing him believable.

He bathed and washed any blood that might have been in his hair or on other parts of his body and dressed in the clothes that he took from Harjes's closet, along with a pair of cuff links for the shirt (that he was still wearing at the DA's office). Next, he ate the "hearty breakfast" prepared for him by Emile Peeters. With the duffel bag in hand, he left the apartment and walked on East 79th, in the direction of First Avenue and the East River.

What he did not know then was that he was seen leaving the building and lugging the duffel bag by a florist named Ruth Forster, who had been introduced to Lonergan by Harjes a year earlier. She was walking her dog from Park Avenue, returning to her shop (and second-floor apartment) at 142 East 79th Street at Lexington Avenue. Forster, who later testified at Lonergan's trial, watched as he carried the duffel bag and headed in the direction of the East River. She lost sight of him after he crossed Third Avenue. In a subsequent police lineup, Forster positively identified Lonergan as the man she saw walking with the duffel bag.

As soon as Lonergan reached the pier, he climbed over the fence that had been erected to protect anyone trying to get too close to the river and flung the bag into the dark water. It floated on the tide and slowly sank. Turning around, he walked west on 79th Street and then to Max Levinson's drugstore at 1440 First Avenue, between 74th and 75th Streets, where he purchased the Max Factor pancake makeup. (In his confession, Lonergan stated that the drugstore was on Second Avenue and 74th Street, but he was mistaken. As far as can be determined, there was no drugstore near that intersection.) Returning to Harjes's apartment, he drank a beer given to him by the maid, Josephine Peeters (who felt Lonergan was nasty to her) and did his best to cover the scratches on his face and neck with the makeup.

His day then continued as if nothing untoward had occurred. He picked up the toy elephant from Sylvia French's apartment and confirmed his lunch date with Jean Murphy Jaburg at the Plaza Hotel, where he also later cashed a check for $25. He took a taxi back to Patricia's at about 12:30 p.m. and left the toy inside in the vestibule. He then met Murphy Jaburg and her young son for lunch and proceeded later to LaGuardia.

In his diligent effort to show inconsistencies in Lonergan's confession, Hamilton Darby Perry, in his 1972 book on the case, suggested it was not plausible that when Lonergan returned with the toy elephant—if he had indeed committed the murder—he did not try to make contact with Miss Black so that he could be seen doing so. This would have strengthened his plea of innocence. Perry had a point, though it was more likely that Lonergan was still in a state of panic and shock about what he had done. Knowing the bloody scene that lay behind the bedroom door, the last thing he would have wanted to do was linger in the vestibule of Patricia's apartment, chatting with the governess or seeing his son—who, as noted, he should have wanted to hand the toy to himself, as most fathers would have done. Yet Lonergan was not thinking straight, and as Murphy Jaburg pointed out, he was disheveled and ornery during their lunch date.

—◦—

At 3:40 p.m. there was a break in the interrogation. Lonergan was permitted to use the restroom and Grumet made a few telephone calls. When they reconvened, Grumet took over the questioning. He wanted to know more from Lonergan about his marriage, and specifically, how much money Patricia had given him on a regular basis.

"While you were living with your wife, did you receive from her a weekly or monthly allowance?" Grumet asked.

"No, not a specific amount," said Lonergan, which was not true.

"You mean there was no definite amount?"

"No definite amount," said Lonergan.

"But you did receive monies from her, from time to time?"

"Yes."

"And was that weekly or monthly, or some other way?"

"Some other way; no status."

"No definite time?"

"No."

"And would that be by way of check?"

"Yes."

"Can tell us how much, on average, she would give you?"

"She would generally give me seven hundred dollars at the beginning of the month."

"By check?"

"Yes."

"And what would you do with that money?" Grumet asked.

"I would pay the household bills out of it."

"And pay your own personal expenses out of that?"

'Yes."

Grumet did not challenge Lonergan's earlier assertion that Patricia did not regularly give him money, since it appeared from what he subsequently said that she did in fact provide him with a $700 check on the first of most months.

"Did you have a means of livelihood?" Grumet asked.

"No," replied Lonergan.

"She was a wealthy woman, was she not?"

"Yes."

"And you had no money of your own."

"No."

Grumet was a traditionalist, like many New Yorkers and Americans in the 1940s. Despite women's participation in the war effort as nurses, factory workers, journalists, and in noncombat positions in the armed forces, many men and women—but certainly not all—maintained that in a marriage, the husband was still the breadwinner. Grumet would have had nothing but disdain for someone like Lonergan who lived off of his wife's money.

He next asked Lonergan about Patricia's will and the fact that she had recently made their son the sole beneficiary.

"Do you know whether or not she stood to inherit any money?" Grumet asked.

"Yes, she did," replied Lonergan.

"How much money?"

"Seven million dollars."

"From whom?"

"From a trust fund of her grandfather's, on the death of her grandmother."

Grumet again went through the details of the murder with Lonergan, ensuring that he had not omitted anything, and that the version he had told Loehr was correct. He also wanted to know more about Dr. Michel and Lonergan's attempt to obtain arsenic and strychnine from him.

His final series of questions dealt with Lonergan's missing RCAF uniform.

"I call your attention to the fact that you state in [the note Lonergan left for Harjes] that you lost your uniform due to a slight case of mistaken trust; that, of course, is not true?" said Grumet.

"No," answered Lonergan.

"And the truth is that you got rid of your uniform as you have already told us?"

"Yes."

"And you got rid of it because of the bloodstains on it?"

"Yes."

"Have you told us the whole truth about this?" asked Grumet.

"Yes," said Lonergan.

Loehr interjected. "Freely and voluntarily?"

"Yes," replied Lonergan.

———

It was after five o'clock by the time Lonergan completed relating his version of the murder. Grumet and Loehr must have been pleased that the details of the narrative he provided them were believable—much more believable than the "cock and bull story," as Grumet had referred to it, of the homosexual encounter with the serviceman Maurice Worcester. Nonetheless, the perception of Lonergan as a "bisexual or homosexual pervert" persisted in the press, and in all probability tainted the jury pool—this, at any rate, is what Lonergan's defense lawyer, Edward Broderick, was to claim.

The "sexual twist can't aid Lonergan's case," a sagacious columnist for the *Daily News* observed. More astute was the prolific Sicilian-born American biographer Frances Winwar (born Francesca Vinciguerra). She later succinctly summed up the dilemma Lonergan faced about the Worcester story in a newspaper feature article entitled "Self-Portrait of Degradation": "True or invented, it has a ring of truth. If such a homosexual adventure did not take place that crucial night, at some time or other, it had occurred, with Lonergan either in the role of Lonergan or the soldier. . . . What is significant is the cunning of the mind that, to ward off suspicion of murder with this wages of death, advanced this shameful alibi, hoping, not implausibly, that the shocked public would accept it, and exonerate him of the killing."

On Friday, October 29, the *Daily News's* entire front page was taken up with a photograph of Lonergan below a large headline in capital letters: "Lonergan Confesses." Inside was the full story of how he had committed the crime based on information DA Hogan had given to the press. For good measure, the tabloid added in its feature about the "slim perverted killer" the statement that detectives had already matched fingerprints taken from the candleholders found at the crime scene to Lonergan's. This was pure fabrication.

The second phase of Lonergan's legal troubles now began.

He was arraigned in homicide court with Grumet charging him with "the brutal and unprovoked killing of his wife." A grand jury then heard the evidence against him, which included his confession, and supported an indictment of first-degree murder. Finally, looking like a deer in headlights—"his bloodshot eyes betrayed his weariness, induced by prolonged questioning," the Associated Press reporter noted—he was brought before Judge Jonah Goldstein in General Sessions Court.

According to what Lonergan later told Perry—still sticking to his story of Loehr promising him a manslaughter plea deal—he was shocked when he was formally charged with first-degree murder for killing Patricia, a crime for which execution by the electric chair was the severest sentence that could be imposed. Though he was not "destitute," as he informed Judge Goldstein, he nevertheless signed a pauper's oath and accepted a court-appointed lawyer. The judge ordered that he would be permitted to consult with his attorney and return to court in five days, at which time he was to offer a plea to the indictment. In the meantime, he was taken to the Tombs and locked in a cell.

Over the next several days, Grumet viewed the scene of the crime and police divers scoured the bottom of the East River, searching for Lonergan's duffel bag with his "bloodstained" uniform. Grappling irons were dropped at the 63rd Street pier and police boats cruised the waters back and forth from the area near 79th to 63rd Streets. Lonergan, who was said to have "rested well" in prison, was also interviewed by the Tombs resident psychiatrist, fifty-seven-year-old Dr. Perry Lichtenstein, who had examined just about every type of criminal and lunatic imaginable over a career that at that point spanned more than three decades. He declared Lonergan "sane," a preemptive move by Grumet to prevent Lonergan's lawyer from using an insanity defense plea.

A day later, on November 2, Patricia's will was filed in probate and the press immediately noted what Lonergan already knew: He had been deleted from the will, and her entire estate was left to their eighteen-month-old son, Billy. From Grumet's perspective, the fact that Lonergan was cut out of the will, coupled with Patricia's threat to not let him see Billy, was the double-edged motive he planned to use to convince a jury of Lonergan's guilt.

⚬⚬⚬

Lonergan had one lucky break. The General Sessions Court found three lawyers willing to defend him: Edward V. Broderick, a fifty-year-old seasoned attorney as chief counsel, with support from Millard H. Ellison and Abraham J. Halprin. Neither Ellison—sixty-five years old, and a staunch Republican who had acted as Thomas Dewey's campaign manager when he ran for district attorney in 1937—nor the younger Halprin, whose legal career up to then had been primarily involved with commercial matters, were to last in their second-chair appointed positions for long. This was solely owing to personality and legal strategy clashes they had with Broderick, a mercurial figure in New York legal circles. (Edward J. Reilly, the Brooklyn criminal attorney who had defended Bruno Hauptmann—who was convicted of kidnapping and murdering aviator Charles Lindbergh's young son—also offered his services to Lonergan.)

A bachelor, Broderick was a big man—"portly" was the adjective the press often used to describe him—who was rarely seen without a fat cigar protruding from his mouth. A stereotypical New Yorker, Broderick was brash, outspoken, had a volatile temper, was unafraid to challenge judges' rulings if he thought they were arbitrary, and a lawyer who put the fear of God into witnesses he was cross-examining. He was arrogant about his courtroom skills and prided himself on doing anything and everything legally possible to defend a client. In a career that had started shortly after he graduated from the Columbia Law School in 1915, he had represented thirty-seven men accused of murder. Of those, thirty-four were acquitted and three were found guilty of the lesser charge of manslaughter. He liked to point out to reporters that he "never had a client go to the electric chair."

Broderick also regarded it as a mark of distinction that he held the record in New York as the lawyer who had been cited the most times, four in all, for contempt of court—and one of the more-notable occasions was to occur at the end of Lonergan's trial. (This record would hold until his death in May 1957, at the age of sixty-four.) In 1927, a judge fined him $100 twice in the same day for disrespecting court rulings. Exactly twenty years later, another judge in another case deemed him guilty of "studied insolence and defiance" by "wilfully disobeying [the court's] lawful mandates." For this transgression, he was fined $200 and sentenced to five days in jail. But as with the other contempt charges, he talked his way out of trouble (in 1947, for instance, he was released from his cell in less than two hours).

His "shenanigans," as Grumet characterized them, were on display throughout the legal proceedings against Lonergan. The *New York Daly Mirror* columnist Thyra Samter Winslow was not one of his fans. "Broderick disappointed me. In appearance, anyhow," she wrote in late February 1944, after watching him in action in the courtroom. "He, of all the principals, seems miscast. His suit fitted badly. He has a double chin and a roll of fat at the back of his neck and the back view, especially, is a trifle plump. He has a thin, hard mouth; his eyes, a cold blue, have deep circles under them. His chin sticks out when he sits in thought—and juts out even more when he talks. His hair is sandy brown, grey at the temples, thinning a little, and [he has a] trifle of an Irish brogue, which sounds too good to be real."

A few days later, she followed this unkind portrait by penning an open letter to Broderick after a particularly nasty confrontation had erupted between Broderick and Grumet during the proceedings. "Dear Mr. B.," she wrote, "I do wish you'd learn to control your temper. Oh, I know how you love to rant about that you're being crucified. And that the Bernheimer millions are trying to disbar you. And that someone—or something—is trying to put an electric chair in the jury box. And screech invectives to the Assistant District Attorney. But dear Mr. Broderick, you're a big boy!" No doubt Broderick chuckled when he read that plea for decorum, but it was never his style to calm down. A winning defense required a lot of anger and indignation and that's exactly how he was going to keep Lonergan from the electric chair.

—

During one of Broderick's first meetings with Lonergan on November 3, Lonergan told him, as well as Ellison and Halprin, that "things are pretty well mixed up, but the truth has not been told." He also asked the attorneys, "What are my chances of an acquittal?" They did their best to reassure him.

The next day, at the appointed time the judge had set for Lonergan to offer a plea, Broderick won an eleven-day stay so that he and his client could consider the matter further. Grumet was livid—Broderick's tactics were continually to aggravate him throughout the duration of the trial—yet Judge George L. Donnellan granted the motion. "What difference do a few days make if the State's rights are not affected?" he asked Grumet. That done, Broderick permitted news photographers to snap more shots of Lonergan before he was taken back to his cell.

Eleven days passed and Broderick requested another week's delay. He also sought the court's permission for Lonergan to see Billy, who was being cared for by his grandmother, Lucille Burton. "I'm very anxious to see my baby," he commented to reporters. "My baby is everything to me." The journalists wondered if he liked the food at the Tombs. "Of course the food is not as good as what a fellow could get at the 21 Club," he told them coolly, "but it's not bad."

The following week, on Tuesday, November 22, Lonergan was briefly in court wearing another suit, one that had been pressed. Reporters noted the "worried" look on his face, compared to the "apathetic attitude" he had displayed up to that point. When asked what his plea was to the charge, he replied, "Not guilty." The visit with his young son was not granted, then or ever, by the court. And if it had been, Lucille would have fought it in any way open to her.

With the preliminary matters settled, it took until mid-January 1944 for the trial to be scheduled. It was set to start on Monday, January 31, with Judge John J. Freschi presiding. A list of 200 potential jurors, selected from a total of 680 people (with only five women among them), was soon presented by Grumet, to which Broderick had no objections. The district attorney's office did ask the Toronto police for more assistance in gathering for them any biographical material they could find about Lonergan—records pertaining to his education, juvenile delinquency, employment, and his alleged "immoral conduct" in Toronto. That assignment was completed over the next several weeks, and the results were forwarded to Loehr and Grumet in New York.

During this period, Lonergan lived day to day in the Tombs, barely tolerating the food, which was a lot worse than he had said it was. He looked forward to the regular exercise period he was permitted and frequent meetings with Broderick and the other lawyers. Broderick warned his client to be wary of who he spoke to in the prison yard, because the defense attorney said he had been told Grumet's office had an informer in the Tombs, another inmate, who reported everything Lonergan was saying and doing. Whether this was true or a result of Broderick's utter distrust for the prosecution is unknown. Nothing, however, was raised about an informer at the subsequent trial, and there is no documentation about any informers in the DA's files.

In the Hippodrome

JUDGE JOHN J. FRESCHI, a sixty-six-year-old veteran jurist and the son of Italian immigrants, had a reputation for being humble and patient. He was going to need all the humility and patience he could muster in the opening stages of Lonergan's murder trial in dealing with Edward Broderick and his court "shenanigans." Broderick, as the *Daily Mirror* so aptly noted, was a "scene stealer"; he had a knack for taking the focus off of clients like Lonergan and putting it on him. But if any judge in the state could handle Broderick, it was Freschi, who had been appointed to the General Sessions in 1931 by Franklin D. Roosevelt prior to the presidential election of 1932, while he was still the governor of New York State.

Freschi had been in the spotlight on other occasions. He had presided over an infamous kidnapping and murder case in 1938, in which a gang of four ex-convicts—including Demetrius Gula and Joseph Sacoda—had kidnapped and presumably murdered Arthur Fried of White Plains, northeast of New York City. Because Fried's body was never found, Gula and Sacoda were convicted of kidnapping only, yet they still received the death penalty under the recently passed Federal Kidnapping Act, or "Lindbergh Law," as it was called, due to the notoriety of the kidnapping and murder of aviator Charles Lindbergh's infant son in 1932.

Two years after the Gula and Sacoda case, Freschi handed gangster Louis "Lepke" Buchalter a thirty-year to life sentence on an extortion conviction. (In another trial held in Brooklyn in December 1941, Lepke was convicted of murder and received the death sentence; he was executed in March 1944.) It had been Freschi, too, who had agreed to the appointment of a lunacy commission to examine Robert Irwin in August 1938, and then accepted its report that Irwin was sane at the time he murdered Mary and Veronica Gedeon and Frank Byrnes.

As an attorney, Broderick was a lone wolf. Over the course of a few months his working relationship with Ellison and Halprin, the other two lawyers assigned to the Lonergan case, went from bad to worse. Broderick wanted Freschi to grant yet another postponement, and on January 24 requested a hearing on the matter. When the motion was discussed, the three lawyers presented a convincing enough argument that Freschi agreed to move the trial start date to February 14. That was acceptable to Ellison and Halprin, but not to Broderick, who wanted another month on top of that, which would have delayed the commencement of the trial to March 15. Freschi demanded to know the reason for this request. Broderick alluded to possible "European complications in this case," and "some occurrences in the Riviera." Freschi, who was as bewildered by this vague excuse as Ellison and Halprin, denied Broderick's request and set the trial date for February 14.

Within nine days, Ellison and Halprin had had enough; working with Broderick on Lonergan's defense proved impossible. Officially, Lonergan requested in a letter to the court that the order assigning him the three lawyers be vacated and that he be allowed to retain Broderick as his private counsel. Broderick was happy to comply. Despite unsubstantiated reports in the *Daily News* that Lonergan's legal fees, which could have run as high as $25,000, were allegedly being looked after by a shadowy Toronto "orchestra leader" or an unnamed "New York society woman," Lonergan was not paying Broderick a dime. The high-profile nature of the case appealed to Broderick's massive ego, and it was great publicity for future business. Once that was decided, Broderick asked for yet another delay, explaining to the court that he had made contact with a witness—the subject of the "European complications"—who could provide relevant information about the Lonergans' marriage.

The mysterious witness turned out to be John Lovelle Massena, a twenty-four-year-old seaman in the merchant marine and would-be actor, who went by the name Jack or "Tach" March. Newspaper reports noted that March was in the Panama Canal Zone working for the US war administration office. Broderick had revealed this fact in a motion he filed on February 11 for a delay of the trial to February 23, which Freschi ultimately granted. Broderick also requested that a government commissioner in Panama interview March.

As soon as Grumet had learned about March, he had his investigators track him down. Broderick had it wrong: March was not, nor had he ever been, in Panama; he was living at his home in the Village of Pelham in West-chester County, twenty-five miles away. He was not on active duty, and was instead performing in a new musical, *Follow the Girls*, which was then in rehearsal at the Adelphi Theatre on 57th Street.

March was also the tennis pro at the Pelham Country Club. He had been introduced to Lonergan after he had moved to New York City. In a letter he sent to Lonergan at the Tombs, March had written disparagingly about Patricia and her café society lifestyle, telling Lonergan about "how Patsy had neglected your child" with "all-night parties, loads of people shouting, while the child lay sleeping." She would, he added, "rush off afternoons and never return until the next day," which was a fairly accurate description of what she had done on Saturday, October 23. In the end, March was not cred-ible—Grumet's investigators also had learned that he had been charged with raping a seventeen-year-old girl in the summer of 1941, though the authori-ties had dropped the case after the grand jury had failed to indict him—and never was called by Broderick as a defense witness.

Coming to Patricia's defense, Grumet stated that Lonergan was "schem-ing to get his hands on the fortune of his dead wife," which, as it turned out, was true, though Lonergan did not attempt to do so until after the trial concluded. Broderick countered with his own accusation that Grumet had reneged on yet another deal in which Lonergan had agreed to plead guilty to second-degree murder. As with the claim about John Loehr offering a plea deal in exchange for Lonergan's confession, Grumet dismissed this lat-est accusation as having no foundation, as did Broderick's former co-counsel, Millard Ellison, who called it a "falsehood."

Broderick then threatened that "Mr. Grumet's veracity will be the subject of sustained attack at the trial," daring Grumet and Loehr to submit to a lie-detector test to prove that neither had offered plea deals to Lonergan. "If this continues," an angry Grumet declared, "I am going to ask that the mentality of Mr. Broderick be examined." This bickering and back-and-forth sniping between Broderick and Grumet tested Judge Freschi's seemingly limitless patience. He admonished both attorneys to cease turning the court into a "hippodrome" with "attacks on personalities and the creation of scenes."

———

The odds of Broderick heeding such a judicial directive were slim. His strat-egy was exactly the opposite: He aimed to push Grumet and Freschi as far as they could be pushed. Within forty-eight hours, Broderick filed two more motions, requesting the disclosure of two documents from the DA's office. He asked for a copy of the New York draft board's 4-F rejection of Lonergan—in which Lonergan declared himself to be a homosexual—and a copy of Dr. Milton Helpern's autopsy report. Since Helpern was an employee of the city of New York, the release of the autopsy results was governed by the city's charter and administrative code, which as of 1936 left it to the medical examiner and district attorney to determine what part, if any, of an autopsy report could be made public. So while Broderick's request seemed straightforward enough, it was not—and certainly not in New York State, which was long included at the top of the list of fourteen states with the most restrictive and one-sided pretrial discovery rules.

In 1944 (and earlier), New York defense attorneys like Broderick were at a decided disadvantage, a reality of the state's legal system which persisted for decades. As lawyer Robert Keith Beck explained in a 1972 journal article, "the steadfast rule in New York was that the accused had no right either to inspection or disclosure except in rare instances where, in the discretion of the court, it was necessary to prevent injustice."

Prosecutors were under no legal obligation to relinquish evidence of any kind to the defense—including autopsy reports, witness names and statements, grand jury testimony, and police reports—and could release such information as the trial proceeded, or not at all. Hence, for decades long before and well after Lonergan's trial, this legal reality had dire consequences, and on occasion led to prosecutorial misconduct, wrongful convictions, and convictions being overturned on appeal. It required a landmark Supreme Court decision in 1963, *Brady v. Maryland*; two versions of the New York State Legislature's Article 240 of the Criminal Procedure Law in 1971 and 1979; and a comprehensive criminal reform law passed in April 2019, to finally give New York defendants and their attorneys pretrial discovery rights that are enforceable.

Broderick and Lonergan were literally at the mercy of the court, the New York City Charter (with respect to obtaining the full autopsy report), and the DA's office for information. And Freschi had no reason, legal or otherwise, to assent to any discovery motions. Hence, on February 21, the judge followed the precedent of the day and denied both of Broderick's motions for the disclosure of Lonergan's military report and the medical examiner's full report—but Grumet consented to provide Broderick with a summary of the autopsy results.

To Broderick this was a pivotal moment in the case. He argued—without any hard evidence, other than Lonergan's speculations—that while the five-page, single-spaced, typed summary he had obtained confirmed the circumstances that led to Patricia's death as Lonergan described in his confession, the full report would have contradictory information proving his innocence.

Broderick was wrong in all respects, although he had no way of knowing this at the time (both documents are in the district attorney's office's Lonergan case file). The summary he received—as compared against the full eight-and-a-half-page, single-spaced, typed (approximately 4,650 words) report—was fairly thorough in its discussion of Patricia's cause of death and the various traumas to her body. In the summary, Helpern omitted sections on her trunk, lungs, gastrointestinal tract, reproductive organs—details that would not have altered Broderick's understanding of the cause of death. In both documents, Helpern indicated that Patricia died of asphyxia by strangulation so severe that it caused the hemorrhaging of her larynx and the lower palpebral conjunctiva (the clear membrane that coats the inside of the eyelid); a contusion on her clavicle; and three deep lacerations on her scalp, caused by the candleholders, which fractured her skull and in turn led to contusion of the brain.

The bottom line of the medical reports—taken together with Lonergan's confession—was that Patricia had died when Lonergan had violently attacked her. A careful analysis clearly shows there were no facts in the full report that would have provided a contradictory narrative which would have led to Lonergan's confession being disregarded (as Hamilton Darby Perry also suggested).

Grumet seemingly was being petty for not providing Broderick with the full report as he requested. Had he handed over to Broderick what he wanted, it would not have changed the medical conclusion of Patricia's death—and indeed, would have supported what Lonergan had stated in his confession. It also would have silenced the defense attorney's loud criticisms.

But that was how the legal game was played in 1944. Grumet had the power to do as he pleased with the report, and he exercised that power lest he set a precedent for future murder trials.

The judge silenced Broderick, too, when he raised the possibility that at the time Patricia was murdered, "a well-known wealthy lawyer was present," who was allegedly the real murderer. This assertion was, as Grumet called it, "unadulterated nonsense," yet it had not stopped the *New York World-Telegram*—a newspaper that did put the war news ahead of the Lonergan trial—from using the sensational and inaccurate headline, "Chum at Killing by Lonergan Hinted, Denied."

Dismissing another attempt by Broderick to delay the start of the trial, Freschi ruled against him; the trial was to begin on Wednesday, February 23—at least, that's what the judge and prosecution believed.

There's Nothing Like a Real Good Murder

IN LATE FEBRUARY 1944, you could forget about standing in line to see such Broadway productions as *Arsenic and Old Lace* at the Hudson Theater, *The Cherry Orchard* at the National, or Rodgers and Hammerstein's *Oklahoma!* at the St. James. The real draw in New York that month was the trial of Wayne Lonergan. The demand for the eighty-five seats inside the thirteenth-floor stately marbled Art Deco–style courtroom in the four-year-old, seventeen-story Criminal Courts Building on Center Street in Lower Manhattan far exceeded the supply (the new $14 million building was close to the old Criminal Courts Building, which had been used from 1893 to 1941). Today the outside of the courthouse is still as imposing as it was then. Above the main entrance in huge block letters it states: "Equal and Exact Justice Equal to All Men of Whatever State or Persuasion." Inside, the building and its decor are showing its age; the wooden benches outside the courtrooms have seen better days.

For weeks, hundreds of New Yorkers inundated the district attorney's office in an attempt to reserve seats for the "Lonergan Show." The only individuals guaranteed spots were the close to sixty journalists from New York and those from cities and towns across the country—some who were correspondents for newspapers in Europe and as far away as Australia—along with sketch artists and "special" writers who were expected to attend, as well as RCAF Squadron Leader J. M. McPherson, who had been ordered to New York to observe the trial. The journalists were all given colored passes by Fred O'Connor of the *New York World-Telegram* and the president of the Criminal Court Reporters Association, allowing them to come and go as they pleased. Once the jury was selected, there were not a lot of seats left for interested spectators in the courtroom. Most New Yorkers and others fascinated by the

Lonergan saga therefore had to be content with reading about daily reports of the intrigues of the case in the press.

The public's obsession with every detail, no matter how trivial, about Patricia and Wayne's private life and the circumstances of her tragic death had been stoked by such syndicated gossip columnists as Walter Winchell and Dorothy Kilgallen, among other tabloid writers. That such newspapers as the *Journal-American* and *Daily News* assigned the Lonergan case to entertainment writers was telling about the type of blanket coverage the case received. Winchell offered the rumor that "a prominent newsman would be called as a witness" (he never was); while Kilgallen, whose Broadway column initially had been launched in 1938 in the *Journal-American* before King Features Syndicate picked it up, informed her numerous readers that Broderick "intends to unfold the whole unsavory past of Bill Burton, the girl's father" (that didn't happen either).

The *Daily News* described Lonergan as a "sex-warped defendant," who the newspaper declared (wrongly) was planning to change his plea to guilty by reason of insanity. The newspaper and its numerous competitors also listed (inaccurately) the witnesses—including "a wealthy prominent Canadian thus far unnamed whose exotic apartment in Toronto Lonergan fled [to] after the killing"—as if they were part of the cast of a bad Broadway melodrama. As Thyra Samter Winslow so aptly put it in one of her numerous Lonergan columns for the *Daily Mirror*, "there's nothing like a real good murder." Keeping the intense focus on Lonergan's personal life, she also added that "Wayne was bi-sexual [*sic*]. He was known not to be completely homosexual. He liked girls too." Above all, these various reporters and writers never failed to remind their readers that Lonergan was accused of "bludgeoning and strangling" his "heiress" wife, Patricia.

⌇

At 10:30 a.m. on Wednesday, February 23, with the large jury pool and everyone else gathered—except for Lonergan, who waited outside the chamber under armed guard—and ready for the start of the trial, Broderick pulled another doozy of a stunt. A day earlier, without informing the court, Broderick took a train to Toronto in search of evidence he could use in his defense of Lonergan. One piece of information he sought was an Ontario psychiatric report on Wayne's mother, Clara Lonergan. Broderick later cryptically told reporters that he had uncovered "surprising evidence," which turned out to be nothing more than documents about Clara's institutionalization in three Toronto-area mental hospitals. In any event, Broderick's actions were unprecedented, and a display of chutzpah and disrespect of the court that Freschi had a difficult time comprehending.

Ten minutes before the trial was to get under way, the judge was stunned when he was handed a telegram Broderick had sent him informing Freschi that the lawyer was in Toronto to investigate further aspects of the case and "respectfully" requesting an adjournment. Once again, Broderick had tested Freschi's patience. As the judge entered the courtroom, his anger was apparent to all. He explained what had occurred and declared for the record that Broderick's absence from the proceedings constituted contempt of court and that he would deal with the attorney at the end of the trial. "He owes an apology," said Freschi, "not only to the court and its officials but to every juror on the panel." He warned Broderick's associate, William Merritt, who was present—caustically described by the *Journal-American* as Broderick's "small, meek . . . whipping boy"—that he expected Broderick to show up within twenty-four hours.

Grumet was equally as annoyed, yet he was curious about exactly what Broderick was attempting to discover in the Ontario psychiatric records. As a precaution, he dispatched Dr. Perry Lichtenstein to Toronto so that he could also investigate further. That mission turned out to be a bureaucratic nightmare, as Lichtenstein spent most of Friday, February 25, trying to track down the right official who could assist him in examining Clara Lonergan's medical records. He went from Toronto City Hall to the Ontario Hospital to the Ontario Legislature and back to City Hall. After interviewing nearly every Toronto police official who had had contact with Wayne, it was Lichtenstein's professional opinion that at no time while Lonergan was in the custody of the Toronto police did he show any "evidence of mental unsoundness."

During his visit, Lichtenstein also spoke with doctors Roy H. Thomas, the chief medical officer for the Toronto Police Department, and Charles Archibald, both of whom had examined Lonergan soon after he had been picked up by the Toronto police. Thomas told Lichtenstein—as Lichtenstein reported to Grumet—that "he saw no marks of any injury on the penis of Lonergan," and that Lonergan "never made any statement that his penis had been injured." Archibald concurred with this assessment that there were "no bruises or other marks on Lonergan's penis, nor did Lonergan make any statement that his penis was hurt."

This line of inquiry was in response to a spicy rumor Grumet had heard, which subsequently became part of the Lonergan case folklore, often repeated in gossip magazines. In this version of the crime, Patricia, while performing oral sex on Lonergan, had bitten his penis so hard that he had struck her with the candlesticks. But as Lichtenstein heard from the two Toronto physicians, this salacious tale had no basis in fact. And, given the animosity between Patricia and Wayne, it is hard to imagine that she would have performed such an intimate act on him under any circumstances.

The person most perplexed by Broderick's gambit was Lonergan, who had been given no prior notice about his lawyer's trip to Toronto. After about thirty minutes of standing around, he was taken back to his cell. The following morning, Lonergan was brought back from the Tombs to the courtroom with the exact same result. Much to Judge Freschi's consternation, Broderick had sent a second telegram indicating he was still in Toronto and required another delay in the proceedings.

Grumet was doubly aggravated, though he had no choice; he told Freschi that he would be agreeable to moving the start of the trial to Monday morning. The judge concurred, but he let the 124 members of the jury pool (by then, 76 of the original 200 had been exempted) know that Broderick's actions should not leave them with a "false impression that might prejudice the rights of the defendant." Back Lonergan went to his jail cell for the weekend.

— —

Broderick returned to New York on Sunday evening. He immediately intimated to reporters that he had obtained "considerable data" on his travels, and that Lonergan, who he had visited, was in "high spirits."

The press also reported that at Grumet's request, Jean Murphy Jaburg had returned from Florida to testify. She had been vacationing there, staying at hotels in Surfside near Miami and farther north at Palm Beach. Her association with Lonergan and the murder had rattled her, and she believed—wrongly, as it turned out—that Grumet or the Miami police had been following her.

In photographs of Murphy Jaburg coming and going from Grumet's office on Sunday night, she looked ravishing, as usual, but she was angry. "This case has ruined my theatrical career," she told the reporters. "Previously, I had been talking with several producers about parts. With the publicity I received in this case, everything stopped. I have a family to consider, including an eight-year-old son, and every time my name is brought into this, they suffer."

Whether or not her show business prospects would have improved was open to question. Yet all available evidence does suggest that her minor connection to Lonergan—a play, dinner, and lunch—did indeed derail her career.

Monday morning, February 28, Broderick was at last in his place in the courtroom in front of Judge Freschi. Leaping to his feet, he launched into a defense of his recent actions and lambasted Grumet's "savagery" at the preliminary hearing. Grumet refused to be baited, however. In a brazen display of courtroom theatrics, Broderick moved that the members of the jury pool be disqualified because they had been privy to the criticisms made about him the past few days, and that Freschi recuse himself for the same reason. In short, he was calling for a mistrial. The judge, who might have erupted in anger, remained calm. He cautioned the prospective jurors that the "defendant must not personally be prejudiced in any way," and then denied Broderick's motion that he grant a mistrial or recuse himself.

Visibly upset with that decision, Broderick charged that his client had been unwittingly brought from Toronto to New York through "deceit and fraud," and once again accused the DA's office of attempting "to sell Lonergan a plea."

Lonergan sat erect at the defense desk, watching and listening intently to his lawyer's latest rant. Dressed in a dark blue pin-striped suit accentuated by a white shirt and navy polka-dot tie, he was in need of a haircut after being locked up for several months. Yet he appeared as neat and confident as ever.

The *Journal-American*, which pulled no punches in its reports of the case, was somewhat harsher in its depiction of the defendant, observing that Lonergan, whose "prison pallor was noticeable," was "now just a seedy show of the bon vivant who once glittered through Café Society." Yet despite his "greasy" tie, the "wilted" collar on his shirt, and his general "shabbiness," Lonergan still "looked cool and impassive," the paper added. In a separate column in the same edition of the *Journal-American*, Broadway writer Louis Sobel wrote about Lonergan that there was "no hint in his strong face of the psychopathological turbulence which [the ADA] would have you believe boils within the cauldron of his emotions."

The most astute observation was from the *Daily Mirror*'s Thyra Samter Winslow. "I hope that (a) people who attend and read about the trial will take a short course in abnormal psychology beforehand; [and] (b) they'll realize that Wayne Lonergan is on trial not because of sexual irregularities, but on a charge of having murdered his young, beautiful wife." The trouble was, few journalists, spectators, or anyone else involved in the trial heeded those wise words. In any assessment of Lonergan, it was fairly impossible to separate perceptions of his sexual identity from the crime he was accused of committing.

———

Apart from Broderick's outburst, the first day was mainly taken up with determining a jury. At the defense lawyer's request, another hundred people had been selected for the pool, which now included a total of six women. Facing the more than two hundred "talesmen," as those who were summoned for jury duty were officially referred to at the time, Grumet stuck to the basics: "What is your business? Are you opposed to Capital Punishment? Have you read about this case? Have you preconceived ideas about this case which would prevent you from listening to the evidence and deciding the case strictly on the evidence?"

Broderick, not surprisingly, was more dramatic. He asked jury prospects if they had read that Lonergan "was a kind of Pittsburgh Phil" who was "gambling his life against two-million dollars (one-third of the [more than] six-million estate) of his deceased wife's share of her inheritance." ("Pittsburgh Phil" was the nickname of astute gambler George Elsworth, who during the late nineteenth and early twentieth centuries made millions betting on horse racing.)

In yet another maneuver, Broderick tried to read a letter that Lonergan had written to the surrogate of Patricia's estate, James Foley, indicating his willingness to waive his rights and his son's rights—which he could not legally do—to her fortune. Grumet immediately objected, expressing his doubt that Lonergan had actually penned it himself. After considering the matter, Freschi consented that jurors could be shown the letter as they were being individually examined by the defense, though cautioned them that they were not to treat any such letter as evidence. The following day, however, he reversed his decision and ruled that the "letter should not be read in public."

Much of Wednesday was another long session in which jurors were examined and accepted or rejected. Broderick's main tactic was to hammer away at the fact that Lonergan's confession was "fake" and threatening that he might call Grumet and John Loehr as witnesses. He also demanded to know the names of the "stool pigeons" the DA had used inside the Tombs, which Grumet rebuffed, and then he addressed the jurors' views on "sexual aberration" and "mental imbalance."

One middle-aged woman who was questioned assured Grumet that she would not be made at all uncomfortable by "sexual aberration with the erotic, exotic and the neurotic." The gallery erupted in laughter at that comment. Asked by Broderick if she was an extrovert, she replied, "I'm no scientist," adding, "but I'd take 'extrovert' to mean I am the reverse of shy, retiring." Broderick approved of her, but Grumet did not, and she was dismissed.

Another issue that was brought to Freschi's attention by Broderick was a *New York Times* article from February 28 in which it was noted that "Lonergan was dishonorably discharged from the RCAF following his confession to the police of phases of his personal life." In fact, this was not true—the *Times* had obtained the information from a Canadian air force official who had no authority to speak on the matter—and the RCAF issued a statement that Lonergan "remains a member" of the RCAF "until the civil case has been disposed of."

This story was bad enough, but it was another news article that precipitated a more serious problem. On the morning of March 2, a page-two story in the *Daily Mirror* noted that Broderick had been informed about "bizarre" (sexual) photographs of Patricia taken by Lonergan, which reportedly were in the possession of Lonergan's sister, June Cummins, in Toronto. (No racy photographs of Patricia were ever published or presented in court.) Freschi and Grumet both wanted to know from Broderick if he had anything to do with the *Daily Mirror*'s report, or if he had such photos.

The interrogation-style questioning made Broderick explode with incredulity. "So help me God and may Christ paralyze my tongue," he declared, "I had nothing to do with that story!"

And he didn't, according to Jack Lait, the tabloid's editor, who wrote to Broderick two days later, indicating that the source of the story "was definitely not him."

For good measure, Broderick added that DA Frank Hogan was "dissatisfied" by the way Grumet was handling the case.

"That is a deliberate lie," shouted Grumet in response. "Mr. Hogan feels the same way as I do about the conduct of the defense counsel." Throwing his arms up in the air, Grumet now indicated that he supported Broderick's call made on Monday for a mistrial.

In an about-face, Broderick changed his mind about a mistrial. His face reddened.

"Mr. Grumet tried to sell the defendant down the river, Judge, on a plea in his chambers," he said, his voice cracking. Grumet, he insinuated, "is responding to the pressure of the Bernheimer-Burton seven millions. He is quitting, and a quitter never wins and a winner never quits."

Before the day was done, Broderick had conjured a vast conspiracy—of mainly wealthy New York Jews—against him and Lonergan, and in that order. The alleged perpetrators included: Arthur Hays Sulzberger, the publisher of the *New York Times*, who was linked to the Berhheimer-Burton family; the banking dynasty of the late Simon W. Straus; and his two former co-defense lawyers, Millard Ellison and Abraham Halprin, both of whom were corrupt, in his view.

"They couldn't crucify this innocent man, Lonergan," Broderick declared, "and now they are trying to crucify me." Looking directly at Freschi, he said, "If you are going to be part of it, we might as well close up the American courts." Broderick urged him to deny any request by Grumet for a mistrial, despite the fact that he had raised the issue first.

Clearly frustrated by Broderick's performance, what he termed "ungentlemanly conduct," Freschi said he would take Grumet's mistrial motion under advisement.

— — —

The evening of Friday, March 3, was not a pleasant one for Judge Freschi. The next morning, he was forced to do what he did not want to do, though he felt he had no choice. He declared a mistrial, dismissed the prospective jurors, recused himself as judge for the next trial, and ordered Broderick to appear before him in one week, on contempt charges. He reproached Broderick, as well, for a "lack of good faith" in his indecisiveness over demanding a mistrial.

"Quite apart from that, however," the judge continued, "the events that have transpired during the last several days have persuaded me that counsel for the defendant has attempted to make of this trial, in which [a] life is involved, a mockery, all for purposes I cannot fathom."

At that, Broderick's face flushed.

More importantly, Freschi ruled that "since a jury has not been impaneled and sworn, jeopardy has not attached. The defendant may legally and properly be put to trial by the State without fear of a possible successful claim of double jeopardy." That is, Lonergan's Fifth Amendment rights, which do not permit being tried twice for the same crime once a verdict has been rendered, had not been violated because he had not been found guilty or acquitted of the murder charge.

As the judge finished speaking, Broderick, who had been uncharacteristically silent, leapt to his feet.

"May I be heard?" he asked.

"No," said Freschi, banging his gavel down on the desk.

Broderick tried again, but before he could get a word out, he was met with "No, No, No" from the judge, who banged his gavel a few more times.

"I take exception to Your Honor's refusal to hear me at this time, on the grounds that it is prejudicial to my client's future trial."

"Your exception is noted," interrupted Freschi.

"And a continuation of Mr. Grumet's promise to harass me during this trial, and—"

"Mr. Broderick, please!" said the judge, hitting his desk with his hand.

Next, Broderick requested that his contempt charge be considered after Lonergan's trial. Freschi refused to grant this request, and as Broderick started talking, the judge cut him off again.

"I am not going to let you, Mr. Broderick, use this court as a vaudeville stage for your purposes," he said sharply.

"Hold up, hold up," cried Broderick.

"You must act as a lawyer," said Freschi. "Please be seated, Mr. Broderick."

The defense attorney did as he was told, then stood a moment later.

"Are you going to let my client rot in jail, while I'm in jail?" Broderick said, assuming he was going to be found guilty of contempt in a week and incarcerated.

Freschi ignored the question, stating that the DA's office would set the next trial date. It was out of his hands. (Four months later, at the end of July, Freschi was to die during an operation for a ruptured appendix.) Frank

Hogan, who was sitting beside Grumet, indicated that the next trial would begin in a few weeks.

Later that day, after visiting with Lonergan in his cell, Broderick emerged to find reporters waiting for him. He held up a statement Lonergan had written and then read it.

"All I want is a fair trial. I am sorry my trial has been delayed. I have complete faith and confidence in Mr. Broderick."

13

Double-Dealing, Double-Crossing, and Double-Talk

JACOB GRUMET DID NOT waste much time. By Tuesday, March 7, he was in General Sessions Court before Judge John Mullen, requesting another panel of jurors for the first-degree murder trial of Wayne Lonergan, who was to be defended by Edward V. Broderick. Despite how adamant Judge Freschi was about Broderick appearing before him at the end of the week on a charge of contempt of court, Grumet anticipated those proceedings would, in fact, not begin until after Lonergan's second trial was finished. And that's what happened: On March 10, Freschi agreed to postpone the contempt case against Broderick until April 15, by which time he anticipated Lonergan's trial would be over.

Meanwhile, Judge Mullen set March 20 as the date for the second trial to get under way. The trial was assigned to a veteran of the New York legal community, Judge James G. Wallace. Broderick commented that he didn't care who the judge was in Lonergan's next trial, but he could not have been thrilled with the choice of Wallace.

Sixty-one-year-old James Garrett Wallace had been a judge since 1935. Like Freschi, he had a link to the Robert Irwin murder trial; it was Wallace who had sentenced Irwin to 139 years in prison. On the one hand, Wallace was entertaining. He was nicknamed the "singing judge" for his superb tenor voice. He was also a good actor, something Broderick might have appreciated. Yet, he had a more serious side, and was still as tough as when he was a lineman for the Columbia University football team in his younger days.

As a lawyer, Wallace became associated with Tammany Hall (the powerful Democratic political machine) and had worked as a corporate attorney before being appointed an assistant district attorney in 1916. He was highly principled and adhered to what today we would consider the conservative values of the era. While some community leaders were critical of the righteousness of the New York Society for the Suppression of Vice (founded by Anthony Comstock in 1873) and the state's 1927 Wales Padlock Law—which did not permit any references or portrayals of "sex degeneracy" or "sex perversion" onstage, including homosexuality—Wallace was not.

"If there were not some sort of restraint there are people . . . who would lower the stage to the very depths for the sake of financial gain," he commented at a Young Democratic Club gathering in March 1929. He had already put those words into action.

On the evening of February 9, 1927, owing in part to the intensive lobbying of John Sumner, who had succeeded Comstock as head of the society, the police shut down three controversial plays: *The Captive*, about a lesbian love affair; *The Virgin Man*, which explored homosexuality; and *SEX*, which had opened a year earlier at the off-Broadway theater, The Daly. *SEX* featured the playwright—the curvaceous Mae West, then thirty-four years old and already a celebrity who thrived on controversy. Sumner had labeled *SEX* "moral poison," and the play had been denounced in the press as "a monstrosity plucked from the garbage can, destined for the sewer." Under the state's obscenity laws (the Wales Padlock Law was not signed until early April 1927), forty-one actors, actresses, theater producers, managers, and workers from all three plays—West, among them—were arrested for participating in "indecent" shows, being a "public nuisance," and "corrupting the morals of youth or others."

The task of prosecuting West fell to Wallace, who was a staunch supporter of the Wales Padlock Law, which by the time the *SEX* trial started at the end of March had been passed by the New York Senate (though not yet signed into law by Governor Al Smith). During the proceedings, West's racy dialogue, her "prolonged" kiss with one of the actors, and the suggestive way she sauntered across the stage were all used as evidence against her and the production. West was not called to the stand, yet she offered to testify. "I would call you if I could," Wallace told her in a display of his humorous side.

The trial lasted less than a week. In his closing argument, Wallace urged the members of the jury to consider the moral ramifications of permitting

SEX to continue. "We have cleaned up the red light district of New York," he claimed. "It's a pretty clean town. But we've got red lights on the stage."

The jury reluctantly found West and the other defendants guilty as charged. Judge George Donnellan fined West, her manager James Timony, and producer William Morganstern $500 and sentenced them to ten days in jail. He stated that *SEX* was "obscene, immoral, and indecent," and that West and her friends had tarnished New York City's reputation—"the most moral city in the universe." West accepted the judgment coolly, but as she left the courtroom, she turned and told the assembled journalists, "I expect it will be the making of me."

It was, and her fame and celebrity grew.

Wallace had long maintained that the state had an obligation to act as moral guardians and that "right-thinking" people had nothing to fear from such regulations as the Wales Padlock Law. "It doesn't seem to me that there is anything in the Wales [L]aw that any normal person could take exception to," he remarked in his 1929 speech. Any "normal person" in 1944 would not have approved of Lonergan's lifestyle—or at least, what was believed to be his lifestyle—and neither did Judge Wallace. As he was about to preside over a case that was to decide Lonergan's fate, he clearly did so with an inherent bias that was difficult to hide.

～

The Lonergan "circus" started up again on Thursday, March 9, with the selection of a new jury panel of three hundred prospects, which included three women. A week after that, Broderick, seeking other "ammunition" he might employ, had Judge Wallace sign an order permitting Dr. Thomas Cusack to examine Lonergan in order to determine if he suffered the same psychological problems as his mother had.

A fifty-nine-year-old psychiatrist and neurologist from Brooklyn, Cusack was an authority on the "degenerative effects of bootleg whiskey" and a favorite of defense attorneys and prosecutors alike for his concise professional testimony in court. In 1927, working with Judd Gray's lawyer, Cusack had examined Gray's lover and co-accused Ruth Snyder—both were on trial for murdering her husband Albert—and in 1936, he had helped the prosecution by testifying that John Fiorenza, who had murdered Nancy Titterton, was not as "wacky" as was believed. (In late March 1944, Loehr received an anonymous letter that Cusack had been convicted of perjury in a case from about seven or eight years earlier. An investigation was conducted, but turned up nothing negative about the psychiatrist.)

On March 18, Cusack spent two and a half hours with Lonergan, only to emerge from the Tombs to tell reporters that "I have not yet formulated any opinion." He visited with Lonergan a second time the following day for several hours, and again, as he departed, said he had nothing to add—just that Lonergan was in "pretty good spirits." In the end, Broderick never called Cusack to testify or submitted his report as evidence, so there is no record of how Cusack judged Lonergan's mental state. It is safe to assume, however, that he did not find him criminally insane; otherwise, Broderick would have attempted to utilize that defense.

On March 20, there was no lack of international and national news for the papers to report. The Germans were on the run in the Battle of Monte Cassino in southern Italy, which ended in an Allied victory two months later; Allied bombers continued their unrelenting assault on southwest Germany; in Algiers, Pierre Pucheau, the former minister of interior in the Vichy government, a puppet of the Germans, was executed by firing squad after being convicted of treason; in New Jersey, a wicked sleet storm caused a bus to plunge from a bridge into the Passaic River, killing at least three people, with many more feared dead; and nearby in Manhattan, New Yorkers were stunned by the snow on the ground that greeted the arrival of spring. Newspapers from New York to Minneapolis to Tampa Bay covered these various stories, yet the start of Lonergan's second trial also rated prominent—in most cases, front-page—coverage in the press.

The trial commenced with Judge Wallace setting the tone: It was all business, and Broderick was on his best behavior, no doubt anticipating that Wallace would be tougher on him than Freschi had. The wily and unpredictable attorney reasoned that dealing with one contempt-of-court charge in the near future was sufficient.

Before the jury selection proceeded, Broderick, as politely as he could, asked the judge to compel Grumet to provide him with the names of witnesses he was planning to call so that he could inquire of the prospective jurors gathered—of the 300 initially called, 66 were immediately exempted for one reason or another—whether they knew of them. Grumet did so, giving him twenty-five names that included Lucille Burton, John Harjes,

Elizabeth Black, Peter Elser, Mario Gabellini, Sylvia French, and Jean Murphy Jaburg. But he did not purposely tell him the names of all of the prosecution's witnesses, and by the disclosure rules of the time, he did not have to.

As Broderick began questioning potential jurors, he asked if they knew or recognized the names on the witness list. His follow-up query was more direct: "Would you be prejudiced one way or another against psychiatric or psychological testimony?" After each juror responded, Broderick glanced at Lonergan to see what his opinion was of the person under scrutiny. Even though this was not the accepted practice, it's what Lonergan demanded. When it was Grumet's turn, he wanted to know if a juror "would accept the court's instruction on testimony trying to fix Lonergan's mental responsibility."

By the end of Monday's session, Grumet and Broderick had agreed on three of the twelve jurors to be chosen, all men—an insurance claim examiner, a banker, and a milk company executive. One man, Don Whiting, an advertising salesman, was dismissed when he admitted that he had wagered "even money" that Lonergan would be found guilty of first-degree murder. The selection continued and was completed on Tuesday. In all, the two lawyers had interviewed only 74 of the 234 jurors available. An all-male and mostly married jury of 12 had been agreed upon. This included John Woodburn, a forty-three-year-old New York editor of Little, Brown and Company, the Boston-based publisher; and William Byrne, the middle-aged, balding, and "dignified" insurance claim examiner chosen on Monday, who would be appointed jury foreman. A photograph of the jury published in the *New York Times* on March 23 shows the twelve (as well as the two alternates) dressed in suits, ties, overcoats, and fedoras, looking very much like the board of directors of a business club.

The one other interesting development from Tuesday's hearing to be revealed was that Grumet had not had Lonergan sign his confession. Despite Grumet's nonchalant comment that "the usual procedure" was followed, the fact that it wasn't signed slightly raised Wallace's eyebrows—but it did not contravene Section 395 of *The Code of Criminal Procedure of the State of New York* (included in the 1936 revised statute). And, indeed, the presence of a signature on the document was not legally necessary, no matter how much Broderick insisted that this lapse undermined the veracity of the admission of culpability.

The much more significant issue about Lonergan's confession that Broderick did legitimately challenge was whether or not it was voluntary, because coerced or involuntary confessions *did* violate the statute, as had been determined in a long list of New York court rulings dating back to 1867. From a purely legal perspective, Lonergan was at a disadvantage, because the trial was held in New York and governed by New York State Criminal Law Procedure.

At the time, there were three essential approaches in the United States to dealing with confessions: the "Orthodox Procedure," adopted by twenty states, in which the trial judge decided whether the confession was voluntary before the jury considered it; the "Massachusetts Procedure," adopted by fourteen states, in which the judge had to initially assess the admissibility of the confession, and if the court found that it met that threshold, the jury then considered the "weight and accuracy" of the confession and its "voluntariness"; and the "New York Procedure," used by New York and thirteen other states, in which the judge left the decision of the "voluntariness" of the confession to the jury—as was the case in Lonergan's trial. It took another two decades before the US Supreme Court ruled that among the three approaches, the New York Procedure was unconstitutional, in that it deprived "the defendant of liberty without due process of law." That Supreme Court ruling in 1964 would become part of Lonergan's legal saga, but in March 1944, that was still far into the future.

It remained cool and rainy in New York on the morning of Wednesday, March 22, when Grumet rose to face the jury and deliver his opening statement. Sitting beside Broderick, Lonergan sat up straight. His fingers were tightly intertwined and rigid on the table in front of him, and his eyes were fixed on Grumet's back as he listened intently to every word the ADA said. The look on Lonergan's face, one journalist present reported, "was calm but serious, with curious intensity in the eyes."

It was not the strongest opening statement Grumet ever gave, though it likely did the trick. He would prove, he declared, that Lonergan had gone to his wife Patricia's residence around nine o'clock in the morning on Sunday, October 24, 1943. An argument erupted between them and then there was a bloody altercation, during which Lonergan struck her hard in the head with the candlesticks, fracturing her skull before choking her to death. Grumet offered no motive for the murder, at least for the moment, but he did have Lonergan's confession to dangle in front of the jury members—as he would do repeatedly throughout the trial. "We have only his statement to what transpired there just before he killed her," said Grumet. "His wife, the only other person in the room at the time, is dead."

He also drew the jury's attention to Lonergan's initial alibi about his encounter with US serviceman Maurice Worcester. "I don't believe it is necessary," Grumet added, "to go into the sordid story of degeneracy that he told [and] later repudiated." Except that now, the link between Lonergan and "degeneracy" was nonetheless planted in the minds of the jury members—if it had not been already—and was to be reinforced when the full "Perversion Alibi," as *Newsday* branded it in a large headline, was read aloud the following day.

"After you have heard all this evidence," said Grumet, concluding his statement, "we shall ask you to find this defendant guilty of first-degree murder, as charged."

No one on the jury moved a muscle or said a thing.

When the judge signaled to Broderick to give his opening statement, the lawyer leapt to his feet, his face red and tight. He was seething with anger and trying hard to control his temper.

"We'll show you," Broderick declared, "that this defendant, Lonergan, from the very start has been the victim of double-dealing, double-crossing and double-talk. It has been illustrated in your own presence by—"

"Objection," said Grumet, on his feet.

Judge Wallace looked at Broderick. "This is the time for opening, Mr. Broderick. The jurors are aware of everything that has happened in their presence."

Broderick nodded and turned to the jury again. "I intend to make this the briefest opening I have ever made in twenty-nine years of practice here. I do that as [a] protective device—not to protect guilt, but to protect innocence against double-dealing, double-crossing and double-talk."

Grumet started his presentation of the evidence strongly by showing the jurors four disturbing black-and-white photographs of the crime scene—including Patricia's limp, bloody, nude dead body—taken by police officer Chris Trauerts of the NYPD's bureau of criminal identification. It was certain that the majority of the jury members, if not all of them, had never before seen such vivid photos of a murder. The collective impact was powerful and lasting.

The rest of the day was taken up mainly by Grumet's questioning of Dr. Milton Helpern, which lasted nearly three long hours. Helpern confirmed the estimated time of death at between about 4:00 a.m. and noon on October

24; in other words, from the time Patricia had returned from her date with Mario Gabellini to the time Lonergan dropped off the toy elephant for his son. Patricia died, Helpern further explained, by "asphyxia by strangulation, laceration of the scalp from the candlestick holders, fracture of the skull and bruise of the brain"—exactly as he had described it in his autopsy report.

Grumet held up the two green onyx candlesticks (which Meyer Berger of the *New York Times* said looked more like green glass) so the jury could see the alleged murder weapons. He did not point out the bloodstain that Helpern had identified on one of the candlesticks in his report of the crime scene, since Dr. Alexander Wiener was unable to positively determine the blood group from the stain sample. In fact, Wiener's entire blood group analysis, though instructive, did not strengthen the prosecution's case for the simple reason that forensic science in 1943 was too primitive (and would remain so until the mid-1970s—still in the pre-DNA era, but when serologists started being able to identify genetic markers in blood). Unlike in the 1936 murder case of Nancy Titterton, in which the perpetrator, John Fiorenza, was tracked down and captured with some "CSI-style" analysis of a piece of rope left at the crime scene, there was no such lightbulb-above-the-head moment in the Lonergan trial.

There were, for example, the cigarette butts Wiener had cataloged at Patricia's residence. He eventually identified the ones in Patricia's bedroom to be from two brands, Old Gold and Philip Morris (today, these also could have been tested for DNA). The Old Gold smoker, Wiener determined, was from a "group A individual," which corresponded to Patricia's blood group or type (there was also a half-eaten LifeSavers candy found by the bed, in which "traces of group A saliva were present"); while the Philip Morris smoker was from a "group B individual." But Wayne Lonergan's preferred cigarette brand—or that of Patricia—was not noted in the DA's case file, or in any other document or press story, so it is impossible to know who exactly smoked those cigarettes. Moreover, neither Helpern nor Wiener's reports identified Lonergan's blood group, because drawing a suspect's blood was not common police procedure at the time. Thus, Grumet never introduced the cigarette butts as evidence at the trial.

If Lonergan had consented to providing a blood sample—and there were various complex legal issues involved in that decision—it might have been possible to rule him out as the person who smoked the other cigarette, if his blood type was "A" or "O" or "AB," which was more infrequent. Yet this seemingly did not occur to Grumet or the police, or Broderick, for that matter.

At the same time, assuming Grumet had been able to prove that Lonergan's blood was indeed "group B," that by itself was hardly sufficient to prove in court that he was the second smoker in the bedroom, or when the cigarette in question was smoked. As the noted forensic scientist Paul L. Kirk put it in a 1954 journal article about linking blood type to a suspect, "how many times the expert testifies to the presence [for example] of O-type blood on a suspect's clothing and then has to admit that nearly half the population has O blood!" Kirk looked forward to the day when blood experts could identify that "the suspect has on his clothes the blood of the victim and nobody else." That day, however, was not in March 1944. When prosecutors did try to use blood grouping evidence, the imprecision of the science in the 1940s and 1950s made it an easy target for defense lawyers to show that blood analysis was often unreliable and too general, and that the conclusions of experts like Wiener were certainly not beyond a reasonable doubt.

(For instance, in 1947 in Los Angeles George Gollum and Beulah Overell, two young lovers, were accused of killing Overell's parents by blowing up her family's yacht. During their trial, the prosecutor used the testimony of a forensic chemist to show that splatters of blood type A—the same blood type as the two victims—were found on Gollum's clothes on the night of the murder. His attorney had no trouble disputing the evidence with the fact that at the time, 42 percent of the human population had blood type A.)

In his discussion of issues about the case against Lonergan, Hamilton Darby Perry—who did not have access to the reports of Helpern and Wiener—was incorrect when he pointed out that the candleholders "that caused the blood and gore, failed to show any blood, tissue, hair or bone on them"—because one of them did; it was only that crime science in 1943 and 1944 could not provide a conclusion about the blood that would have held up in court.

In his cross-examination, Broderick peppered Helpern with a variety of technical queries—and was warned by Wallace to stop "the dissertation on anatomy" and getting into the "realm of metaphysics"—and speculated about Patricia being hit on the head by a whisky bottle or suffering the blood loss from an abortion. It was all conjecture, and Helpern stood his ground, as per his reputation when testifying at a trial.

⌣

Elizabeth Black was visibly nervous as she sat down in the witness box on Thursday morning. She shifted in the chair and fiddled with her glasses, which she held tightly in her lap. As Grumet began questioning her about the fateful weekend in October—about how she had taken Billy for a walk to Lucille Burton's on the October Sunday afternoon, and then was dismayed upon her return to not find Patricia there and her bedroom door still shut—she spoke so softly that the judge and jury could barely hear her. Impatient with the pace of the examination, Judge Wallace intervened, as was his right.

"At any time, at any place in the house, before you discovered the body, did you hear any unusual noise or anything like that?" he asked her.

"No, sir," she replied a little more loudly.

"You sleep pretty soundly, do you?" the judge continued.

"Yes, sir, I do," answered Black.

Broderick did not want to cross-examine her, so Lucille Burton was called as the next prosecution witness. Every set of eyes in the courtroom turned to stare at her as she walked into the courtroom, attired in an elegant ankle-length fur coat and a small black-veiled tilt (or toy) hat, which was regarded as high fashion in 1944. Even in her immense sadness, she exuded wealth, privilege, and style. With a stoic determination, she ignored the collective gaze of the spectators and looked straight ahead.

She, too, only testified for a few minutes as to how Black had summoned her to her daughter's residence. Lucille spoke clearly. She fixed her gaze on Lonergan, but he refused to acknowledge her. There was little point questioning a grieving mother, and Broderick wisely opted not to cross-examine her either.

Captain Peter Elser, dressed in his formal blue marine uniform and holding his white cap, was the next to be called to the stand. He recited his story of how he had had to use tools to open Patricia's bedroom door, and once inside, about the grisly scene he found.

John Harjes followed Elser, and he testified about Lonergan's arrival at his apartment late on Friday, October 22. He read aloud the note that Lonergan had left for him, explaining that he had had to borrow Harjes's clothes because his uniform had gone missing (which he and his friend Harold Le Mon, who had driven with him back to New York that weekend, thought was "fishy"). Harjes identified the makeup compact that had been found in his bathroom, and the fact that an iron dumbbell, one of four that he owned, was missing from his apartment. Grumet contended that this was used to weigh down Lonergan's duffel bag containing his uniform and watch so that it would sink into the East River.

At that moment, Harjes likely regretted the day he had ever laid eyes on Lonergan. Yet, when Broderick asked him if he had ever heard "anybody say anything bad about [Lonergan]," he was honest and replied, "No." Harjes also agreed with the defense lawyer that he had no idea if a dumbbell was taken from his apartment, or by whom—the implication being that it could have been misplaced or lost.

More significant during Thursday's session was the testimony of Toronto Police officials who had traveled to New York for the court proceedings. First, Detective Hedley Ashley of the Toronto department's criminal identification bureau verified photographs taken of Lonergan in Toronto, which clearly showed the scratches on his face.

Then, Toronto detective William J. Wall read his thirty-eight-page typed transcription of John Loehr's examination of Lonergan on October 25, 1943, at the Toronto police station. The courtroom was silent and the jurors, journalists, and spectators were immediately riveted by the narrative of Lonergan's nightlife with Patricia as active members of café society, their elopement in Las Vegas, the birth of their son, and the breakdown of their brief marriage. Wall was forced to stop reading at five o'clock.

Judge Wallace, who tolerated no nonsense in his courtroom, was aware of the so-called "depravity" described in Lonergan's statement, and he did not want to make a bad situation worse. The following morning, anticipating that the story of Lonergan and his "unnatural advances"—as the *New York Herald-Tribune* delicately phrased it—toward Maurice Worcester was included in the section of the Toronto transcript to be shortly read by Detective Wall, he banned spectators from the court. Hence, the only people who heard the "unsavory passages" (to use Meyer Berger's words) of this tale—along with the details of Lonergan's date with Jean Murphy Jaburg—were the lawyers, jury members, journalists (who were allowed to remain in their seats), and Lonergan himself, who appeared more anxious than he had a day earlier. Wallace did not interrupt Wall's reading, and to his credit, refrained from any commentary on morals and values.

Lonergan's official confession was the next order of business. As of yet, Grumet had not introduced any fingerprint or blood evidence or an eyewitness who could place Lonergan inside Patricia's suite at the time of the murder—and nor would he. Apart from circumstantial evidence, yet to be brought to the jury's attention, and the fake alibi about Lonergan's encounter with the US soldier Maurice Worcester that portrayed Lonergan as immoral, the prosecution's entire case rested on the jury accepting the confession as an accurate account of the killing.

Thus, Broderick attempted one more time—and what did he have to lose?—to have the confession suppressed. This motion led to an almost unprecedented scene in the courtroom. With the jury excused, Broderick— in an audacious move, and arguably a last-ditch effort to help his client— called as witnesses, one after the other, DA Frank Hogan, ADA Grumet, and Deputy ADA Loehr to respond to questions about the treatment accorded Lonergan by Toronto and New York police and district attorney officials between October 25 and 28, 1943. The day's antics delayed the testimony of Jean Murphy Jaburg, who had arrived in New York from Palm Beach, Florida, at Grumet's behest.

Hogan, who stayed behind the scenes during this period, did not have much to add.

Grumet, on the other hand, was decidedly annoyed by Broderick's grandstanding. Asked repeatedly by Broderick if Lonergan had been abused during this interrogation, Grumet responded "No" each time. The only point he conceded was that Lonergan did not have much sleep from 5:00 p.m. on October 27 to 2:00 p.m. on October 28.

Judge Wallace's patience had also run out.

"Did you threaten, strike, or otherwise molest him?" Wallace asked, interrupting Broderick.

"Not at all," stated Grumet, clearly aggravated by the question.

Grumet vehemently denied, too, that Lonergan had asked to speak to a lawyer, had been force-fed brandy, and, as Broderick alleged, that he had said to Lonergan that he would die by the electric chair and that Grumet would be "glad to turn the juice on you."

"Didn't you flaunt a picture of Lonergan's dead wife before him and say, 'See what you did to your wife?'" asked Broderick.

"I did nothing of the kind. I don't believe we had those pictures at the time. No such thing happened," Grumet stated.

It was Loehr's turn next. He admitted that when he was in Toronto, he witnessed Lonergan sleeping in two chairs that had been pushed together. But, he, too, denied that anything inappropriate had been done to Lonergan, by him or the various police officers. Like Grumet, he firmly refuted the notion that Lonergan had been forced to drink brandy, or that Loehr had used a copy of *Gilbert's Annotated Code and Penal Law* (the "bible" of

New York State law by law librarian Frank B. Gilbert, which was originally published in 1918) to explain to Lonergan how he might be able to "escape extreme punishment" if he confessed to a lesser crime.

"Did you tell him," asked Broderick, "that you would not prosecute him for murder in the first degree if he talked?'

"I did not," Loehr declared.

Once the three had been cross-examined, Broderick urged the judge to disallow Lonergan's confession on the grounds that it was obtained under duress. And, once more, Wallace refused to do so.

The court session ended on Friday afternoon. Lonergan's confession was to be introduced to the jury on Monday, March 27, when the trial continued.

Back at his office, Grumet, exhausted from a hectic day in court, poured himself a shot of Scotch whisky and ruminated about what he regarded as Broderick's deplorable antics.

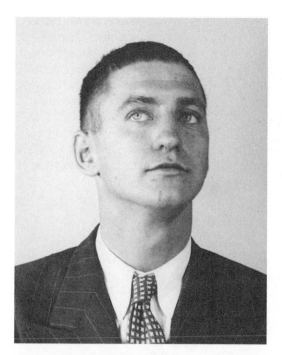

Manhattan district attorney's office photograph of Wayne Lonergan in October 1943 with scratches visible on his chin. Lonergan first claimed that he had received the scratches after he had returned to Toronto on the evening of October 24, 1943. NEW YORK CITY MUNICIPAL ARCHIVES

Mario Gabellini and his wife Drusilla Dunn followng their elopement in Las Vegas in September 1935. The couple divorced a year later. Gabellini escorted Patricia Burton Lonergan on a date to the Stork Club on the last night of her life. LOS ANGELES TIMES PHOTOGRAPHIC ARCHIVES (COLLECTION 1429) UCLA LIBRARY SPECIAL COLLECTIONS, CHARLES E. YOUNG RESEARCH LIBRARY UCLA

John Loehr, the Manhattan deputy district attorney, who traveled to Toronto to interrogate Wayne Lonergan and escort him back to New York City. Loehr subsequently was involved in eliciting a confession from Lonergan. COURTESY OF JOHN G. LOEHR AND JUSTICE GERALD LOEHR

Dr. Milton Helpern, the deputy medical examiner of New York City in 1943, who performed the autopsy on Patricia Burton Lonergan. Later, Helpern was appointed the chief medical examiner. He had a reputation as "Sherlock Holmes with a microscope." NEW YORK UNIVERSITY LILLIAN AND CLARENCE DE LA CHAPELLE MEDICAL ARCHIVES

Dr. Alexander Wiener, an expert on blood type and a member of the Department of Forensic Medicine at New York University Medical School. He surveyed the murder scene at Patricia Burton Lonergan's suite, but was unable to offer any firm conclusions that could be used during Wayne Lonergan's trial. NEW YORK UNIVERSITY LILLIAN AND CLARENCE DE LA CHAPELLE MEDICAL ARCHIVES

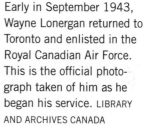

Early in September 1943, Wayne Lonergan returned to Toronto and enlisted in the Royal Canadian Air Force. This is the official photograph taken of him as he began his service. LIBRARY AND ARCHIVES CANADA

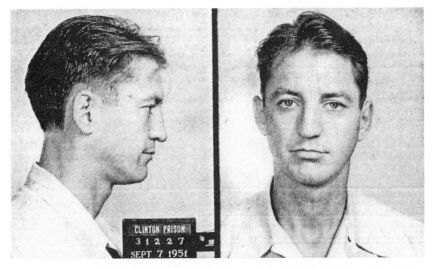

Wayne Lonergan's inmate photographs at Clinton Prison in Dannemora, New York, in September 1951. After seven years of incarceration, Lonergan was worn out and no longer the charming café society "playboy." NEW YORK STATE ARCHIVES

Edward V. Broderick, the flamboyant attorney who defended Wayne Lonergan. Broderick regarded it as a mark of distinction that for a time he held the record in New York City as the lawyer who had been cited the most times, four in all, for contempt of court.
NEWSPAPERS.COM (FROM *DAILY NEWS* ARTICLE APRIL 15, 1944)

Governess Elizabeth Black, who lovingly looked after young William "Billy" Lonergan, Patricia and Wayne's son. The young boy was eighteen months old when his
mother was murdered. NEWSPAPERS.COM (FROM *DAILY NEWS* ARTICLE NOVEMBER 2, 1943)

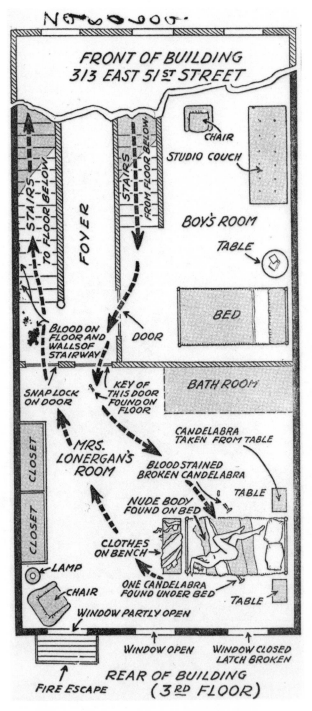

Diagram of the interior of Patricia Burton Lonergan's apartment at 313 East 51st Street in Manhattan. BETTMANN

Wayne Lonergan, "Glamor Boy." Wayne had worked as a lifeguard in Toronto before he moved to New York City in 1939. He was always in great shape and "Hollywood" handsome. BETTMANN

Patricia Burton and her father William O. Burton a few months before his death in October 1940. William had introduced Patricia to Wayne Lonergan and encouraged them to date.
NEWSPAPERS.COM (FROM *DAILY NEWS* ARTICLE SEPTEMBER 1, 1991)

Flier-Husband Held in Heiress' Slaying; Her Nails Yield Clue

COSTELLO TELLS HOW HE DICTATED AURELIO'S CHOICE

Patricia Burton Lonergan's slim, tapering fingers may point the way to her slayer, detectives revealed yesterday following arrest of her RCAF husband in Toronto.

From the start of the police investigation into Patricia Burton Lonergan's murder, her husband Wayne Lonergan was the prime suspect—as this story from the *Daily News* on October 26, 1943 indicates. NEWSPAPERS.COM (FROM *DAILY NEWS* ARTICLE OCTOBER 26, 1943)

Lonergan Here Today To 'Help Solve Killing'

Wayne Lonergan, RCAF aircraftman, early today crossed into the United States from Canada on his way to be questioned here about the bedroom murder of his beautiful heiress wife, Patricia Burton Lonergan. He was due to arrive in New York shortly before noon.

While Lonergan was being cleared by Canadian customs officials at Fort Erie, Ont.,

The late Patricia Burton Lonergan   Wayne Lonergan at Toronto police headquarters

where he was taken from the train because of border technicalities, detectives here delivered a mysterious package to the E. 51st St. station and with great secrecy put it securely under lock and key.

Key to Slaying Mystery

New York Police detectives traveled to Toronto and brought back Wayne Lonergan for quesitoning. Lonergan willingly agreed to accompany them. NEWSPAPERS.COM (FROM *DAILY NEWS* ARTICLE OCTOBER 27, 1943)

DAILY NEWS

LONERGAN ALIBI: TWISTED SEX

Telltale Mark? Wayne Lonergan, husband of the slain Beekman Hill beauty, arrives at LaGuardia airport—with scratch on his chin plainly visible. Police are interested in that scar. Lonergan, who was classified 4F in the U.S. draft because of homosexuality, insists he would was the result of a scuffle with a sailor friend who repulsed his advances in a N.Y. apartment. Assistant District Attorney Gremel was grilling the suspect late last night. —Story on page 4

The *Daily News* on October 28, 1943, with a front page photograph of Wayne Lonergan arriving back in New York escorted by detectives. The lurid headline refers to Lonergan's statement to Toronto and New York police detectives and legal officials that he had been involved in a homosexual encounter the night Patricia was murdered. Owing to such press coverage, the portrait of Lonergan was solidified in the public eye as a dangerous "homosexual." NEWSPAPERS.COM (FROM *DAILY NEWS* ARTICLE OCTOBER 28, 1943)

LONERGAN REVEALED AS 4F, REJECTED ON SEX GROUNDS

A Long, Hard Struggle, But . . .

As lanky, boyish Wayne Lonergan returned to New York, the scene of his wife's murder, at 4:25 P.M. yesterday, it was learned that he had been sent twice to Grand Central Palace for induction into the U. S. armed forces and both times had been rejected and placed in 4F for homosexuality.

The revelation followed a startling report that, while being questioned in Canada, Lonergan confessed to making unnatural advances to the soldier he "befriended" Saturday

End Dimout In All U.S. On Monday

Washington, D. C., Oct. 27 (U.P.)—Dimout regulations that have been operative since the Spring of 1942 will be lifted next Monday, the Government announced tonight.

Wayne Lonergan arrives at LaGuardia Field flanked by Detectives Lonergan (left) and Prendergast.

night. Repulsing these advances, the soldier, whom he named as Maurice Worcester, clawed at his face, Lonergan said in explaining the scratches on his chin and cheek.

Worcester, generally thought to be a figment of Lonergan's imagination after a check at an eastern camp failed to turn up a soldier by that name, actually does exist. But he is believed to have been discharged from the Army in accord with, although he was still wearing his uniform, according to Lonergan.

The 26-year-old RCAF aircraft man arrived at LaGuardia Field aboard an American Airlines flagship from Buffalo and was promptly whisked downtown to the office of District Attorney Frank S. Hogan.

Randolfo Omitted.

He walked from the plane confidently, with Detectives William Prendergast and Nicholas Long

coat, who had accomplished his trip from Canada. He was embarrassingly still a free man—merely in voluntary custody to answer a few questions on the inglorious murder of his beautiful brewery-wife, 22-year-old Patricia Burton Lonergan.

"What are you going to tell 'em, Wayne?" someone called as he strode across the field. Lonergan, hatless, turned and gave a faint smile, then moved. Two scratches, no wider more than three-quarters of an inch long, were visible upon his chin.

At 5:10 P. M. he arrived at Hogan's office and was promptly *(Continued on page 27, col. 2)*

On October 28, 1943, the *Daily News* and other newspapers revealed that Wayne Lonergan had been classified by the US Selective Service Board as "4-F" because he claimed to be a homosexual. Despite later denials, news coverage continued to focus on Lonergan's sexual orientation throughout his trial. NEWSPAPERS.COM (FROM *DAILY NEWS* ARTICLE OCTOBER 28, 1943)

The *Daily News* headline of October 29, 1943. Following a lengthy interrogation, Wayne Lonergan confessed to murdering his wife, Patricia. Later, he and his lawyer claimed the confession was coerced. NEWSPAPERS.COM (FROM *DAILY NEWS* ARTICLE OCTOBER 29, 1943)

Lucille Burton, Patricia Burton Lonergan's mother, and Elizabeth Black, the governess who tended to young Billy, both testified at Wayne Lonergan's trial. NEWSPAPERS.COM (FROM *DAILY NEWS* ARTICLE MARCH 24, 1944)

Mario Gabellini, whose name was misspelled by the *Daily News*, was one of the last people to see Patricia Burton Lonergan alive. Initially, he was a person of interest in the murder investigation and held in custody, but was eventually released.

NEWSPAPERS.COM (FROM *DAILY NEWS* ARTICLE OCTOBER 26, 1943)

Jean Murphy Jaburg, a former show-girl, was Wayne Lonergan's date on the evening of Saturday October 23, 1943. She later said that being linked to Lonergan and the murder case had "ruined" her theatrical career.

NEWSPAPERS.COM (FROM *DAILY NEWS* ARTICLE FEBRUARY 23, 1944)

Willam O. Burton, Patricia Burton Lonergan's father and scion of a wealthy New York family, may have had an intimate relationship with Wayne Lonergan.

NEWSPAPERS.COM (FROM *DAILY NEWS* ARTICLE OCTOBER 26, 1943)

Manhattan assistant district attorney Jacob Grumet was the lead prosecutor at the murder trial of Wayne Lonergan and was frequently exasperated by the antics of Lonergan's lawyer Edward Broderick.
NEWSPAPERS.COM (FROM *DAILY NEWS* ARTICLE FEBRUARY 17, 1944)

Wayne Lonergan on December 2, 1965, at the Royal York Hotel in Toronto following his release from prison.
JAMES LEWCUN/*THE GLOBE AND MAIL*

Brutal, Cold-Blooded, Deliberate Murder

LATE ON SATURDAY NIGHT, March 25, Broderick emerged from the Tombs after spending two and a half hours with Lonergan. He intimated to the reporters waiting for him outside the prison walls that he was seriously thinking of allowing Lonergan to testify. He never did. Instead, he gambled Lonergan's life on one key issue: Despite how the judge ruled, he could convince the jury that Lonergan's confession was false and coerced by unwarranted police and DA tactics. In hindsight, this was merely wishful thinking on his part, and an imperfect defense strategy.

It is true that in the past three decades since DNA testing has been utilized in American court cases, hundreds of convicted individuals have been exonerated. And among this large group have been defendants who confessed to their crimes, many of whom were forced to do so by unscrupulous police officials. Most notable were the so-called "Central Park Five," four African-American boys and one Hispanic teen ranging in ages from thirteen to sixteen. They were targeted by the police and Linda Fairstein, head of the sex crimes unit of the Manhattan district attorney's office, and were coerced into confessing to the rape of a young white woman jogging in Central Park during the evening of April 19, 1989. While they soon declared their confessions to be false, they were nevertheless found guilty and received sentences between five and fifteen years in prison. It took until 2002 to free the Five after a convicted rapist confessed to the crime and DNA evidence proved that he had indeed assaulted the jogger.

It has been equally true that police and district attorneys—who succumb to "tunnel vision" and insist a suspect is guilty, deliberately ignoring possible evidence to the contrary—can, through psychological manipulation and physical browbeating, if not abuse, then obtain a confession from an innocent person.

The case of Wayne Lonergan is not one of those instances, however.

After reviewing the DA and police records and the statements of every legal official Lonergan came into contact with in Toronto and New York and given the specifics of his confession and the manner in which he told it, the only reasonable conclusion that can be arrived at is that he related a story of a murder that was entirely believable. His statement of the events of October 24, 1943, at Patricia's residence fit the pattern of his behavior and simply made too much sense. Though Lonergan was no fool, he was also not clever enough to have devised a confession with such attention to detail—much more detail than the fabricated parts of his Toronto statement. Why confess at all if he was innocent, as he said? Yes, over a period of many hours Loehr and Grumet and the other police officials berated him—if you could call it that—but this treatment was hardly vicious or abusive.

If Lonergan was innocent, and the confession (as well as his initial alibi) was false, as he claimed, what, then, happened to his RCAF uniform?

According to Lonergan, it was not stolen, as he first claimed, nor was it apparently tossed in the East River, as he stated in his alleged coerced confession. So where was it? Even author Hamilton Darby Perry, who told the story of the murder from Lonergan's perspective, conceded that Lonergan never adequately answered this question or offered any opinion as to why anyone else besides him would have wanted to kill Patricia. Because, simply put, there was no one else. It is thus understandable that after all was said and done, the members of the jury did not accept Broderick's coercion argument. It was a reasonable conclusion to have arrived at.

Lonergan was somewhat more nervous as court convened on Monday, March 27. He repeatedly rubbed his chin and ran his fingers through his hair. More than half the day was taken up by Broderick's cross-examination of Toronto and New York police officers—including Detective Sergeant Arthur Harris from Toronto and Captain Daniel Mahoney and Detective William Prendergast from New York, who described how he and his partner Nicholas Looram had traveled to Toronto and escorted Lonergan back with them and John Loehr. When asked by Broderick and Judge Wallace if Lonergan had been under duress or coerced into giving a confession—Broderick continually referred to it as the "so-called confession"—each of the officers said "No." They also reiterated that no promises were made to Lonergan; no one referenced his sexual orientation; no one forced him to drink liquor; and no one taunted him about being executed in the electric chair.

Finally, the moment the jury and gallery members had been waiting for arrived at 4:00 p.m.: the reading of the confession by DA stenographer Henry Edward Vaccaro, who had originally taken Lonergan's statement on October 28, 1943. Before Vaccaro could utter a word, Broderick was at it again, testing Wallace's patience by making yet another motion to have the confession thrown out. The judge quickly denied his request. Vaccaro then began to read the confession in a clear voice, the tragic tale of how Lonergan had fought with and murdered Patricia. Vaccaro was nearly finished when Wallace abruptly ended that day's session. Yet the significant parts of Lonergan's confrontation with Patricia had been covered and had presumably made an impression on the jury members.

The next day the story was described in all of its grisly detail in dozens of US and Canadian newspapers: the torrid argument; Patricia struck by the candlesticks; Lonergan choking her to death; his futile attempt to clean up the blood; and then, how he disposed of his uniform and watch by throwing them in the duffel bag into the East River.

As soon as the proceedings resumed on Tuesday, March 28, Vaccaro finished the reading, which included the revelation that Lonergan may have contemplated suicide in the months before the murder. His visit with Dr. Isidore Michel in New York and his efforts to obtain arsenic and strychnine from him were described, as well.

Grumet saved his strongest witnesses—as well as the most glamorous—until the end.

The glamour was first. No matter her peevish mood about being dragged from Florida to testify, Jean Murphy Jaburg smiled and was delighted to pose for photographers on the steps in front of the courthouse. Suntanned from her trip, she looked radiant as she strode into the courtroom in a chic blue suit with silk lapels, a white frilly scarf, and wearing a soft purple felt hat that amply displayed her lustrous blonde curls. She was a woman who commanded attention, and she got it from the men in the jury box and among the male reporters on the far side of the room. She duly related the details of her introduction to Lonergan and their Saturday-night date, followed by the Sunday lunch at the Plaza when Lonergan showed up wearing John Harjes's pants and jacket. Her testimony did not offer much, other than confirming that Lonergan had told her that his uniform allegedly had been stolen. When the attorneys were finished with her, she smiled at Lonergan as she walked past him, though he did not reciprocate, nor did he even look at her. It was the last time either of them ever saw each other.

More damaging to Lonergan's hope for an acquittal was pharmacist Max Levinson. He identified Lonergan as the customer who had come into his First Avenue store on Sunday, October 24, 1943, to purchase a $1.50 Max Factor makeup compact. Lonergan's face slightly reddened as Levinson pointed him out. In Broderick's cross-examination, he did get Levinson to admit that when he saw Lonergan that day, he did not recall whether he had any scratches on his face. Nor, more importantly, could he state with absolute certainty that the compact found in Harjes's apartment was the one he had sold to Lonergan.

Annaliese Schonberg, the Ray family's nurse, was the first of two surprise prosecution witnesses Grumet called. She told the court how she had stood outside Patricia's bedroom door and more than likely heard a murder being committed. Grumet asked her to imitate the screams she had heard, but she said she could not. She did state that she was about to knock several times on the bedroom door, though she never did. Why she did not call the police—as she surely should have—was not addressed. She said she returned to reading the newspaper, but did hear one last loud and shrill scream before the shouting stopped. It was at this moment that Lonergan, according to his confession, stood over Patricia and realized that she was no longer moving. "I stepped back," he had related, "and I was horrified at this mess of blood all over the place."

Despite Broderick's best efforts to poke holes in Schonberg's story, he could not do it, and she merely repeated herself, reinforcing the horror of what she had experienced in the minds of the jury. Of course, she did not see Lonergan in the residence, yet there was a strong connection between what she had heard and how Lonergan had described what had happened.

Grumet's final witness was another surprise: Ruth Forster, the florist who ran a shop on the corner of East 79th Street and Lexington Avenue beside Harjes's apartment. She identified Lonergan as the man she recalled seeing on Sunday, October 24, at around 11:00 a.m., walking toward the East River, holding a duffel bag. She had also identified this individual as Lonergan in a police lineup. She pointed him out again in the courtroom. As soon as Grumet was finished with Forster, he rested his case at 3:15 p.m.

In what can only be regarded as a desperate ploy—in a long list of desperate ploys—Broderick made a series of motions to have the jury not consider first-degree murder, second-degree murder, manslaughter in the first, or manslaughter in the second. Wallace denied each one as fast as Broderick made them.

For all of Broderick's strategic moves, he came up with no defense at all on Wednesday, March 29. He had examined Detective Prendergast before the completion of the session on Tuesday. He questioned Dr. Isidore Michel about Lonergan's efforts to buy poison. But Wallace determined that this incident and Michel's testimony were not relevant to the murder charge and instructed the jury to disregard it.

Broderick called Mario Gabellini to the witness stand, who told about his immigration to the United States, his life as an interior decorator, and the fact that he had been married twice. He reviewed that last night out with Patricia, as well. Gabellini, however, added nothing to what was already known about his Saturday-night date with her. If it was Broderick's intention to further besmirch Patricia's reputation for dating a swarthy Italian divorcé twenty-one years her senior and cast doubt on Lonergan's culpability in her death, it failed miserably.

Broderick opted not to put Lonergan on the stand—which Lonergan later maintained was a huge mistake—or offer a rebuttal testimony from the psychiatrist he had hired to examine the defendant. When he attempted to submit a medical report documenting Lonergan's mother Clara's troubled medical history, Wallace denied it because he ruled that Broderick "had not laid out a foundation for admission of the report."

As a last Hail Mary, Broderick asked the judge if the jury could go on a field trip to the foot of East 79th Street to ascertain whether it was possible for Lonergan to have thrown the duffel bag into the water. Wallace denied that request, too. Though it was true that there was a fence on the pier at that spot, it was possible to climb over it, which is what Captain Daniel Mahoney said Lonergan had told him he had done.

In any event, a visit by the jury to the end of 79th Street wouldn't have made a difference. The police had brought Lonergan to the pier, accompanied by an entourage of journalists and news photographers, so that he could demonstrate how it was possible to get close enough to the water's edge to toss the duffel bag into the river. One of the photographers present, Lawrence Froeber of the *Daily News*, had snapped a picture of the gathering, which was widely distributed.

On Thursday, March 30, the jury listened to closing arguments. As was the recognized procedure in the State of New York, the defense offered the first summation, followed by the prosecution.

Like a veteran Broadway actor, Broderick moved about the courtroom, speaking for more than an hour and a half. His voice was hoarse by the time he was done. He offered the jury other murder scenarios, as improbable as they were: that Patricia had been killed by a burglar, that she was so drunk she had injured herself, or that Mario Gabellini or Peter Elser were somehow involved in her death.

His main point, however, was that Lonergan was a victim of police abuse and a "terrible indictment." He heaped scorn on Hogan, Grumet, Loehr, Mahoney, and every other person in the DA's office and the New York police force who had had contact with Lonergan. His client, he asserted, had been coerced into giving a false confession by a combination of "no rest, no sleep, fatigue and liquor wearing him out."

Finally, he came to the weapons used at the scene: the candleholders. If they were used to bludgeon Patricia Burton Lonergan, he asked, why was there no blood on them? He suggested, with zero evidence, that the candlesticks might have been planted by the police

"I say to you," Broderick declared, "that you can figure out for yourselves in the jury room, could you possibly, with the short grasp you have upon this candleholder, hit anybody a blow on the head that would cause that candlestick base to take the shape it is in?" He held up one of the candlesticks. "Isn't that distorted shape," he asked, "the result of pressure such as stamping on it, or throwing it down and stamping on it, rather than from contact with a human skull? The skull wasn't a brick wall. It wasn't a cement foundation. This looks more like something ran over it, and that becomes important, because there isn't a single drop of blood on these candlesticks, or on any part of it. . . . If that scalp was opened by these candlesticks, there would be blood on these candlesticks. These candlesticks were placed in that room on the bed after Mrs. Lonergan had stopped bleeding."

On this point, Broderick was wrong, though he did not (and couldn't possibly) know it. Helpern had found a "thick bloodstain" near the upper rim of the base of one of the candleholders, but for some inexplicable reason, Grumet and Helpern decided not to share this finding with Broderick. Had they done so, it might have opened the door to questions about the blood type found on the holder, and the fact that Wiener was unable to identify that. Perhaps Grumet did not want to complicate matters. Still, it was a debatable legal decision to not draw attention to the bloodstain, as well as to permit Broderick to make this accusation that must have had some jury members wondering about this anomaly.

The prosecution had, moreover, not proved, Broderick added with gusto, that Lonergan was at Patricia's residence on the Sunday morning in question. And there was no way to determine if the skin found under her fingernails belonged to him. It was true, too, that no witnesses were found who had seen Lonergan walk back to Harjes's apartment after the murder took place, wearing his bloodstained uniform. These were all relevant points—if not for the confession.

Grumet would have none of Broderick's showmanship or his casting of doubts on the case or the confession. "This was brutal, cold-blooded deliberate murder," he said, pacing in front of the jury like a caged tiger. "The defendant . . . picked up the first candleholder which was on the table where his wife was lying. Now I told you at the very beginning that Mr. Broderick said that every witness was lying, that all the evidence was manufactured, that we placed the candleholders, the dumbbell, and the makeup compact in the room. I won't even dignify that with an answer."

Police officials had determined that the distance was about seventeen feet from the table to the bed. He paced off that distance and stood between the lawyer's table and the judge's bench. Broderick was on his feet, objecting that the distance was only seven feet, but to no avail.

"Now, gentlemen," Grumet continued, "from the jury box to this point is approximately seventeen feet. The defendant has said he picked up the candleholder and went over to the bed where his wife was lying and hit her head with the candleholder. He struck her with such tremendous force that it broke into pieces." (Again, here is where he might have mentioned the bloodstain found on the rim of the candleholder.)

Then Lonergan, Grumet said, having hit Patricia with the second candleholder, grabbed her by the throat and strangled her for a full three minutes until she was dead.

"The killing of Patricia Lonergan by this defendant was from deliberate and premeditated design to accomplish her death and is murder in the first degree. He had plenty of time to think about it, plenty of time to reflect and consider opportunity to decide whether to kill or not to kill."

Grumet disputed Broderick's characterization of Lonergan as a "country boy from the far reaches of Canada, cheated [into a confession] by smart city slicker attorneys on the public payroll." No, Grumet argued, Lonergan was "just a parasite" living off of his wife's money. He did not mention anything about Lonergan's sexual orientation, yet it is reasonable to assume that it remained fixed in the back of the minds of most members of the jury nonetheless as they listened to Grumet's summation.

Since the burden of proof was on the prosecution to prove guilt beyond a reasonable doubt, Grumet denied that Lonergan was forced to drink liquor before he confessed or that he had been subject to any physical or mental abuse.

"Gentlemen," he concluded after addressing the jury for an hour, "decide this case on the evidence, and just on the evidence. On behalf of the people of the State of New York, I ask you to find this defendant guilty of murder in the first degree."

The obvious point that Grumet glossed over was that the only real evidence, as noted, was the confession. Everything else—the story about the makeup compact; Ruth Forster's eyewitness account of seeing Lonergan on the street with a duffel bag—were circumstantial at best. That would be the main issue the jury would have to weigh in its deliberations.

In his charge to the jury on Friday, March 31, Judge Wallace reviewed the facts of the case. He pointed out that there was no evidence introduced that Patricia was drunk at any time Saturday night when she was out with Gabellini, or on the Sunday morning of the murder, but that she did have several drinks during that twelve-hour period. There was also no evidence, he added, repeating what Grumet had said, that Lonergan had been "plied" with liquor by the DA and police before he had confessed.

The jury began deliberating at 12:46 p.m. on Friday, March 31. At 3:45 p.m. foreman William Byrne asked for further instruction: The jury wanted more information about duress as it pertained to a confession obtained by the State.

With the two opposing lawyers and Lonergan present, Wallace reviewed the facts of the case again and how the confession was secured. He explained that the key issue to consider was the difference between a confession given voluntarily and one obtained under duress. Was the confession coerced out of Lonergan? If they believed this, they should disregard the confession and must then deliver a verdict of not guilty, since, as he pointed out, "the People's case depends in large measure on the confession."

A few hours after that, at 6:51 p.m., the jury members had a second query about the different degrees of murder and manslaughter. Wallace offered them a short lesson in the criminal code and the options they had—from finding the defendant guilty of murder in the first degree to a verdict of not guilty. He explained the difference between first-degree premeditated murder and second-degree murder (in the latter, that he murdered her, but in the heat of the moment, without planning to do so in advance). He also explained the difference between first-degree, or voluntary, manslaughter—that he killed her as a "crime of passion" in an argument that escalated—and second-degree, or involuntary, manslaughter—in which Patricia was killed in a negligent way, but with no specific intent to do so.

This fourteen-minute exchange later became the basis of one of Lonergan's appeals, because unlike the first time the jury had asked for more information, Broderick and Lonergan were not in the courtroom when Wallace spoke to the jury on this second occasion, which they should have been, according to clause 427 of *The Code of Criminal Procedure of the State of New York* (1936 and 1940). This clause stipulated that if the jury was deliberating and was brought back to the courtroom with a request for information, notice had to be given to the district attorney and to the counsel for the defense, "and in case of felony, in the presence of the defendant."

Court officers informed Lonergan—as well as Grumet—that the judge was to speak to the jury a second time (why Grumet chose not to be present is unknown). Broderick had left the courthouse and Lonergan was eating his dinner. Lonergan told the court officers he wanted to finish his meal. Broderick, Lonergan, and another lawyer who later represented him (following Broderick's death in 1957) argued that the court had failed in its legal duty to ensure that the defendant and his attorney were present for a conversation the judge had with the jury. The appeals court was to consider this issue, but on the last day of March, 1944, that was still far off in the future.

At 10:22 p.m., ten hours after they had begun deliberating, the members of the jury reached a verdict. Once everyone involved was gathered back into the courtroom, the clerk asked the jury to rise and "look upon the defendant," and for Lonergan to rise and "look upon the jury." Foreman William Byrne, when prompted, announced that the jury had a verdict.

"We find the defendant, Wayne Lonergan, guilty of murder in the second degree," said Byrne.

This meant that while Lonergan would not face a possible death sentence in the electric chair, he would be sentenced to at least twenty years, if not life, in prison. As Byrne's words sank in, Lonergan, according to Meyer Berger of the *New York Times*, who was present, bowed his head, "bit his lip, his knuckles went white on the counsel table and his eyes batted almost in a flutter. Some thought they heard him sob." No other journalist stated that Lonergan cried, but several others did note that he was visibly upset.

Judge Wallace did not comment one way or the other on the verdict as he dismissed the jury, reminding them not to speak with the press about the verdict.

Grumet declared to the reporters that the jury's finding was "fair and intelligent," an assessment shared by Hogan and Loehr.

Broderick, on the other hand, refused to comment about the jury's decision. "Lonergan's a soldier of fortune," he said. "It's his belief that if his number's up, it's up."

The sentencing was set for Monday, April 17. A day later, Broderick still would not state if he planned to appeal. Having watched the trial unfold, RCAF officials finally acted: They announced that as a result of the verdict, Lonergan was to be discharged from the Canadian air force effective April 6, 1944.

———

During the next week, the verdict attracted the expected number of headlines and commentaries. Some pundits like Leonard Lyons remarked about how Lonergan had escaped the "chair." The high-and-mighty editors of the *Philadelphia Inquirer* pointed fingers. They not only blamed Lonergan for the crime, but they also cast an evil eye at Patricia's lifestyle, as well. In their view, the decadence of New York's café society was the true culprit. "Both Lonergan and his wife had long trodden the path of conduct, or rather misconduct, which inevitably leads to ruin and disaster," the editors wrote. "They had surrounded themselves with equally careless companions, who seemed to believe that the laws of common decency and morality were not for them and could be flouted with impunity."

Syndicated columnist George E. Sokolsky put the case in a broader perspective. Known for his conservative anti-Communist views, Sokolsky wondered in a column published on April 5 how it was possible that at that moment, twenty million human beings were engaged in fighting a terrible war with "countries disappearing and reappearing," yet the great headline was

"Lonergan Beats Chair." (Lonergan's murder trial was one of two sensational news stories that consumed the press during the last week of March and the first few weeks of April 1944. The other was whether famed comedian Charlie Chaplin had fathered the child of his onetime girlfriend Joan Barry, who had filed a paternity suit against him. He was acquitted on April 4.)

Meanwhile, *Time* magazine connected the trial and its verdict with homosexuality. "The trial was . . . a clinical study of unusual interest to doctors and psychiatrists," an unsigned article about the case noted. "For it was obvious last week that Defense Attorney Edward V. Broderick would make some plea of insanity involving homosexuality. . . . The defense would apparently try to prove: 1) that Lonergan was too unstable to commit premeditated murder; or 2) temporary insanity. . . . Headlines billed Lonergan as a homosexual who seemed utterly unmoved by his wife's murder. . . . To most people Lonergan does not look like a homosexual. Contrary to popular legend, homosexuals are not necessarily physically abnormal, though sometimes a glandular disturbance is involved. As a rule, homosexuals are made, not born." Such was the daft thinking of the era, which was accepted as sound analysis.

Lucille Burton, who defended her daughter's honor for the rest of her life, announced that she was seeking custody of her grandson, Billy, now twenty-one months old. On June 16, 1944, this custody was approved and she was named the boy's general guardian.

Billy was the sole beneficiary of his great-grandmother Stella Bernheimer Housman's estate, which was valued on August 1943 at $6.9 million. The young boy had already received $180,000 from Patricia's estate, and after administrative deductions, was left with $120,000. By then, he was also the recipient of about $6,000 a year from a separate trust fund that had been established by Stella; Lucille could use that money to look after him, as well. In December 1944, the Surrogate's Court granted Lucille a further $300 per month from the infant's estate for help in raising the boy. Early in 1947, to further protect her grandson from the notoriety of the terrible crime, Lucille petitioned the court to officially change the boy's name to "William Anthony Burton"—the name he still uses to this day.

Stella died in Palm Beach, Florida, on January 25, 1954, at the age of eighty-five. Less than two weeks later, eleven-year-old Billy officially inherited her nearly $7 million estate ($66.6 million today) and was told the tragic truth about his parents.

— ◦ —

On Friday, April 14, Broderick was scheduled to answer for the contempt-of-court charges from the first Lonergan trial. Yet because Lonergan still had not been sentenced, he was granted another week's reprieve.

At long last, on Friday, April 21, Broderick appeared before Judge Freschi, whose anger had not subsided. As soon as the proceedings started, Freschi berated Broderick for twenty minutes for what he termed the lawyer's "wild, reckless, impertinent, abusive, scurrilous, vituperative and irrelevant" behavior and actions. Broderick's "unprofessional" conduct, Freschi added, "was dictated by a desire to delay the trial, confuse the jury and intimidate the court."

Freschi found him guilty on four counts of contempt of court: for failing to appear in court on February 23 and 24, for disobeying the judge when he read a juror a letter Lonergan had written to Surrogate James Foley, for "uproariously rant[ing]" after Grumet requested the initial jury panel be discharged, and for being "outrageously contemptuous" of the court when Freschi remarked that he "hoped the trial would not continue before him." For these transgressions, the judge sentenced Broderick to thirty days in jail on each of the four charges, but to be served concurrently—which meant he had to spend a month in jail. Freschi decided not to impose the sentence immediately, giving Broderick the opportunity to appeal the decision to a higher court.

The Appellate Division took more than a year to adjudicate Broderick's case and opted for leniency. The higher court only fined him $250. The appeals judges concluded that Broderick was defending someone on trial for first-degree murder and assumed that was the reason he had acted with "excessive zeal." In June 1947, in another murder trial before Judge Wallace, Broderick was found guilty yet again of contempt. Wallace fined him $200 and sentenced him to five days in prison at the Tombs. That incarceration lasted only a few hours, after another attorney won his release through an order signed by a higher court justice.

— ◦ —

A week before Broderick stood before Judge Freschi, Wayne Lonergan had stood before Judge Wallace for his sentencing. Prior to the judge rendering his decision, Broderick wanted to list the reasons why he believed there was insufficient evidence to convict his client. Wallace denied his motion.

Standing in the court, Lonergan appeared "indifferent," as the *New York Times* described him. Wallace was tougher than he had to be: For the crime of murdering his wife, Lonergan was sentenced to thirty-five years to imprisonment for the rest of his natural life. He would not be eligible for parole for twenty-three years, until April 22, 1967—though this was later revised to December 22, 1963. The entire sentencing hearing took less than a minute.

Outside the Manhattan courtroom, Broderick told reporters that he was planning to launch an appeal. At 1:00 p.m., "Playboy Wayne Lonergan," as he was dubbed by some reporters, was hustled out of the courtroom through a crowd of three hundred onlookers, into a bulletproof limousine. He was driven to Sing Sing, a maximum-security prison, which at the time used the electric chair for executions, in the village of Ossining, New York, about thirty miles north of New York City on the east bank of the Hudson River. The prison's unique name is based on the name of the indigenous tribe, which had sold the authorities the land in 1685, the "Sinck Sinck," or "Sint Sinck." In 1901, the town, which was then called Sing Sing, changed its name to Ossining, so that it would be distinguished from the prison.

On Lonergan's intake form, he listed as his "nearest relative" his lawyer, Edward V. Broderick. And on the line, "Criminal Acts Attributed to" was written: "Killed wife Patricia Burton Lonergan by beating, choking, and strangling her."

15

Inmate 31227

AS LONERGAN WAS ADAPTING to life inside Sing Sing Prison, Broderick remained committed to protecting his client's interests. On May 16, 1944, in what can only be described as beyond the pale and transparently desperate, Broderick filed "a right of election" in Surrogate's Court in which Lonergan made a claim to one-third of Patricia's estate (at the end of November 1947, the net value of the estate was deemed to be $228,798, or $2.6 million today). He also made good on his promise to launch an appeal of the second-degree murder verdict, since Lonergan could only obtain part of Patricia's estate if his conviction was overturned.

Predictably, the main legal issue of the appeal was that Lonergan's confession was obtained under duress and therefore inadmissible. Broderick contended that Lonergan's constitutional rights had been violated from the moment he had been detained in Toronto to his arraignment in New York City, during which time he was coerced into confessing to the murder. A secondary appeal point was that Judge Wallace had exceeded his authority in his sentence, which Broderick claimed should have been twenty years to life.

Broderick based his primary appeal argument on a recent case that had been adjudicated on March 1, 1943. The US Supreme Court had reversed the conviction of twin brothers Freeman and Raymond McNabb and their cousin, Benjamin McNabb, hillbillies from Marion County, Tennessee, a mountainous eastern area of the state. The three had been convicted of second-degree murder and each sentenced to forty-five years in jail.

On July 31, 1940, four Internal Revenue Service agents—Samuel Leeper, among them—had carried out a raid on the NcNabbs for selling seventy-five gallons of bootleg and untaxed whiskey. In the confrontation that ensued between the agents and the McNabbs, Leeper was fatally shot. The other three agents arrested the twins at the scene. Benjamin McNabb had fled, but he turned himself in the next morning.

FBI agents locked up the defendants and questioned them separately and together from early in the morning hours of August 1 to late in the afternoon of the same day. During that long period, they were deprived of food and proper beds in their cells. Ultimately, confessions were extracted from all of them. The court later ruled that these statements were inadmissible because their confessions had been obtained before they had been arraigned in court; in addition, they had not been given the opportunity to speak to a lawyer. Following the appeal, the sentences of the twins and Benjamin McNabb were reduced to ten years each on charges of voluntary manslaughter.

Broderick was convinced the manner in which the McNabbs were treated mirrored Lonergan's experience. But it was a leap of logic, as the Toronto and New York authorities had not deprived Lonergan of food or a place to rest. And Lonergan had never asked to speak to a lawyer—at least, according to the official record.

In February 1945, Broderick appeared in the Appellate Division to argue his case. ADA Whitman Knapp represented the State and denied the assertion that Lonergan had been mistreated or questioned for longer than seven hours. Five months later, the New York Appeals Court agreed with the State's argument, and without writing an opinion—which surely must have irked Broderick—upheld Lonergan's thirty-five-year prison sentence.

In a last attempt, Broderick requested that the Supreme Court review the conviction, but his application was rejected. This was, as the *New York Herald-Tribune* noted, the "final legal episode" of Lonergan's journey through the system—at least, as it turned out, for the next two decades. Six months after that, the Surrogate's Court officially denied Lonergan's claim on Patricia's estate, basing its decision on the fact that "no one shall be permitted to profit by his own fraud . . . or to acquire property by his crime."

Sing Sing Prison "sprawls over several rolling hills and affords an unrestricted view of the Hudson River," wrote Michael Carter, a journalist for the Baltimore-based *Afro-American* newspaper in May 1943. From anywhere in the town of Ossining, the view was "cheerful," he added, except from inside a cell. "Every window . . . screens in light through a pattern of bars," he noted after a visit to the prison. "You see the river though that pattern and the town and the sky and the sun. The sun repeats the iron bar motif in a pattern of shadow on the floor."

By the time his appeals had been exhausted in 1945, Lonergan had settled into prison life. It could have been worse; at least Lonergan was not one of those inmates condemned to death in Sing Sing's infamous electric chair.

From 1891 to 1963, 606 men and 8 women were executed in Sing Sing's "Death House." Among the most notorious were gangster Louis "Lepke" Buchalter, who died in March 1944 (as the Lonergan trial was under way), and Julius and Ethel Rosenberg, in June 1953, who were executed two years after being convicted of espionage in a controversial trial. (Declassified documents have shown that while Julius was guilty of spying for the Soviet Union, Ethel's role was minimal.) The prison's Jewish chaplain had asked New York State governor Thomas Dewey that Lepke not be executed on March 4, a Saturday, the Jewish Sabbath, but Dewey refused to change the date. In 1943, half of the 22 men on death row were African-American.

Though he likely did not appreciate it, Lonergan benefited from the progressive vision of Warden Lewis Lawes, who had served in that position from 1919 to 1941. In his day, Lawes was considered a prison reformer. He introduced athletics, education and trade school programs, and the installation of radio and motion picture showings for the prisoners' enjoyment, and ensured that the cells were expanded and kept sanitary. Lawes was not a supporter of capital punishment, yet during his long tenure, he supervised 303 executions.

When he first arrived, Lonergan endured a month of hard labor before Warden William Snyder, a veteran of the prison system—Robert Kirby had succeeded Lawes, but died in January 1944, and Snyder was then appointed warden—recognized Lonergan's intelligence and business acumen. He transferred him to the prison's purchasing office. He was seemingly a model prisoner and stayed out of trouble.

While the press eventually lost interest in Lonergan, occasionally his name still made it into gossip columns. "Convicts at Sing Sing report that Wayne Lonergan . . . is one of the most popular prisoners up there," wrote Dorothy Kilgallen in her column of March 7, 1947. On July 12, 1948, columnist Ed Sullivan, who had been recently appointed the host of a television variety show that was to make him an international celebrity, pointed out that Lonergan was "wrangling for a parole." But "for what?" he wondered, failing to acknowledge that Lonergan was not eligible for parole. Danton Walker, the Broadway columnist for the *Daily News*, noted in June 1949 that

Lonergan was spending his time in prison "making notes for a novel about café society." That book, if it actually was contemplated, was never written.

In mid-May 1950, Lonergan was mentioned indirectly in a story about the suicide of Patricia Stousland, a twenty-five-year-old red-headed show-girl who had died at Bellevue Hospital after ingesting poison. The Lonergan connection was that at the time of her death, she was staying at the apartment of Mario Gabellini on East 60th Street. She left a suicide note, which the New York police described as "rambling and almost completely beyond understanding." Gabellini had let her use the apartment while he was out of the country, but once again his name and Lonergan's were linked to the death of a young woman.

As in any large institution in which lots of money changes hands, greed and get-rich scams are prevalent in a prison. In early April 1948, for example, Martin Pomeranz, Sing Sing's principal clerk, was found guilty of smuggling $150 to William Benjamin, who was serving a ten- to twenty-year sentence for swindling credit firms out of $550,000. A similar charge was made against a guard, Morris Diamond, for smuggling in $200 for Benjamin, as well as money for other prisoners, for a fee of 20 percent.

Lonergan was unwittingly accused by another prisoner, who seemingly did not like him, of embezzling $100,000 from the Sing Sing purchasing office in a scheme with two other inmates. In this instance, the charges were false, since Lonergan and the other prisoner clerks never handled any cash. Though he was by all accounts innocent, the warden decided it would be best if Lonergan was transferred. Thus, on September 5, 1951, he was moved to Clinton Prison in Dannemora, New York, 281 miles to the north.

A photograph of Lonergan taken two days after he arrived at Clinton Prison shows a man worn out by seven years of incarceration. Though he was only thirty-three years old when it was taken, he looked much older; the bon vivant "playboy" who once charmed café society was a distant memory. He was now inmate 31227, and would be for the next fourteen years. Yet, he was just as angry; even more so. On his intake form, his criminal act was listed as it was at Sing Sing—"killed wife Patricia Burton Lonergan by beating, choking, and strangling her." Yet, for "criminal act attributed to," officials at Clinton noted: "Denies guilt. Claims he was blackmailed by D.A. Grumet."

That resentment and feeling of victimization, as delusional as it may have been, likely kept Lonergan going.

Sing Sing was bad enough; Clinton Prison in the village of Dannemora—the prison was and still is referred to simply as "Dannemora"—was far from the civilization of Manhattan. Located in the Adirondack Mountain region close to the New York–Quebec border, the locals and inmates referred to the prison as "Little Siberia." The old joke was that the prison only had two seasons, winter and July.

Built in 1844, Clinton Prison was expanded after 1887 when the original wooden walls were replaced by sixty-foot concrete walls that still stand at the present time. In the nineteenth and early twentieth centuries, the prisoners classically wore black-and-white-striped uniforms and were shackled during the day with heavy chains. In July 1929, a riot erupted mainly because of the inmates' anger about overcrowding; three prisoners were killed in a raucous confrontation with guards who tried to quell the disturbance. In the years that followed, progressive reforms were instituted at Clinton, as they were in Sing Sing and other New York prisons.

Lonergan was given a job as a mail clerk and spent a lot of his time reading magazines and books and playing bridge and sports. Over the years, he also befriended two career criminals, Isadore Schwartzberg—aka Irving Shwartzberg, Israel Schawartzberg (adding the "a" in his last name), Louis Siegel, Irving Ace, the Fat Tiger, Mr. Israel, and the Big Mizo—and Moe Auswaks—aka Morris Auswaks and Harry Singer.

A big man at 250 pounds, Schwartzberg's criminal record dated back to 1930 when he was sixteen years old and arrested for grand larceny. He beat that charge and was given a conditional discharge. After that, he was involved in robbery, bookmaking, and forgery. In 1951, he and his younger brother Benjamin pleaded guilty to conspiracy to commit bribery, for trying to fix a college basketball game at Madison Square Garden. Irving was sentenced to a year in jail. Not long after he was released, he was arrested again, this time for being the head of a gang which attempted to "fleece" New York City banks out of $30,000 through false loans. He was released on $20,000 bail. As he liked to jest, "You've heard of a record as long as your arm? Well, my record is as long as two arms."

In January 1954 Schwartzberg was arrested for acts of sodomy; the charge was dismissed by the judge. A year later, while he was out on bail for the 1953 forgery charge, he was arrested again after the police apprehended him driving a stolen car. He was in possession of a priest's robe, leading the officers to believe that he had planned to rob a bank disguised as a priest. Within five months, he violated his bail requirements and was sent to Clinton Prison for four years, where he and Lonergan kept each other company and Schwartzberg transformed himself into a "jailhouse lawyer." There was no denying his talents. Even one ADA commented that Schwartzberg had "a brilliant criminal mind, one that in other circumstances would have made him into an ornament of the bar." Schwartzberg was released on February 25, 1959. He was to interact with Lonergan again in the near future.

Lonergan's other prison pal, "Little" Moe Auswaks, was a veteran felon who arrived in Dannemora in early December 1960, though this was his second stint; the first time he had been incarcerated there was more than three decades earlier. Born in 1902 in Warsaw, Poland (then under Russian control), Auswaks came to New York with his mother, Lena, younger brother Max, and half-sister Fannie in 1912, when he was ten years old. Another brother, Philip, was born in New York. Auswaks's father Meyer, a jewelry salesman, had been in the United States for about five years by that point. Auswaks's first run-in with the law occurred in 1917. There were subsequent arrests for theft and burglary in which he received short prison terms—this included a year and a half in Clinton Prison during 1926 and 1927, for third-degree burglary.

That changed for the worse in January 1929 after Auswaks was charged—together with a New York police officer and three other accomplices—in the robbery of $20,000 worth of jewelry from a Bronx couple. For that crime, he was given a twenty-five-year jail sentence. (His brother Max followed in Moe's footsteps: In 1925, Max, who liked to frequent the Cotton Club, was convicted of forcing a thirteen-year-old girl into prostitution and received a ten- to fifteen-year sentence in Auburn Prison, near Syracuse, New York.)

In late December 1937, while working at a barn outside of Great Meadow Prison at Comstock, New York, where he was incarcerated, Moe escaped, along with another prisoner, Hendryk Reszka. Both men hid out in the New York City area and managed to elude capture for nearly two years, until they were eventually arrested after they robbed a bank of $27,000 in Norwalk, Connecticut, on February 27, 1938. Next, they robbed a Fifth Avenue jewelry store of $72,000 worth of merchandise on August 31. At the end of January

1940 Auswaks received a sentence of thirty to sixty years in Clinton Prison from Judge James Wallace, who would also sentence Lonergan.

Following his release in 1960, Auswaks was sent back to Sing Sing on a parole violation in November of that year, and a month later was transferred to Clinton Prison, where he came into contact with Lonergan. The two men must have traded stories about their experiences in Wallace's courtroom. Auswaks died in prison in December 1977.

<hr>

Convincing himself that he had been wronged by the New York State justice system, Lonergan devoured whatever law books he could find in the prison library and tried to come up with new, creative ways to appeal his sentence. Those efforts were temporarily halted in May 1957 when his ever-determined lawyer, Edward Broderick, died at the age of sixty-four.

Not to be denied, he soon connected with Frances Kahn, who in 1959 was a thirty-one-year-old lawyer with a penchant for challenging the system—no matter what it took. She had grit. At the age of three, she had contracted polio and was thereafter confined to a wheelchair most of the time. That, however, did not stop her. She went on to graduate from the New York University Law School in 1951, got married, and gave birth to a son.

With her thick Bronx accent, blonde hair, and buxom figure, she was attractive, and was otherwise engaging and pleasant, but opposing counsel quickly learned that in a courtroom she was tough and not to be underestimated. She was willing to defend almost anyone who she believed had gotten a "raw" deal from the State. Among her clients was the notorious bank robber George "The Eel" Larned, who had been paralyzed as a result of a shootout with a police officer in 1957 and sentenced to a fifteen- to twenty-year prison term. Kahn appealed his conviction on the grounds that his constitutional rights had been violated because he had been denied representation by the lawyer he had requested. Kahn also later fought for the Brooklyn gangster Joseph Gallo, who was serving a seven- to fourteen-year sentence in Attica State Prison on an extortion conviction. In August 1964, Kahn filed a lawsuit on his behalf, charging that he was being mistreated in prison owing to the fact that he had attempted to integrate black and white prisoners (he had permitted an African-American inmate barber to cut his hair). The deputy corrections commissioner, William Leonard, called Gallo's charge "fictitious," and accused Gallo of being "an agitator and belligerent prisoner."

A year earlier, in January 1963, Kahn had won freedom for thirty-four-year-old Walter Adams by having the court reduce his thirty-year to life sentence for the holdup and killing of a Harlem pharmacist to twenty-five years. Since by then Adams had already served sixteen years in prison, he was eligible for parole. The New York Appellate Court supported her argument that a technical error had been committed by the presiding judge, none other than James Garrett Wallace. When he pronounced sentence, he had failed to ask Adams, as required by law, "What have you to say for yourself, why the judgment of the court should not be pronounced against you?" It was ruled that Adams had been denied his constitutional rights and he was granted parole.

In a lively law career, Kahn made one costly error: She hired the con man Irving Schwartzberg as her law clerk. This odd couple started working on a solution to Lonergan's legal predicament. Kahn was soon to rue the day she became involved with Schwartzberg. (After his release from prison in 1959, Schwartzberg had officially adopted the name "Israel Schawartzberg." But for the purposes of clarity, the spelling of his last name will be kept as "Schwartzberg.")

16

Coercion and Collusion

FRANCES KAHN'S INITIAL strategy for winning Lonergan a new trial was the principle of *coram nobis*—a Latin term meaning "error before us." In filing a writ of *coram nobis* in October 1959 in the Appellate Division of the Supreme Court of New York (the second-highest court in the state), Kahn was attempting to convince the court that there had been a fundamental error at Lonergan's trial. During that second brief discussion Judge Wallace had had with the jury, in which he explained to its members the differences between first- and second-degree murder and manslaughter, he had committed an error, because Lonergan and his lawyer, Broderick, were not present in the courtroom.

Kahn got nowhere with this argument in 1959, or in a subsequent petition for a writ of *habeas corpus* in late July of 1961. The second writ was based on a Court of Appeals of the State of New York decision in a case that had been considered a few months earlier. In October 1952, George Bartlam, a nineteen-year-old movie usher, had been charged in the killing of a twenty-two-year-old man in a brutal attack with a baseball bat that took place in Central Park. Eight months later, Bartlam was convicted of murder and sentenced to life imprisonment. Early in 1961 his lawyer appealed with a writ of *habeas corpus* on the grounds that during Bartlam's trial, the judge and jury had had a discussion at which Bartlam and his lawyer were not present—or so an examination of the trial minutes at first seems to suggest. In a decision of May 1961, the appeals court sent the issue back to the superior (and lower) court, the Cayuga County Supreme Court, for further hearings. (Three years later after this judicial reconsideration, this appeal was rejected when the courts determined that Bartlam, in fact, had been "present at all stages of his trial," and thus his constitutional rights had not been violated.)

In both writs filed by Kahn, however, her arguments were spurious, and the Bartlam decision of May 1961 did not strengthen her case. As was later determined by the Appellate Division of the Supreme Court of New York, First Division, Judge Wallace seemingly had not violated clause 427, or Lonergan's constitutional rights. A court reporter was present during this second interaction with the jury, and the transcript of the discussion (by folio numbers) was referenced in Kahn's writ of *habeas corpus*. A detailed summary of Wallace's explanation about first- and second-degree murder and manslaughter was also included in Meyer Berger's trial report in the *New York Times* the next day, on April 1, 1944. Presumably, Berger and other journalists were in the courtroom when Wallace addressed the jury a second time. And, as noted in chapter 14, court officers insisted that they had told Lonergan about the second meeting; he had simply opted not to return to the courtroom because he wanted to finish eating his dinner. His lawyer was not able to advise him, since Broderick had left the courthouse. It was possible that the court was guilty of neglect in not compelling Lonergan to be present in the courtroom, though this matter was not raised in either of Kahn's appeal submissions—only that Wallace had addressed the jury without Lonergan and Broderick being present.

In December 1962, the Appellate Division of the Supreme Court of New York ruled against Lonergan. The judges affirmed DA Frank Hogan's motion to dismiss the writ of *habeas corpus* that Kahn had submitted on Lonergan's behalf, without offering a written decision and explanation. In light of the initial Bartlam decision of May 1961, sending the case back to the lower court for reconsideration, the judges' lack of a decision for a similar reassessment of Lonergan's case on the same grounds was indeed puzzling. It can only be speculated that the appeals judges, having reviewed the court transcript and the statements about the court's notification to Lonergan, decided that Wallace's directive on the differences between first- and second-degree murder and manslaughter, though perhaps "imperfectly given," were "perfectly accurate" (to use the words of Columbia Law School professor Daniel C. Richman) and did not violate Lonergan's constitutional rights or New York State criminal procedural rules. And even if they had determined his rights had been violated, the appeals judges presumably concluded that Wallace's actions were deemed not to have influenced the final outcome of the trial.

Two years later, a significant US Supreme Court decision, followed by a ruling in the Court of Appeals of the State of New York, provided Kahn with yet another opening to attempt to overturn Lonergan's conviction.

—◦—

On June 14, 1960, at around 1:00 a.m., thirty-four-year-old Nathan ("Satan") Jackson and his girlfriend Nora Elliot, twenty-seven years of age, both of whom were African-American, entered the ICU Hotel on Fulton Street near the corner of Franklin Avenue in Brooklyn and asked to register for a room. Before the clerk could accommodate them, Jackson pointed a gun at him and demanded money. The pair made off with $60. As they fled, the couple encountered twenty-eight-year-old rookie patrolman William Ramos, who was also African-American. Ramos had heard the sound of a window breaking as he walked by the ICU Hotel. It had been smashed by a hotel employee in order to alert the police that there had been a robbery. Ramos saw Jackson and Elliot fleeing and instructed them to stop. When they did not, he pursued them. As he caught up to them, Elliot somehow grabbed his nightstick and began striking Ramos in the head. The constable fell to the ground, yet managed to fire two shots at Jackson, hitting him in the stomach. Jackson then fired back at Ramos—as Elliot, according to witnesses, screamed at Jackson to "kill him, kill him." Ramos was hit and died a short time later at the hospital.

Alerted to Jackson seeking aid at another local hospital for his wounds, Brooklyn detectives questioned him, and he confessed to the robbery and to shooting Ramos. A few hours later, after Jackson had been given sedatives for his pain and nausea—Demerol and scopolamine (or hyoscine)—an ADA arrived at the hospital and interrogated him more thoroughly about the crime. Jackson and Elliot were put on trial together. He was found guilty of murder in the first degree, a verdict that automatically meant the electric chair, and she was convicted of manslaughter in the first degree and received a sentence of five to twenty years in prison.

At the trial, Jackson's lawyer attempted to have his second confession to the ADA disallowed because Jackson was so heavily medicated when he was questioned. Following the "New York Procedure," the judge left the voluntariness of the confession to the jury—as Judge Wallace had done in Lonergan's trial—and the jury, likewise, had accepted it. With Jackson due to be executed at Sing Sing Prison on January 8, 1961, his lawyer appealed the conviction and the planned execution was stopped—for the moment, at any rate. Ultimately, the appeal reached the Supreme Court early in 1963 as *Jackson v. Denno* (Wilfred Denno was the warden of Sing Sing Prison from 1950 to 1967).

The main question for the Supreme Court justices was whether the New York Procedure in dealing with confessions at trial violated Jackson's constitutional rights. The case was argued on December 9 and 10, 1963. Six months later, on June 22, 1964, by a six-to-three majority, the court held that the New York Procedure did not, in fact, provide "an adequate and reliable determination of the voluntariness of the confession" and did not "adequately protect the petitioner's right not to be convicted through the use of a coerced confession." It was, therefore, according to the majority opinion, "violative of the Due Process Clause of the Fourteenth Amendment."

The decision somewhat helped Jackson. He was retried and convicted a second time, even without the prosecution using the confession he had made to the ADA that night in the hospital. And once again, he received a death sentence. But the delay saved him from the electric chair: In November 1967, a month before his day of execution, his life was spared by New York governor Nelson Rockefeller, who commuted his sentence to life imprisonment.

Jackson v. Denno had more immediate consequences for the New York appellate courts and district attorney's offices, because the decision raised critical questions about every trial in which a confession was a crucial issue. Four months after the Supreme Court rendered its ruling, the Court of Appeals of the State of New York heard arguments about the second key case that was to offer Lonergan a glimmer of hope, *People v. Huntley* (1965).

In 1960, Charles Huntley and two accomplices were convicted in a payroll robbery case. Huntley did not testify at his trial, but an oral confession he gave was used against him, despite the fact that a witness claimed he had heard the police roughing up Huntley in order to extract his statement. In 1962, Huntley's lawyer appealed his conviction on the grounds that his confession was not voluntary—that the police had beaten his client until he told them what they wanted to hear. Nonetheless, the appellate court judges saw it differently and denied him the right to appeal. Huntley tried again following the *Jackson v. Denno* decision.

On January 7, 1965, Huntley's second appeal attempt led to an immediate reconsideration of how confessions were dealt with in New York. In a five-to-two ruling (three months before a final decision was given specifically about Huntley), the New York Court of Appeals decided—in light of

Jackson v. Denno—that the voluntariness of confessions had to be determined using the "Massachusetts Procedure." Thereafter, before a jury in the state of New York was to consider a confession as evidence, the judge in a pretrial hearing was required to determine beyond a reasonable doubt whether it was voluntary. As Court of Appeals chief judge Charles Desmond wrote, "[T]he burden of proof as to the voluntariness is on the People." If the jury was permitted access to the confession, its members were also given the right to review how the judge had arrived at his decision about it.

Huntley, himself, did not benefit from the January 1965 decision—though subsequent appeals in other cases about possible coerced confessions were referred to as "Huntley Hearings." He was again denied a new trial. On April 7, 1965, State Supreme Court justice Abraham Geller found "that no force or threats were used by the police and that the confession is voluntary beyond a reasonable doubt."

Frances Kahn was impatient and did not wait for Judge Desmond's decision to be announced. On January 4, 1965, she submitted another *coram nobis* application to obtain a hearing as to the voluntariness of Lonergan's confession. Ten days later, and despite the ruling of January 7, her application was denied. She was persistent, however. In early March, she appeared before Justice Gellinoff to argue that in light of *Jackson v. Denno* and the Huntley case, Lonergan was entitled to a new trial. This time she got the decision she wanted: Gellinoff agreed that a Huntley Hearing to determine the voluntariness of Lonergan's confession was appropriate. He ordered that Lonergan be transferred from Clinton Prison to the Tombs in New York City so that he could be in court for the proceedings.

This decision spurred the district attorney's office to action. In charge was twenty-nine-year-old ADA Thomas J. Hughes Jr. of the homicide division. He and his colleagues began tracking down the key players from the 1944 trial: John Loehr, who was practicing law in Farmington, New Mexico; former detective William Prendergast, who was an investigator for a New York law firm; his former partner, Nicholas Looram, who was working as an insurance investigator in Queens; Toronto detective Arthur Harris, who had retired and was living in England; and former Toronto detective Alex Deans, who was now the chief security officer for the T. Eaton Company department stores.

The easiest person to locate was one of Hughes's predecessors, Jacob Grumet, the former ADA of the homicide division who was still in the news as a member of the State Investigation Commission, charged with the task of uncovering government corruption. Now sixty-four years old, Grumet had mellowed, at least a little. "Human beings are frail creatures," he said in an interview in January 1965, "and it's easy for them to give in to temptation . . . I can't help it, but I feel sorry for people." That sentiment, however, did not extend to Wayne Lonergan, who Grumet maintained was as guilty and culpable for Patricia's death as he had been two decades earlier.

Kahn wanted to relitigate the entire case. To that end, she noted in her submission the witness statement of October 27, 1943, from Harriet Naylor, the Trans-Canada Airlines stewardess who had worked on Lonergan's return flight to Toronto on October 24. Years earlier, she had claimed that there were no scratches on Lonergan's face; that he may have covered the scratches with makeup was not addressed. Kahn also asserted that Annaliese Schonberg, the German nurse, had testified that she had only heard a female voice emanating from Patricia's bedroom on the day of the murder. Although Kahn must have known this was curious, it hardly exonerated Lonergan.

There was also the affidavit Kahn submitted from Harvey Kelley. He was the driver of the ambulance who picked up Patricia's body from her residence and delivered it to the city morgue. Kelley, who was fired from his job, stated that he had "dropped" Patricia's corpse twice: once in her bedroom, as he was attempting to put her on a stretcher, and a second time outside the residence, when her head allegedly hit the sidewalk. No one—not the police, journalists, photographers, or people in the neighborhood standing outside 313 East 51st Street—had seen this or reported it. Moreover, a photograph published in *PM* newspaper showed two attendants—presumably one was Kelley— carrying her body wrapped in a heavy canvas blanket. A second photo from the *Daily News* showed the blanketed body after it had been placed inside a wooden coffin that had no top on it, being loaded into an ambulance. Had Kelley truly dropped her, the blanket itself would have protected the body. It is even harder to believe that if Kelley had done what he said he did, Broderick, as diligent a defense attorney as there was, would not have learned about it and introduced this fact at the 1944 trial.

Notwithstanding that these incidents—if they happened at all—were not included in medical examiner Milton Helpern's report, or that a postmortem injury is generally different than one incurred while a person is still alive (antemortem), these issues were not pertinent and therefore not considered at the 1965 hearing. The only fact that State Supreme Court justice Charles Marks, who was to preside over Lonergan's Huntley Hearing, regarded as relevant was whether or not the confession was "obtained by force, inducement, fraud or anything else that bears on the voluntariness of the confession."

Marks had a well-deserved reputation for being a tough judge. In 1961, he had sentenced a confessed rapist and robber to sixty to one hundred years in prison, the longest sentence ever meted out in New York at the time. Still, during the hearing, he gave Hughes and Kahn a lot of latitude in their examination of the witnesses, permitting them to delve into areas of the case that had little to do with Lonergan's confession and the process by which it was obtained.

Lonergan had had plenty of time to think about what he wanted to say, and presumably had been coached by Kahn to make his statement as colorful as possible. He was in fine form. His affidavit of April 30, 1965, was a masterpiece of victimhood that could have been delivered by a survivor of the Spanish Inquisition. He claimed that he was "tortured" by Toronto and New York police officers; that they "continually beat" him after he had been detained in Toronto; that they had deprived him of food, sleep, and cigarettes; and that he had been "beaten by relays of police officers with the open palms of their hands on the back [of his head]. This torture was worse than a Chinese torture."

Lonergan's statements and the hearing, of course, received plenty of press coverage. Of particular note was the interest in the case by Toronto *Globe and Mail* columnist Scott Young (whose real claim to fame was that he was the father of rock star Neil Young). For Young, a journalist, author of fiction and nonfiction, and a writer admired for his "style and wit," Lonergan was too great a story to ignore. Young traveled to New York to cover the hearing, visited the scene of the crime on East 51st Street, asked pointed questions about how the case unfolded, and produced more than a dozen columns and articles about it.

Lonergan's Huntley Hearing began on Tuesday, May 11, 1965. That first day, and for the duration of the proceedings—it went on from May 11 to June 8 because there were delays for several witnesses, including Loehr and Deans, who had to travel to New York—Hughes and Kahn repeatedly challenged each other, testing Judge Marks's patience. It was reminiscent of the bitter battle between Grumet and Broderick in February and March 1944. Called to testify first, Grumet was uncharacteristically coy, stating that he could not recall precisely the events of October 1943 when Lonergan's confession was given, and suggested that Kahn examine the court record.

Lonergan was on the stand two days later, the first time he had ever testified in a courtroom about what had happened that October weekend in 1943. Young wryly observed that he "looked like [1964 Republican presidential nominee] Barry Goldwater and sounded like [stoic Hollywood actor] Gary Cooper." Like a dog owner trying to teach a puppy how to get used to a leash, Kahn took Lonergan slowly step by step through the events of twenty-one years earlier, when the Toronto detectives showed up at his friend's apartment on Bloor Street West.

"Did they advise you of your right to remain silent?" Kahn asked him.

"No," replied Lonergan.

"Did they advise you of your right to have an attorney?" she asked.

"No," he repeated.

Lonergan stated that he had tried to contact his old friend, lawyer Michael Doyle, and his uncle, Joe Lonergan. He did eventually see his uncle, but not Doyle. Then he told the same contrived story from his latest affidavit: the abuse and deprivation of food and sleep; that detectives Prendergast and Looram had supposedly hit him on the train ride from Toronto to Buffalo; the threats that he was headed to a date with the electric chair; how Loehr had promised him that if he confessed, he would be charged with second-degree manslaughter and that the negative publicity about his sex life would stop; and finally, that Loehr and the detectives had instructed him on what to say in his confession. The assertion about the plea and the publicity even raised the eyebrows of Scott Young, who was skeptical about Lonergan's conviction and prone to giving him the benefit of the doubt. "The idea of anyone's pleading guilty to manslaughter to stop publicity is rather hard to swallow," he wrote.

"What publicity was it you wanted to have stopped?" asked ADA Hughes, during his cross-examination. "The publicity about murdering your wife, or about your sexual habits?"

"I'd say both," replied Lonergan.

A few days later when Hughes continued his cross-examination, he probed further about this aspect of Lonergan's life, asking him questions to which the ADA already knew the answers. He queried Lonergan about his rejection by the US forces in 1942.

"I was classified 4-F," said Lonergan.

"Why?" asked Hughes.

"For psychiatric reasons," Lonergan replied.

"Because you were an alcoholic?" asked Hughes. He did little to disguise his mocking tone.

"No," declared Lonergan, "because they said I was a homosexual. At least, they said so after I volunteered that information."

More telling was that Lonergan had invoked his Fifth Amendment rights against self-incrimination on three occasions when Hughes queried him. The first time occurred when Hughes asked him about the scratches on his face. Pressed about it, Lonergan said that he had gotten scratched in Toronto late on the night he had returned from New York. When Hughes inquired who had scratched him, all Lonergan said was that "there is someone I don't want to identify here." Other than Kahn and Schwartzberg, no one in the courtroom likely believed him. He took the Fifth again after Hughes asked him about his RCAF uniform and then a third time following a question about the Max Factor makeup compact he had bought at Max Levinson's drugstore.

The following week, Prendergast and Looram were both questioned, and both categorically denied, as they had back in 1944, that they had mistreated Lonergan when they had accompanied him from Toronto to New York and while he was in custody preceding his confession. So, too, did John Loehr, who flew into New York from New Mexico.

Loehr was the last witness called to testify on June 3. He had a more precise recollection of the events than his former colleague, Jacob Grumet. Loehr firmly repudiated every claim Lonergan made. There was no collusion, coercion, or mental and physical abuse, he declared.

Asked by Hughes why he had brought up the fact that both he and Lonergan were Catholic, Loehr stated: "Because, Lonergan earlier had told me of acts of perversion performed with a man on the night that his wife was murdered. As a result, definite admissions of homosexual activity were known to police and the district attorneys. During questioning I pointed out to him that this made him look like a rather poor person and a degenerate, and [. . .] that this would have a serious effect on [. . .] his son's future life."

In her cross-examination, Kahn attempted to prove that Loehr had handed Lonergan a written script of his confession, based on what Lonergan had initially told him. But he denied that charge.

Having sat through the starts and stops of the three-week hearing, Scott Young suggested that Lonergan had a fifty-fifty chance of having his original confession thrown out and getting a new trial. The consensus among Young and the other reporters in the courtroom was that the police probably did rough Lonergan up and that he had been denied his civil rights after he had been detained in Toronto. Not only was the possibility of a retrial at stake for Lonergan, but a verdict in his favor from Justice Marks would also mean that he could legally assert his rights to one-third of Patricia's estate, which by 1965 was an estimated $3 million (about $24 million today).

Marks reserved his judgment and took another two weeks to deliver his decision. The news was not good for Lonergan. The judge found that Lonergan's constitutional rights had not been violated by Canadian or American authorities. He ruled that there was no evidence that Lonergan had been beaten or coerced into making his confession, that he had not asked to speak to a lawyer; and that he had "suffered no undue delay in arraignment." In short, stated Justice Marks, Lonergan's confession was voluntary, and by implication, Lonergan was a liar—his testimony was not to be believed.

Tom Hughes was delighted with the decision. Marks "has completely and unequivocally denied the motions in all respects," he wrote to Loehr two days later. "His decision is a strong one, [especially given] all the questions raised by Lonergan, Kahn, etc."

Frances Kahn, on the other hand, was discouraged, but stated that she was not giving up. She told reporters that an appeal to the New York Supreme Court would be next, and if that failed, she would take the case all the way to the federal Supreme Court. Kahn did launch her appeal to the New York Supreme Court, yet on January 19, 1967, the court affirmed the decision of the Court of Appeals. And that was the end of the line for Lonergan's efforts to declare his confession coerced.

Even if the State Supreme Court had consented to consider another Lonergan appeal, Kahn would have had difficulty proceeding. In November 1965, Kahn, Schwartzberg, and Vincent Pacelli, a convicted drug dealer who was serving an eighteen-year prison sentence in a narcotics conspiracy, were indicted on charges of attempting "to intimidate and bribe a government witness not to testify in a narcotics conspiracy case." Kahn and Schwartzberg were already being investigated by a federal grand jury on another charge:

that they had brought a prostitute to visit a federally held prisoner, Harold Konigsburg, who was serving a ten-year sentence on a theft conviction at the Hudson County Jail in Jersey City. Henry McFarland, the seventy-year-old warden of the prison, also got in trouble for operating a "blue room"—a jail suite for pampered prisoners, which had a television, refrigerator, stove, and telephone.

In April 1966, Kahn and Schwartzberg (and Pacelli) were found guilty of conspiring to obstruct justice and given two-year prison sentences. Assistant US attorney John Martin called Kahn a "disgrace to [the legal] profession." Schwartzberg, meanwhile, refused to accept the court's judgment. "How could you do this!" he yelled at the judge. "After all, I am innocent, but she [Kahn] is really innocent."

Kahn served her sentence from March 1967 to October 1968. She was suspended from practicing law in July 1967, and disbarred in July 1969. The following year, Schwartzberg died at the age of fifty-six from a heart attack while he was visiting Montreal.

By the time Kahn and Schwartzberg were serving their jail sentences in 1967, Wayne Lonergan was a free man, released from Clinton Prison and back rebuilding his life in Toronto.

17

Nothing to Hide

BY THE BEGINNING OF DECEMBER 1965, Wayne Lonergan had served nearly twenty-two years of his thirty-five-year sentence. He had been eligible for parole since December 1963, but at that time the members of the parole board decided they were not prepared to convene a hearing for him. It took another two years until he was brought before them. During his long period of incarceration, he had stayed out of trouble. Though he had never stop blaming Jacob Grumet and John Loehr for "railroading" him, he was, nevertheless, granted his freedom and immediately deported to Canada. He could never return to the United States.

Lonergan was now forty-seven years old. The only money he had was from his fifteen-cents-a-day job in prison that had been deposited in a local Upstate New York bank. At the most, this was about $1,200, and likely less. He not seen his son, Billy—now William Anthony Burton—since he had visited with him on Saturday, October 23, 1943. The boy had grown up without both of his parents. He was twenty-three years old and a graduate of Harvard University.

Scott Young and James Lewcun, a *Globe and Mail* photographer, had traveled to Dannemora as soon as Young had gotten word that Lonergan was to be released. Young had spoken to warden Daniel McMann and offered to drive Lonergan back to Toronto. But McMann informed him that prison officials were responsible for Lonergan until he crossed the US–Canada border and was declared deported.

On December 2, 1965, at about 11:00 a.m., Lonergan was driven to Lacolle, Quebec, forty-five miles north of Dannemora. At that point, Young and Lewcun offered him a lift to Toronto. Lonergan initially refused; he was not interested in speaking to journalists or having his picture taken. After the proper documents were filed, Canadian immigration agents then drove him another sixty-six miles north to St. Jean, where they dropped him off in the midst of a rainstorm. He was to take a bus another ninety-four miles to Montreal and then travel to Toronto. Young and Lewcun were waiting for him again, and this time, Lonergan—who had no wish to be stuck on a bus for many hours, accepted the ride. The 432-mile trip to Toronto took more than ten hours, with a stop in Montreal for a much-anticipated steak dinner.

Lewcun got the photograph he wanted once they arrived in Toronto and chauffeured Lonergan to the majestic Royal York Hotel on Front Street, across from Union Station. Lewcun's photo of Lonergan that ran on the front page of the next day's *Globe and Mail* portrayed him coolly stepping into the hotel in an "ill-fitting suit," as Young described it, with a gray scarf slung around his neck.

As Lonergan entered the hotel, other reporters and photographers were also waiting for him. They surrounded him and began shouting questions. Walking across the lobby minding his own business was Toronto mayor Philip Givens, somewhat curious about what was going on. Young, in a mischievous act, called out to him, saying, "Mr. Mayor, I'd like to introduce you to Wayne Lonergan." The mayor, polite Canadian that he was, extended his right hand to Lonergan, who shook it. "Hello," he said. "Yes, I heard about [you] on the news." Photographers snapped some pictures that were published in a few New York papers in the days that followed, touting how a friendly Toronto mayor had welcomed back a paroled murderer.

Lonergan's plan for the future, he had told Young during the long car trip, was to obtain a Canadian passport (which his US felony conviction did not prevent) and visit England, possibly relocating there. His brother and sister, William and June, who both occasionally had journeyed to see him while he was incarcerated, still lived in Toronto, and he was looking forward to spending time with them. Asked a question about his son, he remarked that he knew where he was, but firmly stated that journalists should "leave that boy alone. He's had enough troubles."

In fact, Lonergan contacted his son within a week. He found him still living at Lucille Burton's apartment in New York. According to what Lonergan told Perry, he claimed the two had a pleasant telephone conversation. He invited William to travel to Toronto to see him. He spoke to his son a second time, and Lonergan believed that William would travel to meet with him. Yet that didn't happen. Instead, Lonergan received a strongly worded letter from a lawyer in New York, informing him that he should cease all attempts to communicate with William. Lonergan told Perry that he did eventually find him, though he never saw William again—even after Lucille Burton died at the age of seventy-three, on November 27, 1966. She was buried in the Wolfe family plot in Chicago.

William vanished from the public record around 1964. When Dominick Dunne wrote about the Lonergan case two decades ago, he decided there was nothing to be gained by tracking down William, who at that time would have been about fifty-eight. On July 1, 2020, he celebrated his seventy-eighth birthday. "Children of a parent who kills their other parent lead dreadful lives," Dunne explained. William doesn't remember his mother, other than what Lucille shared with him, and presumably he has negative feelings about his father. It is believed that William married and lived in Florida for a number of years. At the present time, he might live in New York.

I followed Dunne's thinking and decided there was nothing to be gained from contacting William for a comment about a mother he does not remember and a father who was found guilty of killing her.

For the first month of freedom, Lonergan called room 3-297 at the Royal York home. Hotel prices in the mid-1960s were much more reasonable than they are at the present time: The cost of a room was $12 to $14 a day, and you could spend less than $10 on three meals a day at the hotel restaurant. During that first week back in Toronto, Lonergan had a haircut, received sunlamp treatment to get rid of his pale prison appearance, and had a shoeshine. He purchased a decent topcoat, new suit, and a hat. He had tossed away the cheap fedora Clinton Prison officials had given him as soon as he had arrived in St. Jean, Quebec.

He bided his time reacquainting himself with his family and friends and waiting for his Canadian passport to be processed.

He spoke to Scott Young every few days and consented to a notable interview on the CBC TV show *This Hour Has Seven Days*, which was a cross between the CBS newsmagazine show *60 Minutes* and the *Jerry Springer Show*. On the episode of October 24, 1965, for example, the show's producers pitted two Ku Klux Klansmen from Georgia—Grand Dragon Calvin Craig and his lieutenant George Sleigh, who were dressed in their white robes and pointed hats—against Reverend James Bevel, an African-American civil rights activist, without informing the Klansmen that they were going to do this. It made for sensational television. Discussed on the floor of the Canadian House of Commons, CBC canceled the show in 1966 amid great controversy.

Not quite as riveting was journalist and producer Ken Lefolii's interview with Lonergan on a program that aired on December 12, 1965. Working with Lefolii and the CBC on this story, Scott Young first interviewed Lonergan for an hour on December 9, and then Lefolii, who was not satisfied with the answers Lonergan provided to Young, questioned Lonergan himself for another hour. The Lefolii segment of the interview that was broadcast on the show was edited down to about ten minutes.

More than fifty years later, Lefolii recalls Lonergan as being "a very plausible guy." Throughout the discussion with both Young and Lefolii, Lonergan continually portrayed himself as the innocent victim of a great injustice. He spoke with a distinctly Brooklyn accent that he presumably acquired after spending more than two decades in New York prisons (he even used the classic phrase "fuggedaboutit" several times). When Lefolii asked Lonergan whether or not he had murdered his wife, Lonergan was deliberately cagey, replying, "My position is no." He again reiterated that his confession and conviction were "bogus" and rightly pointed out that there was no physical evidence found at the scene that directly tied him to his wife's murder. (At no time during the two-hour conversation did he mention Patricia by name.)

Lefolii probed Lonergan about the 4-F designation by the US Selective Service Board and his homosexual excuse to evade the draft in 1942. He dismissed it as a premeditated ruse. He also came up with a new story for which there is absolutely no evidence. He told Young that in the fall of 1942, Patricia was ill, and he did not want to leave her alone with their baby. He stated that when he informed Patricia that he might enlist in the US Armed Forces—again, this is a highly debatable assertion—she became upset and started to cry. None of their friends or the people who worked for the couple mentioned this episode in their statements to the district attorney or police.

Lonergan accused medical examiner Dr. Milton Helpern of deliberately leaving out crucial details in the summarized report he had supplied to his lawyer Edward Broderick, which Lonergan maintained would have exonerated him—a mistaken conclusion. He noted correctly that there was no fingerprint evidence introduced at his trial. He conveniently failed to add, however, that the fingerprints that were found at Patricia's residence could not be identified according to the forensic techniques available in 1943. Typical of Lonergan, he speculated that the prosecution had found other fingerprints that they "couldn't explain" and that this would have ruined their case.

This accusation was allegedly part of the DA's devious conspiracy against him, which he had conjured in his mind. Lonergan blatantly made up facts that fit his contrived narrative of the events of October 1943—that Jacob Grumet, John Loehr, and the NYPD had smeared him as a homosexual in the press and then framed him for a crime that "someone else" had committed.

Lonergan received his Canadian passport in the new year and left Toronto for London, England, on January 5, 1966. His plan was to live there permanently. For a short time, he stayed with an old friend in the entertainment business, the British-born Major Donald Neville-Willing, then sixty-four years old. Known as "the Major," the wealthy and influential Neville-Willing once had lived in New York City at an apartment on 70th Street, across from Central Park, and had socialized with both Wayne and Patricia. A small man, he was well-known for being a snob and was rarely seen without his bowler hat and a red carnation in the buttonhole of his suit jacket.

Neville-Willing had tried to join the Home Guard, the British armed citizen militia, but was rejected, likely because he was gay. For a time, he was an avid fund-raiser for the British Armed Forces, serving as the president of the British Sailors Book and Relief Society, which collected books, magazines, and games for sailors on British naval ships. After the attack on Pearl Harbor, he enlisted in the American Field Service and was stationed in Cairo during the latter part of World War II.

In 1965, Neville-Willing owned a luxurious residence in Belgravia, the exclusive neighborhood in central London. For some years, he had been the manager of the popular nightclub Café de Paris, where such luminaries as Marlene Dietrich, Dorothy Dandridge, and dance band leader Harry Roy performed.

Lonergan had told Scott Young of the *Globe and Mail* that he did not like publicity, nor did he want it. As photographers followed him around Toronto and then London, however, he embraced his celebrity status—as notorious as it was. "I don't mind the publicity about my past," he said in one interview carried over the United Press wire service. "Hell, I'm immune to it, good or bad. I've got nothing to hide. Everything is out in the open."

Yet another tall tale that Lonergan told Perry was that Lucille Burton had allegedly offered him $300,000 (out of his son's estate) so that he could take care of himself and that she had supposedly spread the word about this while visiting France and England. He never received this money for the simple reason that the story was almost certainly another of Lonergan's falsehoods.

England did not pan out for Lonergan. He lasted about seven months. The *Globe and Mail* reported on July 13, 1966, that he had returned to Toronto and was looking for work. It is unknown whether he found a job, but he did find something better: a well-off woman to take care of him, emotionally and financially.

At some point in 1971 or 1972, Lonergan was introduced to Toronto actress and comedienne Barbara Hamilton. He was fifty-three then; she was forty-five and had never married. Hamilton was a charming, pretty, and zaftig blonde, a high-spirited woman who had been born and raised in Toronto by her father, Harry. Her mother had died when Barbara was only four years old. She had an older sister, Mary, who also cared for her as she was growing up.

Barbara had attended a girls' boarding school in Cobourg, Ontario, seventy-three miles east of Toronto. There, she discovered that she loved being onstage, and loved even more the fact that she could make the audience laugh. Following her graduation, her practical father, who believed show business was "immoral," insisted that Barbara take a business typing course, which she endured, though she eventually studied drama at the Toronto Royal Conservatory of Music.

Starting in 1949, she embarked on a successful career in theater in Toronto and New York. She was a staple of the Toronto theater scene, appearing in numerous musical revues where her comedic talents were featured. A newspaper in Charlottetown, Prince Edward Island, dubbed Barbara "the funniest woman in Canada." She could play the "bratty child, frumpy housewife or gauche siren" with skill and humor. Her most memorable role onstage was as Marilla Cuthbert in the London West End production of *Anne of Green Gables: The Musical* that premiered in 1969 and ran for six months. She also starred in Canadian films and TV shows.

When she met Lonergan, she was ready for a serious relationship and perhaps a bit desperate for love. His dashing good looks immediately won her over. Most curiously of all, she unreservedly accepted his story that he was an innocent man who had been sent to prison for a crime that he did not commit. They both smoked heavily and enjoyed drinking. Eventually, Lonergan moved in with her. He had found another generous woman with a healthy bank account.

She lovingly called him "Waynie." And when Lonergan made her laugh, she'd say "You kill me, Wayne," recalls veteran actor Gordon Pinsent, who was a good friend to Hamilton for many years, as was his wife, actress Charmion "Charm" King. Pinsent and King lived in the same downtown Toronto condominium building as Hamilton and Lonergan. The four of them often went out to dinner together.

From the perspective of Pinsent and King's daughter, actress Leah Pinsent, who was a preteen in the late 1970s—Hamilton was her godmother—Lonergan was usually quiet and didn't say much. She did not know then about his past, but she does remember that "Wayne had a creepy factor to him."

Lonergan "fashioned himself a producer for her," said Gordon Pinsent. It wasn't a legal arrangement, but Lonergan tried to assume "that kind of booking role for her," and she was happy to have a steady man by her side. Lonergan "never talked about his past," added Pinsent. "He drank a lot of Drambuie and smiled."

Pinsent states that nothing was ever said about Lonergan's bisexuality. This was the same point made by the late New Zealand–born Canadian actor Tom Kneebone, who was also acquainted with Hamilton and Lonergan, in an interview with Dominick Dunne conducted around 2000. "[Lonergan] was very attentive and charming to her publicly," Kneebone said. "They were out socially a great deal—parties, openings, that sort of thing. I was disarmed by him. He was a well-mannered, gracious gentleman, the epitome of charm and elegance, and he was enormously literate. He was up on everything. He read voraciously. And I never saw a second of his bisexuality."

Meanwhile, Hamilton Darby Perry told Dunne that Lonergan always dressed elegantly, but that he was "strange"; he would speak to Perry about the book Perry was writing on the case only if they met in a public place. The more Perry got to know Lonergan, the more he wondered about the truthfulness of the stories he was telling to him.

In those years, Barbara Hamilton had only one condition when she sat down for an interview: The journalist or TV commentator was not allowed to ask her about her relationship with Lonergan. In 1984 or 1985, Lonergan became ill with cancer, probably lung cancer from years of smoking cigarettes. He died on January 2, 1986, a few weeks before his sixty-eighth birthday, taking all of his secrets with him. The *New York Times* story about his death had the headline "Wayne Lonergan, 67, Killer of Heiress Wife." The *Globe and Mail* was slightly more tactful: "Wayne Lonergan: Jailed for Killing Wife After Sensational Trial." Both obituaries chronicled Lonergan's murder conviction and legal ordeals.

The *Toronto Star* identified Hamilton as "a close friend for many years." When asked about him, she said that "he was the most kind, gentle and wonderful person I have ever known. I loved him very much." Thereafter, she had a framed black-and-white picture of Lonergan on her dressing-room table. In early July 1994—a year and a half before she died from breast cancer, at the age of sixty-nine—a reporter from the *Star* inquired further about the photograph. "Yes, that's Wayne," Hamilton remarked matter-of-factly. "Oh, he was handsome, handsome as a prince. Fourteen years we were together."

Epilogue

"Wife Killer or Fall Guy?"

IN OCTOBER 1948, Raymond Chandler, the great detective fiction writer, wrote a feature article for *Cosmopolitan* magazine entitled "10 Greatest Crimes of the Century." Number one was the heartbreaking 1932 kidnapping and murder of Charles Lindbergh Jr., the infant son of famed aviator Charles Lindbergh and his wife Anne. Number nine was the murder of Patricia Burton Lonergan by her husband Wayne.

Given the intense press coverage of Lonergan's trial a few years earlier, it was not all that surprising that the case made Chandler's list. There was something about the story that continued to fascinate Americans for decades. Two years after Lonergan had been convicted, poet and novelist Kenneth Fearing loosely based his 1946 novel *The Big Clock* on Patricia and Wayne's strained relationship (subsequently made into a movie of the same name in 1948, starring Charles Laughton and Ray Milland).

The fast-paced novel was a "psycho-thriller" about the murder of Pauline Delos, a beautiful and outspoken woman—"tall, ice-blonde, and splendid"—by her boyfriend Earl Janoth, a wealthy magazine publisher with a bad temper, who may or may not be having a homosexual relationship with a close friend. One day, Janoth sees Pauline on the street with a man he does not realize is one of his editors, George Stroud, who is married and indeed having an affair with Pauline. Janoth soon accuses Pauline of cheating on him with this man (as well as with several women). They have a nasty argument about their lifestyles, and in the heat of the moment, Janoth hits Pauline in the head with a brandy decanter—rather than the two candleholders Wayne used to strike Patricia—and keeps on hitting her until she is dead. Fearing is a master storyteller—he cleverly uses multiple narrators—and the novel holds up well more than seventy years later. Despite the allegations of homosexual, lesbian, and bisexual impropriety, however, its connection to the Lonergan case is tentative.

A much more precise fictional account of the case can be found in a less-satisfying novel, *A Nearness of Evil*, by Carley Mills, published in 1961. This was Mills's first and only book. He was a composer and musical arranger who died a year later, in October 1962, at the age of sixty-five. Mills blatantly shaped his narrative—his dialogue has a "soap opera-ish" quality—around the facts of the Lonergan case, without disguising this appropriation or the personalities of the main characters. Patricia became Diane Randall, a woman who was "tall [and] beautifully formed," and whose "skin glowed [and] dark eyes glowered." Wayne was given the Lonergan-sounding name of Neil Hartigan, who at twenty-two years of age is "tall, broad of shoulder, narrow of waist, with powerful wrists and hands . . . [who] moved gracefully in a catlike manner." Lucille Burton was Florence Randall, the spurned wife and doting mother; and William Burton became Bobby Randall, the scion of a prominent German-Jewish New York family and a bisexual adventurer who enjoys partying in the South of France.

Exactly like William Burton, Bobby Randall, following the death of his father, Hugo Rindshauer, which occurs early in the novel, changes his last name. "I'm cutting out the so-called chosen people," Bobby explains to a friend about his new Gentile surname. "I've had them. They're just a small group of smug, self-satisfied bores who revolve around a tiny axis and think they're the solar system. Not a bad simile, eh?"

Adhering to the details of the Lonergan story, Randall meets Hartigan at the New York World's Fair and they embark on a torrid affair before Hartigan eventually marries Diane. Mills fully explores the sexual triangle between Bobby, Diane, and Neil—in essence, the alleged triangle between William Burton and Patricia and Wayne Lonergan. Except in the novel, the father does not die—as William did—before Diane and Neil marry, over Bobby's strenuous objections. Mills even has Diane use the same words about her relationship with Neil that Patricia was supposed to have said—at least, according to *Daily Mirror* columnist Thyra Samter Winslow: "And, if he's good enough for Daddy, he's good enough for me." In the book, a fictional columnist named Chauncey James (who resembles the *New York Journal-American*'s Cholly Knickerbocker) wryly observes that "Hartigan is going steady with both Randalls."

As this chronicle of café society proceeds, Diane eventually complains that Neil has not given up his homosexual lifestyle. Like Lonergan, Neil joins the RCAF, and Diane is killed on October 17, 1943—rather than October 24, the day Patricia Lonergan was murdered. The subsequent investigation and trial then follow the Lonergan case nearly verbatim, with some literary license.

Rightly or wrongly, Wayne Lonergan became a poster boy for sociopaths. In a May 1949 *Newsday* feature article, Jo Coppola, who was the newspaper's television critic, wrote about the various connections between family, parental influence, and the "evil of warped, abnormal lives." According to Coppola, psychiatrists postulate that "love, the backbone of family relationships," is the "medicine" to cure this growing problem. Quoting Viennese psychiatrist Dr. Wilhelm Stekel, a follower of Sigmund Freud, she notes that happy marriages produce "emotionally healthy children."

She was not as certain, however, about the dynamics of abnormal behavior, though she did add that "perversion is a variance from the normal. Its causes were either social or pathological. Pathological causes are many," she explains. "They include overprotection of children, the rejection of one parent by the other, a fixation on one parent and a repression of the other by the child, environment, glandular disturbances or a sadistic tendency toward the opposite sex. Wayne Lonergan, who brutally beat his wife to death, is an example of the latter." And that was that.

Over the years, the story of the murder, with the requisite number of theories about Lonergan's sexual identity, has been told and retold in countless tabloid newspapers and magazines and remains a favorite topic of crime and mystery bloggers.

The story of the murder of Patricia Burton Lonergan and Wayne Lonergan's alibi, confession, and conviction is two tales in one. The first tells of the tragic death of a young mother—a wealthy woman, who at twenty-two years of age was not prepared to alter her café society social life—nor did she have to. Access to trust funds provided her with the freedom to hire a full-time nanny who cared for her child, as she and many other children of the wealthy did, and still do. Whatever Wayne's relationship had been with her father William—and the available evidence and gossip, for whatever that's worth, strongly suggests they were intimate—Patricia never should have married Lonergan. It was a match that was destined to fail for the simple reason that Wayne could not be trusted. Bisexual or not, he was a born liar with only one true objective: to move up the social ladder and live the good life. Money and status were what he needed, and this drew him to William, as well as Patricia. In all probability, it also cut her life far too short.

The second aspect to this New York tale is best summed up by a headline about Lonergan in the July 1965 issue of Toronto-based magazine *Maclean's*: "Wife Killer or Fall Guy?" Though Lonergan was found guilty by a jury of his peers, legitimate questions were raised about his guilt mainly because the trial took place in an era before DNA was utilized in legal proceedings (making the identification of a suspect nearly 100 percent accurate). In 2018, for instance, owing to DNA testing and a genealogy database, police in California were finally able to arrest the "Golden State Killer," seventy-two-year-old Joseph James DeAngelo, who has been linked to at least thirteen murders, more than fifty rapes, and over a hundred burglaries committed in the 1970s and 1980s.

But in 1944, with no blood or fingerprint analysis possible (because of poor samples and lack of required DNA technology), the only real incriminating evidence the prosecution had against Lonergan was his confession, which the all-male jury ultimately believed. The various judges in the lower and appellate courts who considered how ADA Jacob Grumet, deputy ADA John Loehr, and the New York Police obtained this account of the murder found that the confession was voluntary and not coerced (despite the passionate assertions to the contrary made for years afterward by Lonergan and his dedicated lawyer Edward Broderick, and later, Frances Kahn).

There is no question that at one time, New York Police constables and detectives, as well as police officers across the United States, meted out to suspects the infamous "third degree." The term may have originated with the late-nineteenth-century New York chief inspector Thomas Byrnes. New York detectives who had a suspect in custody abused and even tortured the alleged perpetrator until he confessed, employing tactics like kicking or whipping them, hanging them up while naked, and depriving them of sleep and food and water.

"Against a hardened criminal I never hesitated," said Cornelius Willemse, who served in the New York Police Department from 1900 to 1925 and rose to become a captain. "I've forced confessions—with fist, black-jack, and hose—from men who would have continued to rob and to kill if I had not made them talk. The hardened criminal knows only one language and laughs at the detective who tries any other. . . . Remember that this is war, after all! I'm convinced my tactics saved many lives."

New York reporter and reformer Emanuel "Manny" Lavine was a witness to the police abuse Willemse described. "The so-called roughneck is hit with everything but the foundation of the building," Lavine wrote in 1930. "I have seen a man beaten on his Adam's apple so that blood spurted from his mouth; I have seen another put in a dentist's chair and held there while the dentist . . . ground down a sound molar with a rough burr." He saw suspects kicked, poked, and hit with blackjacks, with lit cigars or cigarettes pushed against their arm or the back of their neck. This brutality, he added, was not unusual or exceptional; it was "simply part of the normal routine" of the New York Police Department.

In 1931, President Herbert Hoover was concerned enough about the ineffective enforcement of Prohibition and the justice system to create the National Commission on Law Observance and Enforcement—more popularly known as the Wickersham Commission, after its chairman, former attorney general George Wickersham. Volume eleven of their report revealed a litany of police abuse that was shocking even back then.

"After reviewing the evidence obtainable the authors of the report reach the conclusion that the third degree—that is, the use of physical brutality, or other forms of cruelty, to obtain involuntary confessions or admissions—is widespread," the section on police tactics concluded. "Protracted questioning of prisoners is commonly employed. Threats and methods of intimidation, adjusted to the age or mentality of the victim, are frequently used, either by themselves or in combination with some of the other practices mentioned. Physical brutality, illegal detention, and refusal to allow access of counsel to the prisoner is common. Even where the law requires prompt production of a prisoner before a magistrate, the police not infrequently delay doing so and employ the time in efforts to compel confession."

The negative publicity from the commission's report was soon followed by a landmark US Supreme Court decision in 1936, *Brown v. Mississippi*, in which it was found that physical coercion by the police to extract a confession was a violation of the Fourteenth Amendment. As Chief Justice Charles Hughes wrote for the majority, "[I]t would be difficult to conceive of methods more revolting to the sense of justice than those taken to procure the confessions of these petitioners." Both of these developments halted—or at least dramatically reduced—the use of police brutality to wring a confession from a suspect.

Hence, by the time Wayne Lonergan was in an interrogation room at the DA's office in Lower Manhattan, giving a suspect the "third degree" was no longer the norm. Moreover, when it happened—and it did—the Supreme Court sometimes set things right, as the justices did in 1945, in *Malinski v. New York*, adhering to the precedent established in *Brown v. Mississippi*. Morris Malinski, who had been convicted of murdering a police officer in 1941 and sentenced to death, had his conviction overturned because the police had violated his Fourteenth Amendment rights in forcing him to confess to the crime.

Malinski had been identified as one of the perpetrators of the murder by a convicted felon, who was bribed by the police into implicating Malinski in a false testimony. When the police apprehended Malinski, they indeed gave him the old "third degree": They stripped him, beat him, and interrogated him relentlessly until he told them what they wanted to hear.

While justice was served in Malinski's case, the system is by no means perfect. Decades later, it took a lot longer for the courts to intervene in the "Central Park Five" case, in which four young African-American teenagers and one Hispanic boy were treated abysmally by the police and DA's office (as noted in chapter 14). In the end, four of them gave what turned out to be false confessions that led to their convictions and incarceration. It took until 2002 for this injustice to be rectified, as vividly shown in two powerful documentaries, Ken Burns's 2012 *The Central Park Five* and Netflix's 2019 *When They See Us*.

It cannot be denied that false confessions, instigated by police and prosecution officials, are still given under duress, leading to terrible injustices. The courts do not always save the day, as the Supreme Court did for Malinski. As of 2019, according to the Innocence Project, of the 360 people exonerated through DNA evidence since 1989, a high percentage "involved some form of false confession."

There were no sound or video recordings of interrogations in 1943, so no one knows exactly what happened between Lonergan and the police and DA lawyers, except for the people in the room with him. Lonergan said one thing; Grumet, Loehr, and the police, another. So which person should we believe?

From the moment he began talking about his weekend in New York after deputy ADA John Loehr had arrived in Toronto, Lonergan told one falsehood after another. His fictitious alibi about his encounter with US serviceman Maurice Worcester reflected his creative imagination, conflicts about his sexual identity, and his desperation. Was there a conspiracy against him, as he alleged? Did Jacob Grumet, an upstanding ADA (and later, a respectable judge) somehow manipulate these events as part of a grand scheme to deprive Lonergan of his freedom? The answer to these questions is a resounding "No."

After reviewing the affidavits in the prosecution archival file of every Toronto and New York police officer, as well as Grumet and his staff of lawyers, including the stenographer who took down the confession—in short, every legal official who had contact with Lonergan in late October 1943—the only reasonable—indeed, the only possible—conclusion is that Lonergan was in no way mistreated. He was not denied food or water or cigarettes, and certainly, he was not physically abused. He was not coerced, but volunteered his detailed confession of what took place between him and Patricia on Sunday morning, October 24, 1943, mainly to put a stop to the negative stories in the press about his so-called perversion.

Notwithstanding the absence of other evidence against him, and acknowledging their likely biases stemming from negative press coverage and caustic comments about his sexuality, it is not difficult to understand why the jurors overlooked questions about reasonable doubt and accepted Lonergan's confession as an accurate account of how he murdered Patricia in a fit of rage.

Suffice it to say that Wayne Lonergan was no "fall guy."

Patricia Burton Lonergan has been gone now for seventy-seven years, a tragic victim of a senseless criminal act committed in a moment of anger, and, more than likely, with no premeditation. Her memory endures at the Salem Fields Cemetery in Brooklyn, where she is buried with the other members of her immediate family—including her father William, who was responsible for bringing Lonergan into her life.

Yes, it was surprising, even peculiar, that neither Elizabeth Black nor Annaliese Schonberg saw Lonergan the Sunday morning of the murder, or that no one witnessed him entering or leaving 313 East 51st Street wearing a blood-spattered air force uniform.

On a Sunday morning, some months ago, I stood outside the brownstone for a few minutes. Although the interior has been renovated over the years—it is now a pricey one-family dwelling with a medical office on the ground floor—the exterior is quite similar to how it appeared in 1943. The building is located in a tree-lined residential neighborhood a few blocks from Lexington Avenue, and in contrast to the typical daily mayhem of Manhattan, it was eerily serene the day I strolled by.

Just like it was on October 24, 1943, when at about 9:00 a.m., Wayne Lonergan, for reasons he likely could not fully explain, purposefully walked up East 51st Street and entered through the main door, kept unlocked.

Climbing the stairs to the second floor, he stood in front of the door he knew led to the master bedroom and knocked.

A minute later, the woman he had married, the mother of his child, Patricia Burton Lonergan—vibrant, loving, and carefree, half asleep from a long night out among the café society glitterati—opened the door. She was barely dressed.

"Hello," she said.

"Hello," Lonergan replied, and he walked in.

A Note on Sources

The main source for this book is the 1,631 pages of the New York District Attorney's *People v. Lonergan* files at the New York City Municipal Archives, dating from 1943 to 1944 and 1964 to 1965. It is a veritable treasure trove of correspondence, witness statements, affidavits, medical examination reports, private memoranda, court transcripts, and judicial decisions, as well as the official transcripts of Lonergan's initial interrogation in Toronto and his subsequent confession in the district attorney's office in New York City. To the best of the author's knowledge, this is the first work on the Lonergan case to make use of this valuable resource.

Other important sources include the in-depth magazine article on the case in 1946 by the accomplished crime writer Edwin Radin, "The Café Society Murder" (whose title I have adapted for my subtitle), published in Mystery Writers of America's *Murder Cavalcade: An Anthology* (New York: Duell, Sloan and Pearce, 1946); and the two earlier books on the case, *The Girl in Murder Flat* by Mel Heimer, a New York City television columnist (New York: Fawcett Publications, 1955); and journalist and magazine publisher Hamilton Darby Perry's *A Chair for Wayne Lonergan* (New York: Macmillan, 1972; 2nd ed., Omaha, NE: Gryphon Editions, 2000). Perry had access to Lonergan himself, whose comments—after Lonergan had spent almost twenty-two years in prison—must be judged judiciously and critically.

Given the extensive press coverage of the case and the significant role it played in shaping the narrative—in particular, articles written by gossip and entertainment columnists—various New York City and other national newspapers and magazines were utilized. Of particular importance were the reports and articles from the *New York Times, New York Herald-Tribune, New York Journal-American, Daily News,* and the *New York Daily Mirror.*

NOTES

Works and sources frequently cited have been identified by the following abbreviations:

ADA	Assistant District Attorney	NYCMA	New York City Municipal Archives
DA	District Attorney	NYPD	New York Police Department
GL	*Globe* (Toronto)		
GM	*Globe and Mail* (Toronto)	NYSA	New York State Archives (Albany)
LAC	Library and Archives Canada (Ottawa)	NYT	*New York Times*
		NWT	*New York World-Telegram*
NDM	*New York Daily Mirror*	PI	*Philadelphia Inquirer*
NDN	*Daily News* (New York)	PIPL	*Philadelphia Inquirer Public Ledger*
NHT	*New York Herald-Tribune*		
NJA	*New York Journal-American*	TS	*Toronto Star*
		WP	*Washington Post*

PROLOGUE: BELLE OF THE EL MOROCCO

xiv. *She was wearing*: NYCMA, 2417–43, *People v. Lonergan*, Milton Helpern, MD, "Autopsy of Patricia Burton Lonergan," October 25, 1943. (Hereafter, the *People v. Lonergan* file is noted as NYCMA Lonergan File.)

xv. *Angry, he sarcastically*: Ibid., "Death of Patricia Lonergan: Wayne Lonergan Confession," October 28, 1943, 4 (hereafter, Lonergan Confession).

xv. *And, on a table*: Helpern, "Autopsy of Patricia Burton Lonergan"; NYT, March 29, 30, 1944.

xv. *Miss Black had risen*: NYCMA Lonergan File, "DA Statement of Elizabeth Black, October 24, 1943 made to John Loehr" (hereafter, Black Statement); "Memorandum of Conversation with Elizabeth Black," November 4, 1943.

xv. *She was a twenty-two-year-old*: NJA, March 28, 1944.

xvi. *Schonberg walked back up*: Gerda Ray (J. Franklin Ray Jr.'s daughter) to Author, April 30, 2019; Archives at Yale University to Author, May 10, 2019.

xvi. *As she reached*: NYCMA Lonergan File, "Summary of Statement of Annaliese Schonberg"; NYT, March 27, 1944.

xvi. *It was a typical Sunday*: Wolcott Gibbs, "The Wayward Press: Five Days Wonder," *New Yorker*, November 6, 1943, 86.

xvii. *In her heightened*: Black Statement.

xvii. *He was visiting*: NYCMA Lonergan File, "ADA Interview of Peter Elser," October 25, 1943.

xvii. *Lucille grabbed the*: Ibid., NYT and NHT, March 24, 1944.

xvii. *Lucille would not listen*: Ibid., "Interview of Elser."

xviii. *Lucius Beebe, who*: Lucius Beebe, "Café Society," *Cosmopolitan* 102:3, Part One (March 1937), 96.

CHAPTER 1: THE MAKING OF A HUSTLER

1. *On Monday, January 14*: NYCMA Lonergan File, "Wayne Lonergan background," Detective Sergeant Arthur Harris to Inspector M. Mulholland, Toronto Police Department, January 20, 1944.

1. *That included an estimated*: CDC, "The 1918 Flu Pandemic: Why It Matters 100 Years Later," May 14, 2018, https://blogs.cdc.gov/publichealthmatters/2018/05/1918-flu; Allan Levine, *Toronto: Biography of a City* (Madeira Park, BC: Douglas & McIntyre, 2014), 144–45.

1. *On January 14, 1918*: TS, GM, January 14, 1918; Levine, ibid., 142.

2. *In international news*: Ibid.; NYT, January 14, 15, 1918.

2. *Norwood was a*: Richard A. Dean, *The Friendly Town, 1821–1963: Sketches of the Birth, Growth, and Development of the Village of Norwood, County of Peterborough* (Norwood, Ontario: Centennial Book Committee, 1978).

2. *By 1918, he*: NYCMA Lonergan File, "Lonergan Parents' Death Records"; Library and Archives Canada (Ottawa) (hereafter, LAC), Census of Canada, 1921, Item 3650344, "Lonergan family."

3. *The most significant fact*: NYCMA Lonergan File, "Clara Lonergan File." The Ontario Health Ministry gave records about Clara Lonergan to James W. McFadden, a special commissioner for New York State. See, NYT, February 21, 1944.

3. *On at least four*: Hamilton Darby Perry, *A Chair for Wayne Lonergan* (New York: Macmillan, 1972), 196. (Unless otherwise indicated, all subsequent references to Perry's book are from the first edition.)

3. *During the nineteenth century*: Donald Harman Akenson, *The Irish in Ontario: A Study in Rural History* (Montreal and Kingston: McGill-Queen's University Press, 1984), 9.

3. *For decades, it was*: Levine, *Toronto*, 63–69.

3. *With the arrival in North America*: Ibid., 72–79.

4. *For grades one through eight*: NYCMA Lonergan File, Detective Sergeant Arthur Harris to Inspector Moses Mulholland, "Wayne Lonergan Report," January 20, 1944; De La Salle College "Oaklands," History, www.delasalle .ca/about-us/history.

4. *Then and now*: Ibid., De La Salle College "Oaklands," History.

4. *In 1932, among the members*: Levine, *Toronto*, 165.

4. *For some reason, he*: Harris to Mulholland, January 20, 1944. See, St. Michael's College Yearbook, 1934, Form IIIC, 76, www.archive.org/ stream/stmyearbookofstmich1934testuoft#mode/2up.

4. *The school and college*: St. Michael's College Yearbook, 1933, 81. www .archive.org/stream/stmyearbookofstmich1933testuoft#mode/2up.

5. *At the end of 1932*: Harris to Mulholland, January 20, 1944.

5. *Five days before Christmas*: Ibid., NYSA, State of New York, Department of Corrections, Sing Sing, 103124, "Wayne Thomas Lonergan Record," April 17, 1944.

5. *Yet when he ran away*: Harris to Mulholland, January 20, 1944; See also, Michael Wilcox, "Cultivating Conformity and Safeguarding Catholicism: The Christian Brothers and their Schools in Ontario, 1851–1962," PhD dissertation, University of Toronto, 2015, 250.

5. *Lonergan and the other boys*: Wilcox, ibid., 252.

5. *In late March 1934*: Harris to Mulholland, January 20, 1944.

5. *Within a few months he had violated*: NYCMA Lonergan File, Lonergan to US Selective Service Board, May 13, 1941.

6. *A minimum-security institution*: Robert M. Stamp, "Early Days in Richmond Hill," http://edrh.rhpl.richmondhill.on.ca/default.asp?ID=s11.13.

6. *Thomas's death and Wayne's ongoing*: Levine, *Toronto*, 159–63.

6. *He attended the Dominion*: Department of Corrections, Sing Sing 103124, "Wayne Thomas Lonergan Record."

6. *"Christ, I hate to leave"*: Hemingway to Isabel Simmons, June 24, 1923, in Ernest Hemingway, *Ernest Hemingway, Selected Letters, 1917–1961*, ed. Carlos Baker (New York: Scribner, 1981), 84.

6. *The brash and bold Hemingway*: Levine, *Toronto*, 146–49.

7. *Anarchist Emma Goldman*: TS, December 7, 1927.

7. *"It must be good to die"*: Leopold Infeld, *Quest: An Autobiography* (Providence, RI: American Mathematical Society, 1980), 324. (Originally published in 1941.)

7. *For several months in 1934*: NYCMA Lonergan File, Wayne Lonergan, "RCAF Application Records, 1942.

7. *According to medical reports*: Ibid., Thurlow Pelton, MD, to Dr. Simon Beisler, October 24, 1942.

7. *In a July 1937 article*: Dr. John B. West, "Gonorrhea Has Preventives," *New York Amsterdam News*, July 24, 1937, 13.

7. *Gonorrhea was not*: NYT, August 31, 1935.

8. *In 1935, many physicians*: *Daily Worker* (New York City), April 17, 1935; Thomas Benedek, "History of the Medical Treatment of Gonorrhea," 2006, http://www.antimicrobe.org/h04c.files/history/Gonorrhea.asp.

8. *To get the job*: Harris to Mulholland, January 20, 1944.

8. *"People believe he is honest"*: LAC, William Lyon Mackenzie King Diaries, R10383-0-6-E, MG26 J13, October 7, 1937.

8. *He was impetuous*: Allan Levine, *King: William Lyon Mackenzie King: A Life Guided by the Hand of Destiny* (Vancouver: Douglas & McIntyre, 2011), 277.

8. *King had no doubt*: Ibid., 277. See also King Diaries, January 5, 1937; November 24, 1934; June 4, 1937; John T. Saywell, *"Just Call Me Mitch": The Life of Mitchell F. Hepburn* (Toronto: University of Toronto Press, 1991), 287; 192.

8. *In the spring of 1937*: Levine, ibid., 277–78; Saywell, ibid;, 239.

9. *"We know what"*: Cited in Adam Mayers, "A Larger than Life Premier," TS, January 2, 2008, www.thestar.com/news/2008/01/02/a_largerthanlife_premier.html.

9. *One of the strapping*: Levine, *Toronto*, 163; Irving Abella, ed. *On Strike: Six Key Labour Struggles in Canada, 1919–1949* (Toronto: James Lorimer & Company, 1975), 112; NYCMA Lonergan File, Inspector Davis, Ontario Provincial Police to Greyhound Lines, Department of Safety and Personnel, April 25, 1939.

9. *Lonergan and his fellow*: GM, April 17, 1937.

9. *In the end*: Saywell, *Hepburn*, 321–26; Abella, *On Strike*, 93–99, 120.

9. *His supervisor, Edward Blair*: NYJA, November 8, 1943; Perry, *A Chair*, 56–57.

9. *Lonergan soon found*: NYCMA Lonergan File, Horace Lapp to Greyhound Lines Department of Safety and Personnel, April 1939.

10. *According to a report*: Harris to Mulholland, January 20, 1944.

10. *And in a revealing moment*: NYCMA Lonergan File "Lonergan's Oral Statement to John Loehr, October 28, 1943, and Transcript of Toronto

Statement," 37 (hereafter, Toronto Statement). See also, "Memorandum: Helen Wing, 1943" (she knew Wayne Lonergan and William and Patricia Burton in New York City); DA Interview of Peter Elser, October 25, 1943; Toronto Police Interview of Sidney Capel Dixon, October–November 1943.

10. *The New York Police*: GM, June 4, 1965.

10. *Unlike other academics*: "Review of Sex Variants: A Study of Homosexual Patterns by George Henry," *California Journal* 70:2 (February 1949), 154.

10. *He concluded that Lonergan*: NYCMA Lonergan File, Memorandum of Conversation with Dr. George W. Henry, November 30, 1943; Henry to Candler Cobb, US Selective Service Board, March 6, 1942.

11. *At the time, he was not*: Perry, *A Chair*, 274.

11. *In 2000, however*: Perry, *A Chair for Wayne Lonergan*, 2nd ed. (Omaha, NE: Gryphon Editions, 2000), 291–94. See also, Dominick Dunne, *Justice: Crimes, Trials, and Punishments* (New York: Crown Publishers, 2001), 274; Charles Kaiser, *The Gay Metropolis* (New York: Grove Press, 1997), 20.

CHAPTER 2: THE BURTONS

12. *That money, and William's*: "United States Census, 1910," "Max E. Bernheimer," Manhattan Ward 22, New York, New York, United States; citing enumeration district (ED) ED 1304, sheet 4A, family 58, NARA microfilm publication T624 (Washington, DC: National Archives and Records Administration, 1982), roll 1045; FHL microfilm 1,375,058.

12. *Though William's sexual orientation*: Perry, *A Chair* (2nd ed.), 294; Perry, *A Chair* 14–15; Dunne, *Justice*, 274; Kaiser, *The Gay Metropolis*, 20; "Memorandum: Helen Wing, 1943."

12. *During much of the twentieth*: See, *Afro-American* (Baltimore), September 28, 1940.

13. *In November 1944*: NHT, November 18, 1944.

13. *In Washington, DC*: WP, July 3, 1946.

13. *And in May 1948*: Ibid., May 28, 1948.

13. *In France, on the other hand*: Gary Chapman, Jazz Age Club, "Queer Paris," www.jazzageclub.com/pink/queer-paris.

13. *The Wolfe family were proud Southerners*: Barry L. Stiefel, "Origins of Jewish and African American Relations of the Baruchs of Hobcaw, South Carolina," Making History Together, March 24, 2016, https://making historybtw.com/2016/03/24/guest-post-origins-of-jewish-and-african -american-relations-of-the-baruchs-of-hobcaw-south-carolina; Bernard

Baruch, *My Own Story* (New York: Henry Holt and Company, 1957), 19–21; Margaret L. Coit, *Mr. Baruch* (Boston: Houghton Mifflin, 1957), 2–3.

13. *They lived in a*: Baruch, ibid., 23; Coit, ibid., 3; Isabelle Wolfe Baruch, "Recollections of Sherman's Raid through South Carolina" in Linda Malone, ed., *Fairfield Remembers* (Fairfield County, SC: Fairfield Archives & History, 2006), 24.

14. *In February 1865*: Robert N. Rosen, *The Jewish Confederates* (Columbia, SC: University of South Carolina Press, 2000), 341. See also, Mark H. Dunkelman, *Marching with Sherman: Through Georgia and the Carolinas with the 154th New York* (Baton Rouge: Louisiana State University Press, 2012); Isabelle Wolfe Baruch, "Recollections of Sherman's Raid through South Carolina," 24–33.

14. *"Indelibly impressed upon"*: Wolfe Baruch, ibid., 24.

14. *In 1867, Isabelle*: *American Hebrew and Jewish Messenger*, December 2, 1921.

14. *Lytton, who lived to be 102*: *Chicago Daily Tribune*, April 1, 1949; NYT, April 1, 1949.

14. *Escaping economic hardship*: Howard M. Sachar, *A History of the Jews in America* (New York: Alfred A. Knopf, 1992), 38–39; Stanley Nadel, "Germans," in Kenneth T. Jackson, Lisa Keller, Nancy Flood, eds. *Encyclopedia of New York City* (New Haven, CT: Yale University Press, 2010), 505–7; Hasia R. Diner, "German Immigrant Period in the United States," *Jewish Women's Archive*, https://jwa.org/encyclopedia/article/german-immigrant-period-in-united-states.

15. *In 1862, he was also*: Amy Mittelman, *Brewing Battles: A History of American Beer* (New York: Algora Publishing, 2008), 28–29.

15. *First was the enormous*: Edwin G. Burrows and Mike Wallace, *Gotham: A History of New York to 1898* (New York: Oxford University Press, 1999), 741.

15. *He was one of*: NYT, March 29, 1890; Jay Brooks, "Historic Beer Birthday: Emanuel Bernheimer," Brookston Beer Bulletin, August 3, 2018, https://brookstonbeerbulletin.com/historic-beer-birthday-emanuel-bernheimer.

15. *The wealthy socialites*: Mike Wallace, *Greater Gotham: A History of New York City from 1898 to 1919* (New York: Oxford University Press, 2017), 372.

15. *Joseph Seligman and his family*: Allan Levine, *Scattered Among the Peoples: The Jewish Diaspora in Twelve Portraits* (New York: Overlook Press, 2003), 267–68; Sachar, *A History of the Jews in America*, 98.

16. *In 1868, the Bernheimers*: Temple Emanu-El, "Our History," www.emanuelnyc.org/about-us/our-history.

16. *Like the Bernheimers*: *American Hebrew and Jewish Messenger* (New York), January 23, 1914; NYT, March 27, 1902.

16. *Max and Stella and*: Wallace, *Greater Gotham*, 1079.

17. *Max was at a courthouse*: NYT, September 25, 1913.

17. *He was laid to rest*: May French, "Salem Fields Cemetery, New York Cemetery Project, January 27, 2011, https://nycemetery.wordpress.com/2011/01/27/salem-fields-cemetery; "Max Emanuel Bernheimer," Find a Grave, www.findagrave.com/memorial/194210177/max-emanuel-bernheimer.

17. *Stella and her sons*: NYT, October 7, 1913.

17. *Elberon and nearby locales*: Sharon Hazard, "Monmouth County: The Jewish Newport of the Jersey Shore," *Two River Times*, July 20, 2012.

17. *The New York weekly*: See, *American Hebrew and Jewish Messenger*, August 17, 1917; August 2, 1918; See also, Robert Khederian, "Elberon, the High-Profile Gilded Age Resort You've Never Heard Of," *Curbed*, July 13, 2017, www.curbed.com/2017/7/13/15964280/elberon-history-gilded-age-newport-mckim.

18. *William later claimed*: See, NHT, March 15, 1925. For a fascinating account of this issue, see Kirsten Fermaglich, *A Rosenberg By Any Other Name: A History of Jewish Name Changing in America* (New York: New York University Press, 2018).

19. *As was the custom*: Mel Heimer, *The Girl in Murder Flat* (New York: Fawcett Publications, 1955), 10.

19. *When the family was*: Dunne, *Justice*, 274.

19. *The trouble began*: NHT, October 20, 1921; NYT, May 6, 1922.

20. *Claire Cornell had other problems*: NHT, December 6, 1925; WP, July 23, 1926.

20. *On the day of his*: NYT, May 10, 1922; April 28 1924.

20. *In 1922, George*: NYT, May 10, 1924.

21. *The sensational story*: NYT, May 10, April 28, 1922; *St. Louis Post-Dispatch*, May 10, 1922; *Philadelphia Inquirer*, May 11, 1922; "Mrs. Astor and the Gilded Age," https://mrsastor.com/content/9.

21. *She later listed*: NYT, March 15, 1925.

22. *As alimony, William*: Perry, *A Chair*, 16.

22. *Lucille took little Patsy*: Heimer, *The Girl in Murder Flat*, 10.

22. *Quite inexplicably*: *Los Angeles Times*, August 12, 1930. Thanks to Lisa Krain for bringing this to my attention.

22. *Lucille later said*: NDN, February 29, 1944.

CHAPTER 3: THE DEBUTANTE AND THE DISPATCHER

23. *They sailed on the Cunard*: William O. Burton and Patricia Burton, 1939; citing Immigration, New York, New York, United States, NARA microfilm publication T715 (Washington, DC: National Archives and Records Administration, n.d.).

23. *The story was*: Perry, *A Chair*, 4; Dunne, *Justice*, 274.

24. *Patricia's social calendar*: NHT, December 11, 1939; June 30, 1940.

24. *In late December 1939*: NYT, December, 27, 1939.

24. *Less than two weeks later*: Ibid., January 9, 28, 1940.

24. *FDR's birthday celebration*: Ibid., February 16, June 30, 1940.

24. *And early in 1941*: Ibid., April 22, 1941.

25. *Financial support totaling*: Grover A. Whalen, "The New York World's Fair of 1939," *Bankers' Magazine* 138:1 (January 1939), 27–33; Bill Cotter, *The 1939–1940 New York World's Fair* (Mount Pleasant, SC: Arcadia Publishing, 2009), 15.

25. *Such exhibits as General*: Cotter, ibid., 7.

25. *The fair "is a more"*: Gardner Harding, "World's Fair, New York," *Harper's Magazine* (June 1, 1939), 194.

25. *About the only issue*: Ibid., 197.

26. *The company also transported*: "The Buses of Exposition Greyhound," *The World's Fair Community*, January 18, 2008, http://www.worldsfaircommunity .org/topic/7498-the-buses-of-exposition-greyhound.

26. *Greyhound management rated him*: NYCMA Lonergan File, William F. Grant, Greyhound Manager Department of Safety and Personnel to H. E. Johnson, Capital Theatre Bus Terminal, February 7, 1944.

26. *He soon found other*: Ibid., Toronto Detective Alex Deans, "Report on Lonergan," October 25, 1943.

26. *Decades later, Lonergan*: Perry, *A Chair*, 11–12.

26. *Sponsored by the American*: "Café Society Murder," *Newsweek* (November, 1943), 46; Dunne, *Justice*, 273.

26. *At the same time*: Perry, *A Chair*, 14–16.

27. *The other and arguably*: See, Edwin Radin, "The Café Society Murder," in Mystery Writers of America's *Murder Cavalcade: An Anthology* (New York: Duell, Sloan and Pearce, 1946), 334; Dunne, *Justice*, 273.

27. *As a* New York Journal-American *story*: Cited in Gibbs, "The Wayward Press," 86.

27. *In 1939, Dixon was*: Toronto Police Interview of Sidney Capel Dixon.

27. *"Lonergan's conversation on"*: Ibid.

27. *Lonergan did spend*: Radin, "The Café Society Murder," 334–35; Perry, *A Chair*, 14.

27. *"Although New York was"*: Ralph Blumenthal, *Stork Club: America's Most Famous Nightspot and the Lost World of Café Society* (New York: Little, Brown & Company, 2000), 159. See also, Hugh Ryan, *When Brooklyn Was Queer: A History* (New York: St. Martin's Press, 2019), 161–63.

27. *Plainclothes detectives stalked*: Ryan, ibid., 156–57; Kaiser, *The Gay Metropolis*, 83.

27. *Violent crime and homosexuality*: Estelle B. Freedman, "'Uncontrolled Desires': The Response to the Sexual Psychopath, 1920–1960," *Journal of American History* 74: 1 (June, 1987), 92; Lillian Faderman, *The Gay Revolution: The Story of the Struggle* (New York: Simon & Schuster, 2015), 4–5.

28. *Typical was this*: J. Paul de River, *The Sexual Criminal: A Psychoanalytic Study* (Springfield, IL: Charles C. Thomas, Publisher, 1949), xii.

28. *Similarly, the respected*: Benjamin Karpman, "The Sexual Psychopath," *Journal of Criminal Law and Criminology* 42: 2 (July–August, 1951), 186–87.

28. *The widely held view*: George Painter, "The Sensibilities of Our Forefathers: The History of Sodomy Laws in the United States," www.glapn.org/sodomylaws/sensibilities/new_york.htm.

28. *In New York it was*: Kaiser, *The Gay Metropolis*, 83–84.

28. *Much more serious*: Painter, "The Sensibilities of Our Forefathers."

28. *It was worse in Illinois*: Faderman, *The Gay Revolution*, 4.

28. *A 1938 study*: George W. Henry and Alfred A. Gross, "Social Factors in Case Histories of 100 Underprivileged Homosexuals," *Mental Hygiene* 22 (October 1938), 599.

29. *Lonergan, who liked to be*: Dunne, *Justice*, 276.

29. *Lucille, who was still*: "William Oliver Burton," www.findagrave.com/memorial/194209852/william-oliver-burton.

29. *He had been fired*: Grant to Johnson, February 7, 1944.

29. *He was undoubtedly aware*: On Patricia Burton Lonergan's finances, see, NYCMA Lonergan File, "Patricia B. Lonergan Account," prepared by Harry Civiletti, Attorney and Counselor at Law, July 31, 1943. In press articles, as well as in subsequent books by Heimer and Perry on the case, there was confusion about how much money Patricia had and lived on each month. The DA's office made no attempt to clarify these details to the reporters.

30. *He borrowed money*: *Minneapolis Morning Tribune*, October 29, 1943; NYT, March 5, 1944.

30. *The city's "newest industry"*: PIPL, November 23, 1941.

30. *Hollywood stars were also*: Ibid.

31. *They stopped at the*: Radin, "The Café Society Murder," 335.

31. *Only the* Daily News: Cited in Perry, *A Chair*, 21.

31. *Wayne convinced Patricia*: NYCMA Lonergan File, "Jacob Grumet's Notes on Cross-Examination of Lonergan, 1944."

31. *As she later was supposed*: NDM, February 20, 1944.

CHAPTER 4: STARRING IN THE MOST EXCITING FLOOR SHOW IN THE WORLD

32. *A rite of passage*: Blumenthal, *Stork Club*, 40.

32. *This Parisian-style designation:* Marilyn Kaytor, *"21": The Life and Times of New York's Favourite Club* (New York: Viking Press, 1975), 1.

32. *She was what Walter*: *Nevada State Journal*, April 11, 1939; Lili Anolik, "Paris, Lindsay, Britney: The Rise and Fall of a Celebrity Supernova," *Vanity Fair*, Holiday Issue, December 2018/January 2019. 71; Neil Gabler, *Winchell: Gossip, Power and the Culture of Celebrity* (New York: Vintage Books, 1995), 265.

32. *Patricia, too, was*: NDM, February 28, 1944.

33. *All evening, like clockwork*: Blumenthal, *Stork Club*, 1, 15.

33. *On a busy evening*: Damon Runyon, "Mr. 'B' and his Stork Club," *Cosmopolitan* 122:5 (May 1947), 25.

33. *If you were deemed*: Blumenthal, *Stork Club*, 1, 15.

33. *On the other hand*: Paul Freedman, *Ten Restaurants that Changed America* (New York: Liveright Publishing, 2016), 309.

33. *In Lonergan's no doubt*: Perry, *A Chair*, 13.

33. *The object was to be seen*: Brendan Gill, "Happy Times: Profile of Jerome Zerbe," *New Yorker* (June 9, 1973), 39; Charles Clegg and Duncan Emrich, eds., *The Lucius Beebe Reader* (Garden City, NY: Doubleday & Company, 1967), 391; Joanna Scutt, "Gentlemen for Rent," *New Yorker*, July 1, 2014, www.newyorker.com/books/page-turner/gentlemen-for-rent.

34. *For a few years, Beebe*: Cited in Brendan Gill, *Here at the New Yorker* (New York: Random House, 1975), 121–22.

34. *"To millions and millions"*: Lucius Beebe, *The Stork Club Bar Book* (New York: Rinehart & Company, 1946), viii.

34. *Or, as another café*: NYT, October 5, 1966; Gill, *Here at the New Yorker*, 13.

34. *It was the reason*: Anthony Young, *New York Café Society: The Elite Meet to See and Be Seen, 1920s–1940s* (Jefferson, NC: McFarland & Company, 2015), 190–92; Gill, ibid., 50.

34. *Though the Stork and El Morocco*: Blumenthal, *Stork Club*, 13; Young, ibid., 182.

34. *They also spied*: Blumenthal, ibid., 132.

35. *Born in rural Oklahoma*: Ibid., 65–72.

35. *He managed to talk*: Ibid., 87–88.

35. *They found liquor*: John Kobler, *Ardent Spirits: The Rise and Fall of Prohibition* (New York: G. P. Putnam's Sons, 1973), 234–35. Allan Levine, *The Devil in Babylon: Fear of Progress and the Birth of Modern Life* (Toronto: McClelland & Stewart, 2005), 213–15.

35. *What Billingsley did not*: NHT, September 20, 1939; Blumenthal, *Stork Club*, 103.

36. *For the café society*: Beebe, "Café Society," *Cosmopolitan* (March 1937), 98.

36. *By this time, he*: Gabler, *Winchell*, 188; Brian Kellow, *Ethel Merman: A Life* (New York: Viking Press, 2007), 76–8, 82–6; Carly Flynn, *Brass Diva: The Life and Legends of Ethel Merman* (Berkeley: University of California Press, 2007), 114–15.

36. *He was also a dictatorial*: Runyon, "Mr. 'B' and his Stork Club," 133; Blumenthal, *Stork Club*, 10, 23; NYT, October 5, 1966.

36. *Working sixteen hours*: Runyon, ibid., 133–36; Blumenthal, ibid., 10, 20.

36. *The daily grind*: Blumenthal, ibid., 57.

36. *If he tugged his left ear*: Beebe, *The Stork Club Bar Book*, x.

36. *"I have to bring"*: Finis Farr, "Sherman Billingsley," *Cosmopolitan* 106:5 (May 1939), 106.

36. *Nothing was too*: Ibid., 106.

36. *"He distributes free"*: Lucius Beebe, *Snoot If You Must* (London: D. Appleton-Century Company, 1943), 190; Young, *New York Café Society*, 183.

37. *In the fingers*: Blumenthal, *Stork Club*, 23. See the photograph, for example, in Farr, "Sherman Billingsley," 106.

37. *Many of Billingsley's patrons*: Blumenthal, ibid., 159.

37. *It would be fair*: Ibid., 159–83.

37. *Born in in 1897*: Young, *New York Café Society*, 185; NYT, June 11, 1961; Levine, *Toronto*, 121–22.

37. *Perona found a job*: NHT, June 22, 1935; Young, ibid., 185–86; Gill, "Happy Times," 50.

38. *In a June 1935 column*: NHT, ibid.

38. *He was "one of the"*: Gill, "Happy Times," 50.

38. *Perona spent years*: Beebe, *Snoot If You Must*, 66–67; Young, *New York Café Society*, 186.

38. *The El Morocco was*: Cited in Doyle Auctions, "Doyle New York's September 16, 2014 Auction of El Morocco: The John Perona Collection Exceeds Estimate," September 16, 2014, http://doyle.com/auctions/14em01-el -morocco-john-perona-collection/doyle-new-yorks-september-16-2014 -auction-el.

38. *The* New York Post's *Broadway*: Jeffrey Lyons, *What a Time It Was!: Leonard Lyons and the Golden Age of New York Nightlife* (New York: Abbeville Press Publishers, 2015), 16.

38. *Added Beebe in*: NHT, June 22, 1935.

38. *"Oh, it was a ritual"*: Cited in Laura Shaine Cunningham, "Ghosts of El Morocco," NYT, September 5, 2004.

38. *One night during*: Diana Vreeland, *D. V.* (New York: Alfred A. Knopf, 1984), 143; Cunningham, ibid.

39. *For those who*: *Pittsburgh Post-Gazette*, July 28, 1945.

39. *"I wore red silk"*: Cited in Cunningham, "Ghosts of El Morocco."

39. *As Beebe aptly*: Beebe, "Café Society," *Cosmopolitan* (March 1937), 26.

39. *Later, the gossip*: NYCMA Lonergan File, "Statement of Harold Le Mon," October 25, 1943.

40. *This subject came up*: Toronto Statement, 27.

40. *For part of the summer*: Heimer, *The Girl in Murder Flat*, 74.

40. *While they were*: NYCMA Lonergan File, Pelton to Beisler, October 24, 1942.

40. *Once the newlyweds*: NYT, October 25, 1943; NHT, March 27, 1944.

40. *Her monthly stipend*: "Patricia B. Lonergan Account," July 31, 1943.

41. *Patricia gave Wayne*: Lonergan Confession, 29.

41. *His usual weekday*: NYCMA Lonergan File, "Memorandum Remis Soucy," October 1943.

41. *Patricia, on the other hand*: NYCMA Lonergan File, Red Cross certificate March 2, 1942; The American National Red Cross, Volunteer Certificate, March 1943; "Memorandum Remis Soucy"; *Minneapolis Morning Tribune*, October 29, 1943; NYT, October 26, 1943.

41. *The mores of*: *Daily Boston Globe*, March 12, 1936.

41. *She offered her*: Ibid., November 10, 1931; March 12, 1936. See also, *The Sun* (Baltimore), July 4, 1932.

41. *Lonergan was often*: NYCMA Lonergan File, DA report, "Patricia Lonergan's Financial Support of Wayne Lonergan"; "Memorandum of Conversation with Lucille Wolfe Burton," November 4, 1943; DA's "List of Lonergan's Possessions"; Radin, "The Café Society Murder," 335–36; Author's interview with Ronda Cooper, the Characters Talent Agency, April 14, 2019.

42. *He had been introduced*: Perry, *A Chair*, 24–25; H. Peter Kriendler, *"21": Every Day was New Year's Eve* (Lanham, MD: Taylor Trade Publishing, 1999), 133.

42. *Lambert had met*: NYCMA Lonergan File, "Memorandum on George Lambert," October–November, 1943.

42. *Her pet name*: Heimer, *The Girl in Murder Flat*, 13.

42. *Lucille paid the price*: NYCMA Lonergan File, ADA Jacob Grumet, "Notes for Cross-Examination of Lonergan," February–March, 1944.

42. *Wayne and Patricia did enjoy*: See, "Memorandum Remis Soucy"; "Memorandum: Helen Wing, 1943"; Perry, *A Chair*, 27.

42. *According to Remis Soucy*: Ibid., Soucy and "Helen Wing."

43. *It was Soucy's job*: Ibid., Soucy.

43. *Sometimes he brought*: Grumet, "Notes for Cross-Examination of Lonergan."

43. *The housekeeper was instructed*: "Memorandum Remis Soucy."

43. *He did meet Lucius*: Perry, *A Chair*, 26; Kriendler, *"21,"* 133.

43. *Thyra Samter Winslow later noted*: NDM, February 29, 1944.

CHAPTER 5: A MARRIAGE MISTAKE

44. *"They fought like"*: Cited in Heimer, *The Girl in Murder Flat*, 12.

44. *After she died*: Toronto Statement, 5.

45. *Remis Soucy later*: "Memorandum Remis Soucy."

45. *Black was slight*: NYCMA Lonergan File, Black Statement.

45. *Katherine Graham, the publisher*: Katherine Graham, *Personal History* (New York: Vintage Books, 1998), 25–26.

45. *The children of the wealthy*: Mary Cable, *Top Drawer: American High Society from the Gilded Age to the Roaring Twenties* (New York, Atheneum, 1984), 148–49.

45. *A maid, Marie*: Ibid., "DA Statement of Marie Tanzosch," November 5, 1943 (hereafter, Tanzosch Statement).

46. *If he had to fight*: Perry, *A Chair*, 30–31.

46. *William was four years older*: GM, May 19, 1965.

46. *By 1942, and likely*: "United States Border Crossings from Canada to United States, 1895–1956," Wayne Thomas Lonergan, October 27, 1942; from "Border Crossings: From Canada to U.S., 1895–1954," citing Ship, arrival port Buffalo, New York, NARA microfilm publication M1480, Records of the Immigration and Naturalization Service, RG 85 (Washington, DC: National Archives and Records Administration, n.d.), roll 73.

46. *As Lonergan had anticipated*: NYCMA Lonergan File, Candler Cobb, Local Board No. 31 to Major B. T. Anuskewicz, Selective Service Headquarters, New York, New York, January 24, 1942.

46. *The regulations identified*: Allan Bérubé, *Coming Out Under Fire: The History of Gay Men and Women in World War Two* (Chapel Hill, NC: The University of North Carolina Press, 2010), 9–15; Kaiser, *The Gay Metropolis*, 28–29.

46. *In one suggested scenario*: Dexter Means Bullard, "Selective Service Psychiatry," *Psychiatry* 4:2 (1941), 231–32; Bérubé, ibid., 16–19.

46. *"We question"*: Carl Binger, MD, "How We Screen Out Psychological 4-Fs," *Saturday Evening Post*, January 8, 1944, 75.

47. *Or, as a headline*: *Afro-American* (Washington, DC), September 11, 1943.

47. *By March 1942*: Cited in Bérubé, *Coming Out Under Fire*, 19.

47. *To this end, thousands*: Ibid., 22.

47. *When word got*: Ryan, *When Brooklyn Was Queer*, 200.

47. *According to the* Afro-American: *Afro-American*, September 11, 1943.

47. *More fuel was added*: See, Ryan, *When Brooklyn Was Queer*, 208–12; NHT, May 12, 1942; PI, May 20, 1942; *Boston Globe*, May 21, 1942.

47. *At his initial induction*: Cobb to Anuskewicz, January 24, 1942.

47. *This time, Lonergan was*: Toronto Statement, 7.

48. *Nearly three decades*: Perry, *A Chair*, 30–31.

48. *In a CBC Television*: LAC, "Lonergan, Wayne," Interview, *This Hour Has Seven Days*, December 1965, 515964 (sound recording) (hereafter, LAC, Lonergan Interview, *This Hour Has Seven Days*); GM, December 13, 1965.

48. *Military officials regarded*: Cobb to Anuskewicz, January 24, 1942.

48. *Psychiatrist Dr. George Henry*: NYCMA Lonergan File, Henry to Cobb, March 6, 1942.

48. *By the summer of 1943*: *Minneapolis Morning Tribune*, October 29, 1943.

48. *He claimed that*: Toronto Statement, 4–5; "Memorandum: Helen Wing, 1943."

48. *On several occasions*: Grumet, "Notes for Cross-Examination of Lonergan."

49. *The hamlet on Fire Island*: Esther Newton, *Cherry Grove, Fire Island: Sixty Years in America's First Gay and Lesbian Town* (Raleigh, NC: Duke University

Press, 2015), 13; Lee E. Koppelman and Seth Forman, *The Fire Island National Seashore: A History* (Albany: SUNY Press, 2008), 12; NYT, August 2, 1996.

49. *When a New York City ADA*: Toronto Statement, 6.

49. *His tuition was generously*: DA report, "Patricia Lonergan's Financial Support of Wayne Lonergan"; Black Statement.

49. *The ads often featured*: NYT, March 5, 1939.

49. *At the photography school*: NYCMA Lonergan File, "Memorandum: Witness George Herascu."

49. *Raised in South Australia*: NYT, August 21, 1982; National Gallery of Australia, "In the Spotlight: Anton Bruehl," 2011, https://nga.gov.au/exhibition/bruehl/default.cfm?MNUID=6.

50. *Alas, Lonergan's apprenticeship*: Sing Sing, "Wayne Thomas Lonergan Record."

50. *The one-year lease*: NYCMA Lonergan File, "Lease Agreement, between Chester Burt Fentress and Wayne and Patricia Lonergan."

50. *"Frightfully sorry about"*: NYCMA Lonergan File, Wayne Lonergan to Patricia Burton Lonergan, August 14, 1943.

50. *She altered the terms*: Ibid., "Copy of Last Will and Testament of Patricia Burton Lonergan, Alexander & Keenan, Attorneys and Counsellors at Law, August 19, 1943; NYT, March 31, 1944.

51. *Built in 1939*: NYT, February 9, 1937.

51. *A second set of stairs*: Archives at Yale to Author, May 10, 2019; *New York White Pages* of 1943.

51. *The young boy was recuperating*: NDN, March 29, 1944.

52. *In 1924, as the brownstones*: NYT, June 25, 2000; Harold Schechter, *The Mad Sculptor* (Boston: Houghton Mifflin, 2014), 4.

52. *The name is derived*: Burrows and Wallace, *Gotham*, 178–79.

52. *In November 1935*: Bernard Ryan Jr., "Vera Stretz Trial," www.encyclopedia.com/law/law-magazines/vera-stretz-trial-1936; Harold Schechter, "Bloody, Bloody Beekman Place: Where the Wealthy Wind Up Dead," *The Daily Beast*, January 22, 2015; Schechter, *The Mad Sculptor*, 7–28.

53. *Several months later*: Schechter, *The Mad Sculptor*, 29–46; *Newsweek*, May 2, 1936, 7, 18; NYT, May 29, 1936.

53. *Robert Irwin was a*: Schechter, ibid., 133–34.

53. *Meanwhile, the shapely*: Ibid., 147.

53. *On Saturday night, March 27*: Ibid., 104–5, 153–54, 243.

54. *Next, Irwin took Mary's*: Ibid., 237–47; Lewis J. Valentine, *Night Stick: The Autobiography of Lewis J. Valentine, Former Police Commissioner of New York* (New York: Dial Press, 1947), 172–82.

54. *After a prolonged*: NYT, June 28, 1937.

54. *At his trial he was*: Schechter, *The Mad Sculptor*, 301.

55. *Twenty-two-year-old Helen*: "Memorandum: Helen Wing, 1943."

55. *He later claimed*: Toronto Statement, 7–8.

55. *As he later wrote*: NYCMA Lonergan File, Wayne Lonergan to Patricia Burton Lonergan, September 4, 1943.

55. *The RCAF medical board*: Ibid., "RCAF Medical Board Report for Wayne Lonergan," September 2, 1943.

55. *The university and the RCAF*: Ibid., "RCAF Form for Canadian Service Personnel Visiting the USA,"; *Christian Science Monitor*, February 18, 1942.

55. *On the recommendation*: Toronto Police Interview of Sidney Capel Dixon; NYCMA Lonergan File, Arthur Harris to John Loehr, November 1, 1943; Gwyn Thomas and Jack Batten, "Wife Killer or Fall Guy," *Maclean's* (Toronto) July 3, 1965, 38–39.

55. *The Belvidere, run by*: GM, September 19, 1940; Toronto Police Interview of Sidney Capel Dixon.

56. *It is possible that Dixon*: NJA, November 8, 1943; Perry, *A Chair*, 54–55.

56. *Dixon later told*: Toronto Police Interview of Sidney Capel Dixon.

CHAPTER 6: WEEKEND FURLOUGH

57. *According to his later*: Lonergan Confession, 38.

58. *Yet once he arrived*: Toronto Statement, 8.

58. *While he had been in New York*: NYCMA Lonergan File, Providence Loan Society of New York, "Wayne Lonergan Loans of $410 and $140," October 7, 1943.

58. *Lonergan later told*: Toronto Statement, 8.

59. *Once Lonergan knew*: Ibid., 10." Memorandum: Helen Wing, 1943."

59. *His grandfather, John*: See, Susie Pak, "The House of Morgan: Private Family Bank in Transition" in Korinna Schönhärl, ed., *Decision Taking, Confidence and Risk Management in Banks from Early Modernity to the 20th Century* (Basingstoke, UK: Palgrave MacMillan, 2017), 15–55; Vincent P. Carosso, *The Morgans: Private International Bankers, 1854–1913*, Harvard Studies in Business History 38 (Cambridge, MA: Harvard University Press, 1987); 16, 1914; NYT, February WP, September 12, 1914.

59. *John's son, H. (Henry) Herman*: NYT, August 22, 1926.

60. *Tragedy struck*: Ibid., January 5, 1923.

60. *This time, Herman was*: Ibid., August 22, 1926.

60. *In August 1936*: Ibid., August 5, 1936.

60. *John attended Cambridge*: Ibid., April 15, 1950.

60. *When World War II broke*: NYCMA Lonergan File, "DA Statement of John F. Harjes," October 25, 1943 (hereafter, Harjes Statement).

60. *Harjes's path crossed*: NYT, May 30, 1941.

61. *Their friendship grew*: Ibid., February 2, 1943; NJA, October 25, 1943.

61. *As reported in*: NYT, February 2, 1943.

61. *By the spring of 1944*: Ibid., March 24, 1944.

61. *Lonergan arrived at Harjes's*: Harjes Statement.

61. *He slept for several*: NYCMA Lonergan File, "DA Statement of Emile Peeters," October 25, 1943 (hereafter, Peeters Statement).

61. *Emile, who was sixty-one*: Ibid.; "Emile Charles Peeters and Josephine Peeters, 1932"; citing Immigration, New York, New York, United States, NARA microfilm publication T715 (Washington, DC: National Archives and Records Administration, n.d.).

61. *Harjes, however, had instructed*: Peeters Statement.

61. *Harjes said he did know*: Harjes Statement.

62. *Harjes assured Lonergan*: Ibid.; NJA, March 28, 1944.

62. *Two years later, she*: NJA, May 17, 1944.

62. *By the fall of 1943*: NYCMA Lonergan File "DA Statement of Jean Murphy Jaburg," October 25, 1943 (hereafter, Jaburg Statement).

62. *Dressed in his RCAF uniform*: Toronto Statement, 33–34.

63. *Once he arrived*: NYCMA Lonergan File, "DA Statement of Sylvia French," November 23, 1943 (hereafter, French Statement); Toronto Statement, 11–12; NYT, February 23, 1956; November 26, 1964.

63. *French was a charming*: Ibid., French Statement; NJA, March 24, 1944.

63. *He stopped by a shop*: Toronto Statement, 14.

63. *Harjes asked her if*: Harjes Statement.

64. *She then called Harjes's*: Jaburg Statement.

64. *Peeters the butler*: Toronto Statement, 17; Peeters Statement.

64. *Patricia was already out*: Black Statement; Tanzosch Statement.

64. *Lonergan said he had to pick*: Jaburg Statement.

65. *Though* One Touch of Venus: Toronto Statement, 20.

65. *Then, Murphy Jaburg and Lonergan*: Jaburg Statement; Toronto Statement, 20–22.

65. *They were hoping to have*: Young, *New York Café Society*, 174; Kriendler, *"21,"* 54.

65. *Lonergan ordered the chicken*: Toronto Statement, 21.

65. *Murphy Jaburg recalled that*: Jaburg Statement.

66. *Later on, Kriendler and Berns*: Kriendler, *"21,"* 132.

66. *Operated by Herbert Jacoby*: *New York City Guide 1* (New York: Random House, 1939), 32.

66. Variety *magazine had*: "Night Club Reviews: Blue Angel, N.Y.," *Variety*, April 21, 1943, 49.

66. *Lonergan and Murphy Jaburg each*: Toronto Statement, 22–24; Jaburg Statement.

66. *While doing so, he claimed*: Lonergan's story about Murray Wooster/ Maurice Worcester and Loehr's questions about it can be found in Toronto Statement, 24–27.

67. *Exhausted, and seemingly*: Thanks to Major William March, retired, Air Reserve and RCAF Historian, Directorate of Air Force History and Heritage, for information about the issue of the missing uniform. March to Author, May 31, 2019.

67. *Peeters later recalled*: Peeters Statement.

68. *She later remembered that*: French Statement.

68. *At approximately 12:30 p.m.*: Toronto Statement, 30.

68. *Taking one look at him*: Jaburg Statement.

68. *When Murphy Jaburg was later asked*: Ibid.

69. *Back at Harjes's at about*: Harjes Statement.

CHAPTER 7: OUT FOR A GOOD TIME

70. *Her standing instruction*: Black Statement; Tanzosch Statement.

71. *Gabellini was a debonair*: NJA, October 26, 27, 1943.

71. *His first wife, Helen*: *Salt Lake City Tribune*, September 14, 1929.

71. *Helen was a widow*: NYT, July 8, 1928.

71. *He had little money*: NYCMA Lonergan File, "DA Statement of George Granata," October 25, 1943 (hereafter, Granata Statement); "DA Statement of Thomas Farrell," October 25, 1943 (hereafter, Farrell Statement).

71. *He was late, and Patricia was not*: NYT, March 29, 1944.

72. *A year earlier, Goodwin*: NYCMA Lonergan File, "DA Statement of Jean Audrey Goodwin," October 25, 1943 (hereafter, Goodwin Statement); Farrell Statement.

72. *Leaving the Peter Cooper*: Farrell Statement.

72. *That Saturday evening*: Ibid.

72. *During the dinner*: Ibid.; Goodwin Statement.

72. *"She was out"*: Farrell, ibid.

73. *Gabellini covered his*: Ibid.

73. *They stopped for a nightcap*: Ibid.

73. *He asked the driver*: Perry, *A Chair*, 277; NYT, March 30, 1944.

73. *On Sunday at about*: Granata Statement.

73. *Black also told Gabellini*: Black Statement.

74. *Joining the police*: NYCMA Lonergan File, Milton Helpern, "Autopsy of Patricia Burton Lonergan," October 25, 1943, 9 (hereafter, Burton Lonergan Autopsy).

74. *He would be appointed*: See, Marshall Houts, *Where Death Delights: The Story of Dr. Milton Helpern and Forensic Medicine* (New York: Coward-McCann, 1967) and Milton Helpern, *Autopsy: The Memoirs of Milton Helpern, the World's Greatest Medical Detective* (New York: St. Martin's Press, 1977).

74. *The scene the police*: Burton Lonergan Autopsy, 9–10.

74. *Two green-glass or onyx*: Ibid., 11; NYCMA Lonergan File, "DA Report on Candlestick Holders."

75. *One of the detectives*: NYCMA Lonergan File, "District Attorney Crime Scene Reports and Memorandum"; "Milton Helpern Testimony, March 20, 1944."

75. *"The [pyramid]-shaped base"*: Burton Lonergan Autopsy, 11–12; Radin, "The Café Society Murder," 319.

75. *"She bled a great deal"*: Burton Lonergan Autopsy, 1; NYCMA Lonergan File, Alexander Wiener, "Report on Patricia Lonergan," Bacteriological and Serological Laboratory, December 13, 1943 (hereafter, Wiener Report).

75. *In fact, the detectives later calculated*: NYCMA Lonergan File, "New York Police Department List of Items from Patricia Lonergan."

76. *He was well-known for his*: NYT, November 7, 1976.

76. *Wiener would analyze cigarette stubs*: Wiener Report.

76. *In addition to the bloodstain*: Ibid.

76. *A bloody fingerprint*: NYT, October 28, 1943.

77. *He had deep roots*: See, Arnold L. Steigman, "Mayor-Council Government: Yonkers, New York 1908–1939: A Study of 'Failure' and Abandonment," PhD Thesis (New York University, 1967), 235–1077; Author's interview with Justice Gerald Loehr, May 6, 2019.

77. *John Loehr, who passed away*: Author's Interview with Justice Gerald Loehr, ibid.

77. *His other son, John G. Loehr*: Author's Interview with John G. Loehr, July 26, 2019.

77. *He was then forty-four*: Newsday, January 21, 1965; NJA, February 29, 1944: NDM, March 6, 1944.

77. *Grumet had previously worked*: NYT, June 9, 1987; January 27, 1966.

78. *One thing Hogan insisted*: Author's interview with Justice Gerald Loehr.

79. *While rummaging through*: Perry, *A Chair*, 114.

79. *Gabellini was questioned*: "DA Statement of Mario Gabellini," October 25, 1943; NYT, October 26, 27, 30, 1943.

79. *The interrogation of Gabellini*: Farrell Statement; Goodwin Statement; NYCMA Lonergan File, "DA Statement of Emilio Tagle," October 25, 1943.

CHAPTER 8: A LIKELY SUSPECT

80. *Convicted, along with her*: Levine, *The Devil in Babylon*, 270–72; Denis Brian, *Sing Sing: The Inside of a Notorious Prison* (Amherst, NY: Prometheus Books, 2005), 139–42.

81. *The* Daily News *offered*: NDN, NHT, NYT, October 25, 1943; Gibbs, "The Wayward Press," 86–87.

81. *By late afternoon*: See the Associated Press story in the *Austin American Statesman*, October 25, 1943.

82. *Harris asked him*: NYCMA Lonergan File, "Detective Arthur Harris Notes," October 25, 1943 (hereafter, Harris Notes).

82. *Lonergan was not surprised*: GM, October 25, 1943.

82. *The detectives first drove*: Harris Notes.

83. *Whatever the reason*: NYCMA Lonergan File, Philip Waite to Grumet, November 17, 1943; NYT, November 5, 1943.

83. *"We want that uniform"*: NYT, October 26, 1943; Harris Notes.

83. *Lonergan, as cool and carefree*: Harris Notes.

84. *Michael Doyle, a Toronto*: GM, May 21, 1965; NYT, May 21, 1965.

84. *Another Toronto lawyer*: NYT, October 26, 1943; GM, October 27, 1943.

84. *As Davis asserted*: NYT, October 27, 1943.

84. *Frederick Malone, an assistant*: GM, October 27, 1943.

84. *"How can anyone"*: GM, October 30, 1943.

84. *The* Globe and Mail's *editors*: Ibid.

85. *"I suppose you want"*: The interrogation of Lonergan by John Loehr and Arthur Harris on October 25, 1943, can be found in the Toronto Statement, 1–38.

85. *"I cannot think of anything"*: Lonergan's comments about Loehr are from LAC, Lonergan Interview, *This Hour Has Seven Days*.

92. *In the days, months and years*: Perry, *A Chair*, 64.

93. *"The story was so revolting"*: NJA, March 24, 1944.

93. *"A guilty man"*: Ibid., October 27, 1943.

93. *"He is a very likely suspect"*: NHT, October 26, 1943.

93. *Grumet later told Lonergan*: Cited in Perry, *A Chair*, 171.

CHAPTER 9: THE SEX-TWISTED PLAYBOY WITH A CREW CUT AND A SNEER

94. *She related the details*: Jaburg Statement.

94. *"It's such a sordid thing"*: NYT, NJA, October 26, 1943; Heimer, *The Girl in Murder Flat*, 14.

94. *One thing was clear*: NHT, October 26, 1943.

94. *Detective Harris, however:* Harris Notes.

95. *At about 9:00 a.m.*: NYCMA Lonergan File, "Report of Patrol Constable Ronald Harrison, Toronto Police Department."

95. *"Lonergan appeared to be rational"*: Ibid.

95. *Lonergan was told about*: Harris Notes.

96. *It was a small gathering*: GM, October 28, 1943.

96. *At the graveside*: Ibid.; Heimer, *The Girl in Murder Flat*, 24; NYT, February 28, 1991.

96. *While tidying up*: Harjes Statement.

97. *He later testified*: NYT, March 29, 1944.

97. *After the family farewells*: Harris Notes; NYCMA Lonergan File, "Loehr to Grumet, October 27, 1943" (from Buffalo).

97. *Despite later suggestions*: NYCMA Lonergan File, "Report of William Prendergast."

97. *Canadian customs officers*: NYT, October 26, 1943.

97. *American immigration officials*: Thomas and Batten, "Wife Killer or Fall Guy," 39.

98. *They checked into the Statler*: "Report of William Prendergast"; Heimer, *The Girl in Murder Flat*, 92.

98. *Loehr and the detectives*: Thomas and Batten, "Wife Killer or Fall Guy," 39; Heimer, ibid., 89–90.

99. *Sure enough, by*: Gibbs, "The Wayward Press," 89–90; NYT, NDN, NJA, October 28, 1943.

99. *Its front page*: NDN, October 28, 1943.

99. *The unrelenting commentary*: NJA, October 30, 1943; Kaiser, *The Gay Metropolis*, 23–24.

99. *Citing research by*: NJA, ibid. See also, "The Lonergan Case," *Time* 43:14, April 3, 1944, 71.

99. *As Charles Kaiser notes*: Kaiser, *The Gay Metropolis*, 24.

99. *Before the last week*: NJA, October 30, 1943; Gibbs, "The Wayward Press," 90-91.

100. *"Murder has driven"*: GM, October 28, 1943.

100. *Wolcott Gibbs, the* New Yorker's: Gibbs, "The Wayward Press," 87–90.

100. *He was given food*: NYT, May 2, 14, 1965.

100. *Lonergan was later to declare*: LAC, Lonergan Interview, *This Hour Has Seven Days*.

100. *Grumet maintained that*: NYT, NHT, GM, March 25, 1944; NYCMA Lonergan File, John Loehr, Typed Report of Interrogation of Wayne Lonergan, October 29, 1943, 3–5.

101. *In the confines of the room*: Loehr, ibid., 5–6; NYT, March 25, 1943; Perry, *A Chair*, 173.

101. *Later that morning, Loehr*: Loehr, ibid., 6–12.

101. *The tale about Maurice*: NYT, October 29, 1943.

101. *Lonergan was present*: Ibid.

102. *Two decades later*: NYT, May 14, 1965; Perry, *A Chair*, 175.

102. *Justice Gerald Loehr*: Author's interview with Justice Gerald Loehr.

102. *Lonergan and Loehr did share*: Loehr, Typed Report of Interrogation of Wayne Lonergan, 12–20.

104. *Thus, it would be difficult*: NYCMA Lonergan File, "Lonergan's Oral Statement to John Loehr," October 28, 1943.

104. *At approximately 2:00 p.m.*: Ibid., Henry E. Vaccaro, Report, October 28, 1943.

CHAPTER 10: NOTHING BUT THE TRUTH

106. *"Are you prepared to tell"*: Much of this chapter is based on NYCMA Lonergan File, "Wayne Lonergan Statement on Death of Patricia Lonergan," October 28, 1943, 1–39; and "Substance of Wayne Lonergan's Oral Statement to Mr. John Loehr, made on October 28, 1943, between 1:30 and 2:10 p.m., prior to his recorded statement."

108. *Patricia might have cried out*: Perry, *A Chair*, 253.

110. *She was walking her dog*: NYCMA Lonergan File, "Miss Ruth M. Forster Interview," John F. Loehr Memorandum, November 22, 1943; NYT, March 29, 1944.

110. *Returning to Harjes's*: Peeters Statement.

110. *In his diligent effort*: Perry, *A Chair*, 243.

112. *Despite women's participation*: Lewis A. Erenberg and Susan E. Hirsch, eds., *The War in American Culture: Society and Consciousness during World War II* (Chicago: University of Chicago Press, 2014), 137; Emily Yellin, *Our Mothers' War: American Women at Home and at the Front During World War II* (New York: Free Press, 2004), xiv, 6. Yellin notes that attitudes about women and marriage were changing in the United States.

113. *Nonetheless, the perception*: NYCMA Lonergan File, "Motion of Edward V. Broderick," March 8, 1944.

113. *The "sexual twist"*: NDN, October 30, 1943.

113. *She later succinctly*: Cited in Perry, *A Chair*, 142.

113. *On Friday, October 29*: NDN, October 29, 1943.

113. *He was arraigned*: NYCMA Lonergan File, City Magistrate Courts, Homicide Court, Borough of Manhattan, *"People of the State of New York vs. Wayne Thomas Lonergan,"* October 29, 1943; WP, October 30, 1943.

113. *A grand jury then*: Ibid., *"The People of the State of New York vs. Wayne Thomas Lonergan,"* October 29, 1943.

114. *Finally, looking like a deer*: WP, October 30, 1943.

114. *According to what Lonergan*: Perry, *A Chair*, 85–86; NYT, October 30, 1943.

114. *Over the next several days*: NYT, October 31, 1943.

114. *He declared Lonergan*: *Austin American Statesman*, November 1, 1943.

115. *Edward J. Reilly, the Brooklyn*: NYCMA Lonergan File, Edward J. Reilly to District Attorney's office, New York, October 27, 1943.

115. *A bachelor, Broderick*: NYT, May 11, 1957; Heimer, *The Girl in Murder Flat*, 30.

115. *He liked to point out*: NYT, November 2, 1943; NDM, March 6, 1944.

115. *Broderick also regarded it*: NYT, May 11, 1957.

115. *In 1927, a judge*: Ibid., March 7 1927.

115. *Exactly twenty years*: Ibid., June 25, 1947.

115. *His "shenanigans"*: Ibid., February 16, 1944.

115. *The* New York Daily Mirror *columnist*: NDM, February 29, 1944.

116. *"Dear Mr. B."*: Ibid., March 3, 1944.

116. *"What difference do a few"*: NYT, November 5, 1943.

116. *"I'm very anxious"*: Ibid., November 16, 1943.

117. *Reporters noted the "worried" look*: Ibid., NHT, November 23, 1943.

117. *The district attorney's office did ask*: NYCMA Lonergan File, Loehr to Inspector Moses Mulholland, January 13, 1944.

117. *Broderick warned his client*: Perry, *A Chair*, 95–97.

CHAPTER 11: IN THE HIPPODROME

118. *Broderick, as the* Daily Mirror: NDM, February 29; March 6, 1944.

118. *He had presided over*: NYT, December 15, 1938; July 30, 1944.

118. *Two years after the Gula*: NHT, April 6, 1940.

118. *It had been Freschi*: Ibid., March 25, 1938; Schechter, *The Mad Sculptor*, 272–76.

119. *Broderick wanted Freschi to grant*: NYT, January 25, 1944.

119. *Despite unsubstantiated reports*: NDN, February 28, 1944; Perry, *A Chair*, 126–27.

119. *The mysterious witness*: NYCMA Lonergan File, Danforth, Investigative Bureau to Grumet, February 21, 1944.

119. *As soon as Grumet*: Ibid.

120. *In a letter he*: NYT, February 12, 1944.

120. *In the end, March was*: Danforth, Investigative Bureau to Grumet, February 21, 1944.

120. *Coming to Patricia's*: NYT, May 17, 1944.

120. *As with the claim*: Ibid., February 16, 1944.

120. *Broderick then threatened*: NHT, February 17, 1944.

120. *He admonished both attorneys*: Ibid.

121. *Since Helpern was an employee*: Laurence A. Tanzer, The New York City Charter adopted November 3, 1936 (New York: Clark Boardman Company, 1937); New York City Charter, "Chapter 2: Medical Examiner," April 28, 2019, http://library.amlegal.com/nxt/gateway.dll/New%20York/charter/new yorkcitycharter?f=templates$fn=default.htm$3.0$vid=amlegal:newyork_ny.

121. *So while Broderick's request*: New York State Bar Association "Report of the Task Force on Criminal Discovery," January 30, 2015, 3 www.nysba.org/workarea/DownloadAsset.aspx?id=54572.

121. *As lawyer Robert Keith Beck*: Robert Keith Beck, "Discovery in New York: The Effect of the New Criminal Procedure Law," *Syracuse Law Review* 23:1, (1972), 91; See also Vincent Stark, "New York Discovery Reform Proposals: A Critical Assessment," *Albany Law Review* 79:4 (2015–2016), 1266–67.

121. *Prosecutors were under no*: Beth Schwartzapfel, The Marshall Project, to Author May 7, 2019. For example, Jabbar Collins, who was found guilty of murder in 1995 in a Brooklyn court, served fifteen years in prison before it was proven that he was innocent. His conviction occurred because a senior Brooklyn prosecutor withheld evidence that would have shown Collins had not committed the crime. See, Joaquin Sapien and Sergio Hernandez, "Who Polices Prosecutors Who Abuse Their Authority? Usually Nobody," *ProPublica*, April 3, 2013, www.propublica.org/article/who-polices-prosecutors-who-abuse-their-authority-usually-nobody.

121. *It required a landmark*: Brady v. Maryland, 373 U.S. 83 (1963), https://supreme.justia.com/cases/federal/us/373/83; New York State Bar Association "Report of the Task Force on Criminal Discovery," January 30, 2015, 1–6, www.nysba.org/workarea/DownloadAsset.aspx?id=54572; Stark, "New York Discovery Reform Proposals: A Critical Assessment," 1266–70; Thomas N. Kendris, "Criminal Discovery in New York: The Effect of the New Article 240," *Fordham Urban Law Journal* 8:4 (1979), 735–36; Joaquin Sapien, "Criminal Justice Legislation Will Force New York Prosecutors to Disclose More Evidence, Sooner," *ProPublica*, April 8, 2019, www.propublica.org/article/criminal-justice-legislation-will-force-new-york-prosecutors-to-disclose-more-evidence-sooner.

122. *The summary he received*: Helpern, "Autopsy of Patricia B. Lonergan," 1–9; Milton Helpern, "Re: Autopsy of Patricia B. Lonergan" (summary), 1–5.

122. *A careful analysis*: For Perry's discussion of the two reports, see Perry, *A Chair*, 252–54.

122. *The judge silenced Broderick*: NWT, February 22, 1944; *Hartford Courant*, February 22, 1944; Heimer, *The Girl in Murder Flat*, 37.

CHAPTER 12: THERE'S NOTHING LIKE
A REAL GOOD MURDER

124. *The only individuals*: NYCMA Lonergan File, Grumet to J. H. Noonan, Executive City Editor, *Boston Record*, January 21, 1944; Canadian Legation, Washington, DC, to Grumet, February 21, 1944.

125. *Winchell offered the rumor*: Cited in Perry, *A Chair*, 116.

125. *The* Daily News *described*: NDN, February 28, 1944; *Brooklyn Daily Eagle*, February 20, 1944; Perry, ibid., 116–17.

125. *As Thyra Samter Winslow so aptly*: Cited in Perry, ibid., 117–18.

125. *Above all, these various*: NHT, February 23, 1944; NDN, February 28, 1944; *Pittsburgh Post-Gazette*, March 4, 1944; *Hartford Courant*, March 26, 1944; *Tampa Bay Times*, March 26, 1944.

125. *A day earlier, without*: NYCMA Lonergan File, "*People v. Wayne Thomas Lonergan*, Stenographer's Minutes, February 24, 1944; Moses Mulholland, Inspector of Detectives, Toronto Police Department to Grumet, April 13, 1944; NYT, February 24, 25, 1944; *Brooklyn Daily Eagle*, February 23, 1944.

125. *Broderick later cryptically*: NYT, February 26, 1944.

126. *"He owes an apology"*: NJA, February 26, 1944.

126. *As a precaution, he*: NYCMA Lonergan File, Grumet to James Weir McFadden, Crown Attorney Office, Toronto, February 24, 1944, Grumet to Inspector Mulholland, February 24, 1944; NYT, February 25, 1944.

126. *That mission turned out*: NYCMA Lonergan File, Dr. Perry Lichtenstein to Grumet, March 6, 1944; GM, October 26, 1944.

127. *But as Lichtenstein*: Lichtenstein to Grumet, ibid.; Dunne, *Justice*, 288.

127. *The judge concurred*: NYT, February 25, 1944.

127. *He immediately intimated*: Ibid., February 27, 28, 1944.

127. *The press also reported*: NYCMA Lonergan File, Jean Murphy Jaburg to Grumet, January 6, 1943; February 9, 1943; Grumet to Murphy Jaburg, February 11, 1944; Murphy Jaburg to Grumet, February 20. 1944.

127. *Her association with Lonergan*: Ibid., Murphy Jaburg to Grumet, February 3, 1944.

127. *"Previously, I had"*: NJA, February 26, 1944.

128. *In a brazen display*: WP, February 29, 1944.

128. *Dressed in a dark blue*: NYT, NDM, February 29, 1944.

129. *The most astute*: NDM, February 29, 1944.

129. *Facing the more than*: NYCMA Lonergan File, "*People v. Lonergan* Jury Questions."

129. *He asked jury prospects*: NYT, February 29, 1944.

129. *In yet another maneuver*: NYCMA Lonergan File, Lonergan to Surrogate James Foley, February 25, 1944.

129. *After considering the*: NYT, February 29; March 2, 1944; WP, February 29, 1944; TS, March 1, 1944.

130. *One middle-aged*: NYT, March 2, 1944.

130. *Another issue that was*: Ibid., February 28, 1944.

130. *In fact, this was not true*: Ibid., March 2, 1944; NYCMA Lonergan File, "*People v. Lonergan*," Proceedings March 2, 1944.

130. *On the morning of March 2*: NDM, March 2, 1944.

130. *"So help me God"*: Ibid.; NYCMA Lonergan File, Jack Lait, NDM, to Broderick, March 4, 1944.

131. *For good measure*: "*People v. Lonergan*," Proceedings, March 2, 1944.

131. *In an about-face*: NYT, March 3, 1944.

131. *"They couldn't crucify"*: Ibid.; NHT, March 3, 1944.

132. *"Quite apart from that"*: NYT, March 4, 1944.

132. *As the judge finished*: Ibid.

132. *Four months later*: Ibid., July 30, 1944.

133. *"All I want"*: Ibid., March 4, 1944.

CHAPTER 13: DOUBLE-DEALING, DOUBLE-CROSSING, AND DOUBLE-TALK

134. *On the one hand, Wallace*: NYT, November 30, 1956.

135. *While some community leaders*: Ibid., April 17, 1927.

135. *"If there were not"*: Ibid., March 3, 1929.

135. *On the evening of February 9*: Cited in Jill Watts, *Mae West: An Icon in Black and White* (New York: Oxford University Press, 2003), 77–78; Levine, *The Devil in Babylon*, 304–6.

135. *Under the state's obscenity laws*: NYT, February 10, 1927.

135. *During the proceedings, West's*: NHT, March 31, 1927.

136. *"We have cleaned up"*: Ibid., April 2, 1927.

136. *He stated that* SEX *was*: NYT: April 20, 1927,

136. *West accepted the judgment*: Ibid.; Levine, *The Devil in Babylon*, 308–9.

136. *Wallace had long maintained*: NYT, April 17, 1943.

136. *"It doesn't seem to me"*: Ibid., March 3, 1929.

136. *In 1927, working with Judd*: Ibid., April 15, 1958; Landis MacKellar, *The "Double Indemnity" Murder: Ruth Snyder, Judd Gray, and New York's Crime of the Century* (Syracuse, NY: Syracuse University Press, 2006), 97.

136. *In late March 1944*: NYCMA Lonergan File, Glynn to Loehr, March 28, 1944.

137. *On March 18, Cusack*: NYT, March 19, 1944.

137. *He visited with Lonergan*: Ibid., March 20, 1944.

137. *Newspapers from New York*: See, for example, NYT, *Atlanta Constitution, Austin Statesman, Chicago Daily Tribune, Tampa Bay Times,* and *Minneapolis Star-Journal,* March 20, 1944.

138. *By the end of Monday's*: NYT, March 21, 1944.

138. *One man, Don Whiting*: Heimer, *The Girl in Murder Flat,* 58.

138. *This included John Woodburn*: NYT, March 22, 1944.

138. *Despite Grumet's nonchalant*: Brandon L. Garrett, L. Neil Williams Jr., Professor of Law, Duke University Law School to Author, May 12, 2019; See also, Brandon L. Garrett, "The Substance of False Confessions," *Stanford Law Review* 62:4 (April 2010), 1051–1118.

138. *The much more significant*: "Admissibility of Confession under State and Federal Standards," *Columbia Law Review* 52:3 (March 1952), 423–25. Among the key cases on this issue were: *People v. Scott*, 195 N.Y. 224, 88 N.E. 35 (1909); *People v. White*, 176 N.Y. 331, 68 N.E. 630 (1903); *People v. Chapleau*, 121 N.Y. 266, 24 N.E. 469 (1890); *Murphy v. People*, 63 N.Y. 590 (1876); *People v. Randazzio*, 194 N.Y. 147, 87 N.E. 112 (1909); *People v. Elmore*, 277 N.Y. 397, 14 N.E. 2d 451 (1938); *People v. Alex*, 265 N.Y. 192 N.E. 289 (1934); *People v. Doran*, 246 N.Y. 409, 159 N.E. 379 (1927); *People v. Trybus*, 219 N.Y. 18, 113 N.E. 538 (1916); *Balbo v. People*, 80 N.Y. 484 (1880); *People v. Wentz*, 37 N.Y. 303 (1867). See also, Faraday J. Strock, "Validity of the Admission-Confession Distinction for Purposes of Admissibility," *Journal of Criminal Law and Criminology*, 39:6 (March–April 1949), 743–50.

139. *At the time, there*: "The Role of a Trial Jury in Determining the Voluntariness of a Confession," *Michigan Law Review* 63:2 (December, 1964), 381–82; Arthur J. Paone, "The New Trial Procedure on Confession in New York," *Cornell Law Review* 50:3 (Spring 1965), 462; Paul Shechtman, "'Jackson v. Denno' and Voluntariness of Confessions 50 Years Later," *New York Law Journal* 251:118 (June 20, 2014), www.law.com/newyorklawjournal/almID/1202660104749.

139. *The look on Lonergan's face*: Cited in Heimer, *The Girl in Murder Flat,* 59.

139. *"We have only his statement"*: NYT, March 23, 1944.

140. *He also drew the jury's*: Ibid.; *Newsday*, March 24, 1944.

140. *"After you have heard"*: NYT, NHT, March, 23, 1944.

140. *"We'll show you"*: Ibid.

140. *"I intend to make"*: Ibid.

141. *Grumet held up*: NYT, ibid.

141. *He did not point out*: Wiener Report. See also, Randolph N. Jonakai, "When Blood Is Their Argument: Probabilities in Criminal Cases, Genetic Markers, and, Once Again, Bayes'Theorem," *University of Illinois Law Review* 2 (1983), 370–71; Laurel Beeler and William R. Wiebe, "DNA Identification: Tests and the Courts," *Washington Law Review* 63:4 (July 1988), 903–55.

141. *He eventually identified*: Ibid.

141. *Moreover, neither Helpern*: See, *New York Police Department, Rules and Regulations and Manual of Procedure of Police Department of the City of New York* (New York: New York Civil Service Commission, 1940), 460. No section on blood or obtaining a blood sample from a suspect is included or indexed.

141. *If Lonergan had consented*: Dariush D. Farhud and Marjan Zarif Yeganeh, "A Brief History of Human Blood Groups," *Iranian Journal of Public Health* 42:1 (January 2013), 1–2.

142. *As the noted forensic*: Paul L. Kirk, "Progress in Police Investigation," *Annals of the American Academy of Political and Social Science* 291 (January 1954), 57. See also, David Lanham, "Blood Tests and the Law," *Medicine, Science and the Law* 6:4 (October 1966), 190–99.

142. *For instance, in 1947*: *Los Angeles Times*, July 23, 25, 1947.

142. *In his discussion of issues*: Perry, *A Chair*, 252–53.

142. *In his cross-examination, Broderick*: NHT, March 23, 1944.

143. *"At any time"*: Ibid., March 24, 1944.

143. *He read aloud the note*: "Statement of Harold Le Mon."

145. *Asked repeatedly by Broderick*: NYT, March 25, 1944.

145. *"Did you threaten, strike"*: Ibid.

CHAPTER 14: BRUTAL, COLD-BLOODED, DELIBERATE MURDER

147. *And among this large group*: Richard A. Leo, "False Confessions: Causes, Consequences, and Implications," *Journal of the American Academy of Psychiatry and the Law Online* 37: 3 (September 2009), 332–43; http://jaapl.org/content/37/3/332.

147. *Most notable were*: See, Sarah Burns, *The Central Park Five* (New York: Knopf Doubleday, 2011).

148. *Even author Hamilton*: Perry, *A Chair*, 273.

148. *When asked by Broderick*: NYT, March 28, 1944.

149. *Her testimony did not*: Ibid., March 29, 1944.

150. *She pointed him out again*: Ibid.

151. *Broderick opted not to put*: Perry, *A Chair*, 176.

151. *When he attempted to submit*: NYT, March 30, 1944.

151. *In any event, a visit*: Ibid., March 30, 1944.

152. *As was the recognized procedure*: Harold St. Leo O'Dougherty, ed., "The Trial," Section 388, *Penal Law and the Code of Criminal Procedure of the State of New York, with 1937 Amendments, Indexed* (Brooklyn, NY: Eagle Library, 1937), 282. Section 338 was included in the revised version of New York State criminal procedure in 1970, which is still used at the present time. See, Frederick J. Ludwig, "Improving New York's New Criminal Procedure Law," *St. John's Law Review* 45:3 (March 1971), 419–20, "Article 260.30," Numbers 8 to 10, *New York State Law Criminal Procedure Law: Consolidated Laws of New York's CPL Code* (Albany: New York State, 2007), http://ypdcrime.com/cpl.

152. *"I say to you"*: Ibid., March 31, 1944.

153. *These were all relevant*: Perry makes the same point. Perry, *A Chair*, 184.

153. *"This was brutal"*: NYT, March 31, 1944.

154. *Was the confession coerced*: Ibid., April 1, 1944.

155. *This fourteen-minute exchange*: NYCMA Lonergan File, "Notice of Appeal, *"People v. Lonergan,"* October 26, 1959, and August 23, 1961; Perry, *A Chair*, 206.

155. *This clause stipulated*: O'Dougherty, *Penal Law and the Code of Criminal Procedure of the State of New York*, 286.

155. *Court officers informed*: Perry, *A Chair*, 206.

155. *"We find the defendant"*: NYT, ibid.

156. *As Byrne's words sank in*: Ibid. Perry doubted that Lonergan would have sobbed. "Wayne Lonergan," he wrote, "showed almost no emotion at any point during the investigation or trial." See, Perry, *A Chair*, 207; NHT, Associated Press, April 1, 1944.

156. *Having watched the trial*: LAC, Royal Canadian Air Force records, R.W. Lightly to Commanding Officer No. 23 PAED, RCAF, Toronto, April 4, 1944; Discharge Certificate, No. 273983 of Wayne Thomas Lonergan, April 6, 1944.

156. *During the next week*: Pittsburgh Post-Gazette, April 7, 1944; PI, April 2, 1944.

156. *Syndicated columnist George*: PI, April 5, 1944.

157. *"The trial was"*: "The Lonergan Case," 71.

157. *The young boy had already*: NYT, June 16, 1944.

157. *In December 1944*: GM, December 2, 1944.

157. *Stella died in*: NYT, February 7, 1954.

158. *At long last*: NHT, April 22, 1944.

158. *The Appellate Division*: NYT, June 28, 1945.

158. *In June 1947*: Ibid., June 25, 1947.

159. *Standing in the court*: Ibid., April 18, 1944.

159. *The prison's unique name*: See ibid., November 19, 1983; Sing Sing Prison Museum, www.singsingprisonmuseum.org/quick-facts.html.

159. *On Lonergan's intake form*: Department of Corrections, Sing Sing, 103124, "Wayne Thomas Lonergan Record."

CHAPTER 15: INMATE 31227

160. *On May 16, 1944*: NYT, May 17, 1944; November 29, 1947.

160. *The US Supreme Court*: See "McNabb v. United States," 318 U.S. 332 (1943), https://supreme.justia.com/cases/federal/us/318/332; Atlanta Constitution, June 8, 1943; Chicago Daily Tribune, August 29, 1943.

161. *In February 1945*: NYT, July 20, 1945.

161. *In a last attempt*: Ibid., November 20, 1945; NHT, November 29, 1945.

161. *Six months after that*: NHT, May 18, 1946.

161. *Sing Sing Prison*: Afro-American, May 1, 1943.

162. *From 1891 to 1963*: Scott Christianson, Condemned: Inside the Sing Sing Death House (New York: New York University Press, 2000), 14; NYT, August 10, 13, 2015.

162. *The prison's Jewish chaplain*: Christianson, ibid., 51.

162. *In 1943, half: Afro-American*, May 1, 1943.

162. *In his day, Lawes*: Brian, Sing Sing, 113–16, 145, Baltimore Sun, April 24, 1947.

162. *When he first arrived*: Perry, A Chair, 214–15.

162. *While the press*: Pittsburgh Post-Gazette, March 7, 1947; NDN, July 12, 1948; PI, June 28, 1949.

163. *In mid-May 1950*: Minneapolis Sunday Tribune, May 14, 1950, NYT, May 14, 1950.

163. *In early April 1948*: NYT, April 3, 9, 1948; February 9, 1950.

163. *Lonergan was unwittingly*: Perry, *A Chair*, 220.

163. *A photograph of Lonergan*: NYSA, Clinton Inmate Record Cards Series. B0097-77, "Warden's Record Card Clinton Prison for Wayne Thomas Lonergan," April 17, 1944, to November 4, 1965.

164. *Sing Sing was bad enough*: "History of Clinton Prison," www.correction history.org/html/chronicl/docs2day/clinton.html.

164. *Built in 1844*: Ibid.

164. *Lonergan was given a job*: GM, April 26 1966; Perry, *A Chair*, 221.

164. *Over the years, he also*: NYCMA Lonergan File, New York Police Department Prisoners' Criminal Records for Isadore Schwartzberg and Moe Auswaks; Warden Daniel McMann to New York Police Chief Inspector Lawrence McKearney, May 5, 1965.

164. *In 1951, he and*: NYT, March 11, 1952; December 23, 1970; NHT, June 18, 1953.

164. *A year later, while*: NYT, January 2, 1955.

165. *Within five months*: WP, December 24, 1970.

165. *Even one ADA commented*: NYT, December 23, 1970.

165. *Lonergan's other prison pal*: NYSA, Clinton Inmate Record Cards Series B0097-77, "Warden's Record Card Clinton Prison for Moe Auswaks," February 2, 1940, to May 6, 1964.

165. *Born in 1902*: Ibid.

165. *Both men hid*: NHT, May 19, July 7, 1939; NYT, January 30, 1940.

165. *At the end of January*: "Warden's Record Card Clinton Prison for Moe Auswaks."

166. *Following his release*: Ibid.

166. *Those efforts were*: NYT, May 11, 1957.

166. *Among her clients*: *Newsday*, January 12, 1963.

167. *The New York Appellate Court*: *New York Amsterdam News*, January 26, 1963.

CHAPTER 16: COERCION AND COLLUSION

168. *Frances Kahn's initial strategy*: "Notice of Appeal, "*People v. Lonergan*," October 26, 1959, and July 20, 1961.

168. *In October 1952*: NYT, October 24, 1952; *People Ex Rel. Bartlam v. Murphy*, 9 N.Y. 2d 550 (1961), https://law.justia.com/cases/new-york/court -of-appeals/1961/9-n-y-2d-550-0.html; *People Ex Rel. Bartlam v. Murphy*, 13 N.Y. 2d 1068 (1963), https://law.justia.com/cases/new-york/court-of -appeals/1963/13-n-y-2d-1068-0.html; *People Ex Rel. Bartlam v. Murphy*, 14 N.Y. 2d 548 (1964), www.leagle.com/decision/196456214ny2d548246.

169. *A court reporter was present*: Notice of Appeal, "*People v. Lonergan*," July 20, 1961. The transcript folio numbers cited were 2735–37.

169. *A detailed summary*: NYT, April 1, 1944.

169. *In December 1962*: *The People of the State of New York v. Wayne Thomas Lonergan*, 18 A.D.2d 634 (1962).

169. *It can only be speculated*: Daniel C. Richman, Columbia Law School, to Author, August 2, 2019. Thanks to Prof. Richman for his comments about the various appellate court decisions.

170. *On June 14, 1960*: *New York Amsterdam News*, October 8, 1960.

170. *A few hours later*: "The Role of a Trial Jury in Determining the Voluntariness of a Confession," *Michigan Law Review* 63:2 (December, 1964), 382–83.

170. *Jackson and Elliot were put*: *New York Amsterdam News*, October 22, December 3, 1960; *Jackson v. Denno*, 378 US 368 (1964), U.S. Reports (October Term, 1963), 368–440. See also Oyez, www.oyez.org/cases/1963/62; Paul Shechtman, "'*Jackson v. Denno*' and Voluntariness of Confessions 50 Years Later," *New York Law Journal* 251:118 (June 20, 2014), www.law.com/ newyorklawjournal/almID/1202660104749.

171. *The case was argued*: *Jackson v. Denno*, ibid., 368–440.

171. *The decision somewhat helped*: NYT, March 23, April 9, 20, 1965; *Atlanta Constitution*, November 21, 1967.

171. *In 1960, Charles Huntley*: NYT, January 8, April 10. 1965; *People v. Huntley*, 15 N.Y. 2d 72 (1965); Donald C. Schupak, "Evidence—*Jackson v. Denno* Ruling Retroactively Applicable in *Coram Nobis* Proceeding Provided Issue of Voluntariness Raised at Trial," *Syracuse Law Review* 16:3 (Spring 1965), 689–92.

171. *On January 7, 1965*: NYT, January 8, 1965; Ibid.

172. *Huntley, himself, did not*: *The People of the State of New York, Plaintiff, v. Charles Huntley, Defendant*. Supreme Court, Special and Trial Term, New York County, April 7, 1965, 46 Misc.2d 209 (1965).

172. *On January 4, 1965*: *The People of the State of New York, Respondent, v. Wayne Thomas Lonergan, Appellant*, Court of Appeals of the State of New York, January 15, 1965.

173. *"Human beings are frail creatures"*: Newsday, January 21, 1965.

173. *There was also the affidavit*: NYCMA Lonergan File, "Affidavit of Harvey Kelley," April 27, 1965.

173. *Moreover, a photograph*: PM, October 26, 1943; NDN, August 12, 2012.

174. *The only fact that*: GM, June 4, 1965.

174. *Marks had a well-deserved*: NYT, April 3, 1976.

174. *His affidavit of April*: NYCMA Lonergan File, "Affidavit of Wayne Lonergan," April 30, 1965.

174. *For Young, a journalist*: Kingston Whig-Standard (Kingston, Ontario), June 8, 2005.

175. *Called to testify*: TS, May 12, 1965.

175. *Young wryly observed*: GM, May 14, 1965.

175. *"Did they advise"*: Ibid.

175. *The assertion about the plea*: Ibid.

175. *A few days later*: Ibid., May 19, 1965.

176. *More telling was*: Ibid., May 14, 1965.

176. *The following week*: Ibid., May 22, 1965.

176. *Asked by Hughes*: Ibid., June 4, 1965.

177. *The consensus among*: Ibid., June 7 1965.

177. *Marks reserved his judgment*: Ibid., June 24, 1965.

177. *Marks "has completely"*: NYCMA Lonergan File, Hughes to Loehr, June 25, 1965.

177. *She told reporters*: GM, June 29, 1965.

177. *Kahn did launch her appeal*: People v. Lonergan, 27 A.D. 2d 707, January 19, 1967.

177. *In November 1965*: NYT, November 9, 1965.

177. *Kahn and Schwartzberg were already*: Austin Statesman, December 3, 1965.

178. *Assistant US attorney John Martin*: NYT, December 23, 1970.

178. *She was suspended*: Ibid., March 2, 1967; July 5, 1969.

178. *The following year*: Ibid., December 23, 1970; WP, December 24, 1970.

CHAPTER 17: NOTHING TO HIDE

179. *He had been eligible*: NYT, December 3, 1965.

179. *The boy had grown up*: GM, May 15, 1965.

180. *As Lonergan entered the hotel*: Ibid., December 3, 1965; January 16, 2002.

180. *Asked a question*: Ibid., December 3, 1965.

181. *She was buried*: See Lucille Wolfe Burton's grave, www.findagrave.com/memorial/122592204. Thanks to Lisa Krain, a distant relative of Lucille Burton, for assisting me in finding this information.

181. *When Dominick Dunne wrote*: Dunne, *Justice*, 294.

181. *Hotel prices in*: GM, August 2, 1966.

181. *On the episode of*: CBC, *This Hour Has Seven Days*, Digital Archives, www.cbc.ca/archives/entry/this-hour-has-seven-days-chuvalo-welles-and-the-klan; NYT, October 13, 2002.

181–82. *Discussed on the floor*: Norman Hillmer, "*Seven Days*: Canada's Most Subversive Television Series," *The Canadian Encyclopedia*, September 20, 2013, www.thecanadianencyclopedia.ca/en/article/the-peoples-seven-days-feature.

182. *More than fifty years later*: Author's interview with Ken Lefolii, June 13, 2019; GM, December 13, 1965; LAC, Lonergan Interview, *This Hour Has Seven Days*.

183. *For a short time*: GM, January 6, 1966; TS, January 6, 1966; *The Guardian* (London), March 16, 1991.

183. *A small man, he was*: *The Guardian*, ibid.

183. *Neville-Willing had tried*: *The Guardian*, ibid.; NYT, May 11, 1940.

183. *"I don't mind"*: Montreal Gazette, January 6, 1966; GM, January 5, 1966.

183. *Yet another tall tale*: Perry, *A Chair*, 226.

184. *Hamilton was a charming*: Shirley Mair, "Barbara Hamilton Afraid of Stardom? She's Earned it, and Won it," *Chatelaine* (October 1964), 28–29, 86–87.

184. *A newspaper in Charlottetown*: Ibid., 86.

184. *Most curiously of all*: Author's interview with Gordon Pinsent, April 30, 2019; Author's interview with Ronda Cooper, July 17, 2019.

185. *And when Lonergan made her*: Author's interviews with Gordon Pinsent, April 30, 2019, and Leah Pinsent, July 24, 2019.

185. *From the perspective of*: Leah Pinsent interview.

185. *This was the same point*: Dunne, *Justice*, 293.

185. *Meanwhile, Hamilton Darby Perry*: Ibid., 291.

185. *He died on*: NYT, January 3, 1986; GM, January 4, 1986.

186. *When asked about him*: TS, January 4, 1986.

186. *In early July*: TS, July 3, 1994.

EPILOGUE: "WIFE KILLER OR FALL GUY?"

187. *In October 1948*: Raymond Chandler, "10 Greatest Crimes of the Century," *Cosmopolitan* (October 1948), 50–53.

187. *The fast-paced novel was*: Kenneth Fearing, *The Big Clock* (New York: New York Review of Books, 2006). See also, Alan M. Wald, *American Night: The Literary Left in the Era of the Cold War* (Chapel Hill: University of North Carolina Press Books, 2012), 39–40; Drewey Wayne Gunn, "Wayne Lonergan's Long Shadow: A Forties Murder and Its Literary Legacy," in Curtis Evans, ed., *Murder in the Closet: Essays on Queer Clues in Crime Fiction Before Stonewall* (Jefferson, NC: McFarland & Company, 2017), 213–14.

187. *A much more precise*: Carley Mills, *A Nearness of Evil* (New York: Coward-McCann, 1961).

188. *Patricia became Diane*: Ibid., 55.

188. *Wayne was given*: Ibid., 102.

188. *"I'm cutting out"*: Ibid., 46.

188. *Mills fully explores*: Ibid., 116; Gunn, "Wayne Lonergan's Long Shadow," 214–15.

188. *Except in the novel*: Mills, ibid., 117.

188. *In a May 1949*: *Newsday*, May 22, 1949.

189. *Over the years*: See, for example, "Murder in Manhattan," *Xtra*, February 8, 2014, www.dailyxtra.com/murder-in-manhattan-57937; "Heiress Murdered by Husband with Candelabra in her Bedroom in 'Twisted Sex' Crime that Captivated New York in 1943," NDN, August 12, 2012; Naben Ruthnum, "Footnotes to a Murder," Hazlitt, https://hazlitt.net/feature/footnotes-murder; "Killers Without Conscience," https://krazykillers.wordpress.com/2015/10/16/twisted-sex-a-beautiful-heiress-and-a-macabre-murder; Gunn, "Wayne Lonergan's Long Shadow," 215.

190. *In 2018, for instance*: Stephen Leahy, "The Real CSI," *National Geographic*, April 25, 2018, https://news.nationalgeographic.com/2018/04/dna-testing-accuracy-golden-state-killer-science-spd.

190. *There is no question*: Richard Leo, *Police Interrogation and American Justice* (Cambridge, MA: Harvard University Press, 2008), 47–48.

190. *"Against a hardened"*: Cornelius W. Willemse, *Behind the Green Lights* (New York: A. A. Knopf, 1931), 354.

190. *"The so-called roughneck"*: Emanuel H. Lavine, *The Third Degree: A Detailed and Appalling Exposé of Police Brutality* (New York: Vanguard Press, 1930), 4–5, 49.

191. *"After reviewing the"*: Cited Edwin R. Keedy, "The Third Degree and Legal Interrogation of Suspects," *University of Pennsylvania Law Review* 85:8 (June 1937), 763.

191. *As Chief Justice Charles*: Brown v. Mississippi, 297 U.S. 278 (1936), https://supreme.justia.com/cases/federal/us/297/278.

191. *Both of these developments*: Leo, *Police Interrogation and American Justice*, 4, 43, 273–76.

192. *Malinski had been identified*: Malinski v. New York, 324 U.S. 401 (1945); NYT, March 27, 1945; National Registry of Exonerations, www.law.umich.edu/special/exoneration/Pages/casedetailpre1989.aspx?caseid=208.

192. *In the end, four of them*: Kate Storey, "'When They See Us' Shows the Disturbing Truth About How False Confessions Happen," *Esquire*, June 1, 2019, www.esquire.com/entertainment/a27574472when-they-see-us-central-park-5-false-confessions.

192. *As of 2019, according to*: Innocence Project, "False Confessions & Recording of Custodial Interrogations," www.innocenceproject.orgfalse-confessions-recording-interrogations.

Selected Bibliography

Abella, Irving, ed. *On Strike: Six Key Labour Struggles in Canada, 1919–1949*. Toronto: James Lorimer & Company, 1975.

Adler, Jeffrey S. "Less Crime, More Punishment: Violence, Race, and Criminal Justice in Early Twentieth-Century America." *Journal of American History* 102:1 (June 2015): 34–46.

"Admissibility of Confession under State and Federal Standards." *Columbia Law Review* 52:3 (March 1952): 423–25.

Akenson, Donald Harman. *The Irish in Ontario: A Study in Rural History*. Montreal and Kingston: McGill-Queen's University Press, 1984.

Allen, Mearl L. *Welcome to the Stork Club*. New York: A. S. Barnes and Company, 1980.

Bakan, Jonathon E. "Café Society: Locus for the Intersection of Jazz and Politics during the Popular Front Era." PhD dissertation, York University, 2004.

Baruch, Bernard. *My Own Story*. New York: Henry Holt and Company, 1957.

Beck, Robert Keith. "Discovery in New York: The Effect of the New Criminal Procedure Law," *Syracuse Law Review* 23:1, (1972): 89–112.

Beebe, Lucius. "Café Society." *Cosmopolitan* 102:3 Part One (March 1937): 26–29, 96, 98; 102:4 Part Two (April 1937): 38–39, 96, 99–100; 102: 5 Part Three (May 1937): 82–84.

———. *Snoot If You Must*. London: D. Appleton-Century Company, 1943.

———. *The Stork Club Bar Book*. New York: Rinehart & Company, 1946. https:// euvs-vintage-cocktail-books.cldbz/1946-The-Stock-Club-Bar-Book-by-Lucius -Beebe/6.

Beeler, Laurel, and William R. Wiebe, "DNA Identification: Tests and the Courts." *Washington Law Review* 63:4 (July 1988): 903–55.

Bérubé, Allan. *Coming Out Under Fire: The History of Gay Men and Women in World War Two*. Chapel Hill: University of North Carolina Press, 2010.

Blumenthal, Ralph. *Stork Club: America's Most Famous Nightspot and the Lost World of Café Society*. New York: Little, Brown & Company, 2000.

Brian, Denis. *Sing Sing: The Inside of a Notorious Prison*. Amherst, NY: Promethus Books, 2005.

Bullard, Dexter Means. "Selective Service Psychiatry." *Psychiatry* 4:2 (1941): 231–39.

Burns, Sarah. *The Central Park Five*. New York: Knopf Doubleday, 2011.

Burrows, Edwin G., and Mike Wallace. *Gotham: A History of New York to 1898*. New York: Oxford University Press, 1999.

Cable, Mary. *Top Drawer: American High Society from the Gilded Age to the Roaring Twenties*. New York: Atheneum, 1984.

Carosso, Vincent P. *The Morgans: Private International Bankers, 1854–1913*. Harvard Studies in Business History 38. Cambridge, MA: Harvard University Press, 1987.

Chandler, Raymond. "10 Greatest Crimes of the Century." *Cosmopolitan* (October 1948): 50–53.

Christianson, Scott. *Condemned: Inside the Sing Sing Death House*. New York: New York University Press, 2000.

Clegg, Charles, and Duncan Emrich, eds. *The Lucius Beebe Reader*. Garden City, NY: Doubleday & Company, 1967.

Clevenger, Joseph R., ed. *Penal Law and the Code of Criminal Procedure of the State of New York, with Amendments Passed by the Legislature to the end of Regular Session of 1940*. Albany, NY: Matthew Bender and Company, 1940.

Coit, Margaret L. *Mr. Baruch*. Boston: Houghton Mifflin Company, 1957.

Cotter, Bill. *The 1939–1940 New York World's Fair*. Mount Pleasant, SC: Arcadia Publishing, 2009.

Dean, Richard A. *The Friendly Town, 1821–1963: Sketches of the Birth, Growth, and Development of the Village of Norwood, County of Peterborough*. Norwood, Ontario: Centennial Book Committee, 1978.

de River, Joseph Paul. *The Sexual Criminal: A Psychoanalytical Study*. Springfield, IL: Charles C. Thomas, Publisher, 1949.

Drizin, Steven A., and Richard Leo. "The Problems of False Confessions in the Post-DNA World. *North Carolina Law Review* 82:3 (2004): 891–1008.

Dunkelman, Mark H. *Marching with Sherman: Through Georgia and the Carolinas with the 154th New York*. Baton Rouge: Louisiana State University Press, 2012.

Dunne, Dominick. "The Talented Mr. Lonergan." *Vanity Fair* (July 2000): 156–69.

———. *Justice: Crimes, Trials, and Punishments*. New York: Crown Publishers, 2001.

Erenberg, Lewis A., and Susan E. Hirsch, eds. *The War in American Culture: Society and Consciousness during World War II*. Chicago: University of Chicago Press, 2014.

Faderman, Lillian. *The Gay Revolution: The Story of the Struggle*. New York: Simon & Schuster, 2015.

Farhud, Dariush D., and Marjan Zarif Yeganeh. "A Brief History of Human Blood Groups." *Iranian Journal of Public Health* 42:1 (January 2013): 1–6.

Fearing, Kenneth. *The Big Clock*. New York: New York Review of Books, 2006. (Originally published in 1946.)

Fermaglich, Kirsten. "Too Long, Too Foreign . . . Too Jewish": Jews, Name Changing, and Family Mobility in New York City, 1917–1942. *Journal of American Ethnic History* 34:3 (Spring 2015): 34–57.

———. *A Rosenberg by Any Other Name: A History of Jewish Name Changing in America*. New York: New York University Press, 2018.

Flynn, Carly. *Brass Diva: The Life and Legends of Ethel Merman*. Berkeley: University of California Press, 2007.

Freedman, Estelle B. " 'Uncontrolled Desires': The Response to the Sexual Psychopath, 1920–1960." *The Journal of American History* 74: 1 (June, 1987): 83–106.

Freedman, Paul. *Ten Restaurants that Changed America*. New York: Liveright Publishing, 2016.

Gabler, Neal. *Winchell: Gossip, Power and the Culture of Celebrity*. New York: Vintage Books, 1995.

Garrett, Brandon L. "The Substance of False Confessions." *Stanford Law Review* 62:4 (April 2010): 1051–1118.

Gibbs, Wolcott. "The Wayward Press: Five Days Wonder." *New Yorker* (November 6, 1943): 86–92.

Gill, Brendan. "Happy Times: Profile of Jerome Zerbe." *New Yorker* (June 9, 1973): 39–68.

———. *Here at the New Yorker*. New York: Random House, 1975.

Goldstein, Richard. *Helluva Town: The Story of New York City during World War II*. New York: Free Press, 2010.

Graham, Katherine. *Personal History*. New York: Vintage Books, 1998.

Gunn, Drewey Wayne. "Wayne Lonergan's Long Shadow: A Forties Murder and Its Literary Legacy." In Evans, Curtis, ed. *Murder in the Closet: Essays on Queer Clues in Crime Fiction Before Stonewall*. Jefferson, NC: McFarland & Company, 2017. Jefferson, NC: McFarland & Company, 2015: 210–16.

Heimer, Mel. *The Girl in Murder Flat*. New York: Fawcett Publications, 1955.

Helpern, Milton. *Autopsy: The Memoirs of Milton Helpern, the World's Greatest Medical Detective*. New York: St. Martin's Press, 1977.

Henry, George W., and Alfred A. Gross. "Social Factors in Case Histories of 100 Underprivileged Homosexuals." *Mental Hygiene* 22 (October 1938): 591–611.

Houts, Marshall. *Where Death Delights: The Story of Dr. Milton Helpern and Forensic Medicine*. New York: Coward-McCann, 1967.

Jackson, Kenneth T., Lisa Keller, and Nancy Flood, eds. *Encyclopedia of New York City*. New Haven, CT: Yale University Press, 2010.

Jentzen, Jeffrey M. *Death Investigation in America: Coroners, Medical Examiners, and the Pursuit of Medical Certainty*. Cambridge, MA: Harvard University Press, 2009.

Johnson, Julie Ann. "Speaking for the Dead: Forensic Scientists and American Justice in the Twentieth Century." PhD dissertation, University of Pennsylvania, 1992.

Johnson-McGrath, Julie. "Speaking for the Dead: Forensic Pathologists and Criminal Justice in the United States." *Science, Technology, & Human Values* 20:4 (Autumn 1995): 438–59.

Jonakai, Randolph N. "When Blood Is Their Argument: Probabilities in Criminal Cases, Genetic Markers, and, Once Again, Bayes' Theorem." *University of Illinois Law Review* 2 (1983): 369–421.

Joselit, Jenna Weissman. *Our Gang: Jewish Crime and the New York Jewish Community, 1900–1940*. Bloomington: Indiana University Press, 1983.

Josephson, Barney, and Terry Trilling-Josephson. *Cafe Society: The Wrong Place for the Right People*. Urbana: University of Illinois Press, 2009.

Kaiser, Charles. *The Gay Metropolis*. New York: Grove Press, 1997.

Karpman, Benjamin. "The Sexual Psychopath." *Journal of Criminal Law and Criminology* 42: 2 (July–August 1951): 184–98.

Kaytor, Marilyn. *"21": The Life and Times of New York's Favourite Club*. New York: Viking Press, 1975.

Keedy, Edwin R. "The Third Degree and Legal Interrogation of Suspects." *University of Pennsylvania Law Review* 85:8 (June 1937): 761–77.

Kellow, Brian. *Ethel Merman: A Life*. New York: Viking Press, 2007.

Kendris, Thomas N. "Criminal Discovery in New York: The Effect of the New Article 240." *Fordham Urban Law Journal* 8:4 (1979): 731–771.

Kingsman, Gary. *The Regulation of Desire: Sexuality in Canada*. Montreal: Black Rose Books, 1987.

Kirk, Paul L. *Crime Investigation: Physical Evidence and the Police Laboratory*. New York: Interscience Publishers, 1953.

———. "Progress in Police Investigation." *The Annals of the American Academy of Political and Social Science* 291 (January 1954): 54–62.

Kobler, John. *Ardent Spirits: The Rise and Fall of Prohibition*. New York: G. P. Putnam's Sons, 1973.

Koppelman, Lee E., and Seth Forman. *The Fire Island National Seashore: A History*. Albany: SUNY Press, 2008.

Kriendler, H. Peter. *"21": Every Day Was New Year's Eve*. Lanham, MD: Taylor Trade Publishing, 1999.

Lanham, David. "Blood Tests and the Law." *Medicine, Science and the Law* 6:4 (October 1966): 190–99.

Lavine, Emanuel H. *The Third Degree: A Detailed and Appalling Expose of Police Brutality*. New York: The Vanguard Press, 1930.

Leahy, Stephen. "The Real CSI." *National Geographic* (April 25, 2018), https://news .nationalgeographic.com/2018/04/dna-testing-accuracy-golden-state-killer -science-spd.

Leo, Richard A. *Police Interrogation and American Justice*. Cambridge, MA: Harvard University Press, 2008.

———. "False Confessions: Causes, Consequences, and Implications." *Journal of the American Academy of Psychiatry and the Law Online* 37: 3 (September 2009), 332–343; http://jaapl.org/content/37/3/332.

Levine, Allan. *Scattered Among the Peoples: The Jewish Diaspora in Twelve Portraits*. New York: Overlook Press, 2003.

———. *The Devil in Babylon: Fear of Progress and the Birth of Modern Life*. Toronto: McClelland & Stewart, 2005.

———. *King: William Lyon Mackenzie King: A Life Guided by the Hand of Destiny*. Vancouver: Douglas & McIntyre, 2011.

———. *Toronto: Biography of a City*. Madeira Park, B.C.: Douglas & McIntyre, 2014.

Ludwig, Frederick J. "Improving New York's New Criminal Procedure Law." *St. John's Law Review* 45:3 (March 1971): 387–433.

Lyons, Jeffrey. *What a Time It Was!: Leonard Lyons and the Golden Age of New York Nightlife*. New York: Abbeville Press Publishers, 2015.

MacKellar, Landis. *The "Double Indemnity" Murder: Ruth Snyder, Judd Gray, And New York's Crime of the Century*. Syracuse, NY: Syracuse University Press, 2006.

Mair, Shirley. "Barbara Hamilton Afraid of Stardom? She's Earned It, and Won It." *Chatelaine* (October 1964): 28–29, 86–87.

Malone, Linda, ed. *Fairfield Remembers*. Fairfield County, SC: Fairfield Archives & History, 2006.

Margolick, David. *Strange Fruit: Billie Holiday, Café Society, and an Early Cry for Civil Rights*. Philadelphia: Running Press, 2000.

Mills, Carley. *A Nearness of Evil*. New York: Coward-McCann, 1961.

Mittelman, Amy. *Brewing Battles: A History of American Beer*. New York: Algora Publishing, 2008.

Mystery Writers of America. *Murder Cavalcade: An Anthology*. New York: Duell, Sloan and Pearce, 1946.

Newton, Esther. *Cherry Grove, Fire Island: Sixty Years in America's First Gay and Lesbian Town*. Raleigh, NC: Duke University Press, 2015.

New York Police Department. *Rules and Regulations and Manual of Procedure of Police Department of the City of New York*. New York: New York Civil Service Commission, 1940.

New York State Law Criminal Procedure Law: Consolidated Laws of New York's CPL Code. Albany, NY: New York State, 2007. http://ypdcrime.com/cpl.

O'Dougherty, Harold St. Leo, ed. *Penal Law and the Code of Criminal Procedure of the State of New York, with 1937 Amendments, Indexed*. Brooklyn, NY: Eagle Library, 1937.

Osborne, Thomas Mott. *Within Prison Walls*. New York: D. Appleton & Company, 1914.

Pak, Susie. "The House of Morgan: Private Family Bank in Transition," in Korinna Schönhärl, ed. *Decision Taking, Confidence and Risk Management in Banks from Early Modernity to the 20th Century*. Basingstoke, UK: Palgrave MacMillan, 2017, 15–55.

Paone, Arthur J. "The New Trial Procedure on Confession in New York." *Cornell Law Review* 50:3 (Spring 1965): 461–71.

Penal Law and the Code of Criminal Procedure of the State of New York: With All Amendments Passed by the Legislature at the Session of 1913. Albany, NY: Matthew Bender and Company, 1913.

Perry, Hamilton Darby. *A Chair for Wayne Lonergan*. New York: Macmillan, 1972. Second edition, Omaha, NE: Gryphon Editions, 2000.

"The Role of a Trial Jury in Determining the Voluntariness of a Confession." *Michigan Law Review* 63:2 (December, 1964): 381–89.

Rosen, Robert N. *The Jewish Confederates*. Columbia, SC: University of South Carolina Press, 2000.

Ryan, Hugh. *When Brooklyn Was Queer: A History*. New York: St. Martin's Press, 2019.

Sachar, Howard M. *A History of the Jews in America*. New York: Alfred A. Knopf, 1992.

Sapien Joaquin. "Criminal Justice Legislation Will Force New York Prosecutors to Disclose More Evidence, Sooner." *ProPublica* (April 8, 2019), www.propublica.org/article/criminal-justice-legislation-will-force-new-york-prosecutors-to-disclose-more-evidence-sooner.

Sapien, Joaquin, and Sergio Hernandez. "Who Polices Prosecutors Who Abuse Their Authority? Usually Nobody." *ProPublica* (April 3, 2013), www.propublica.org/article/who-polices-prosecutors-who-abuse-their-authority-usually-nobody.

Schechter, Harold. *The Mad Sculptor*. Boston: Houghton Mifflin, 2014.

Schupak, Donald C. "Evidence—*Jackson v. Denno* Ruling Retroactively Applicable in *Coram Nobis* Proceeding Provided Issue of Voluntariness Raised at Trial," *Syracuse Law Review* 16:3 (Spring 1965), 689–92.

Shechtman, Paul. "'*Jackson v. Denno*' and Voluntariness of Confessions 50 Years Later." *New York Law Journal* 251:118 (June 20, 2014), https://www.law.com/newyorklawjournal/almID/1202660104749./?slreturn=20200103091837.

Stark, Vincent. "New York Discovery Reform Proposals: A Critical Assessment." *Albany Law Review* 79:4 (2015–2016): 1265–1305.

Strock, Faraday J. "Validity of the Admission-Confession Distinction for Purposes of Admissibility." *Journal of Criminal Law and Criminology* 39:6 (March–April 1949): 743–50.

Thomas, Gwyn, and Jack Batten. "Wife Killer or Fall Guy." *Maclean's* (Toronto), July 3, 1965, 20, 38–39.

Valentine, Lewis J. *Night Stick: The Autobiography of Lewis J. Valentine, Former Police Commissioner of New York.* New York: The Dial Press, 1947.

Vreeland, Diana. *D. V.* New York: Alfred A. Knopf, 1984.

Waggoner, Susan. *Nightclub Nights: Art, Legend and Style 1920–1960.* New York: St. Martin's Press: 2001.

Wald, Alan M. *American Night: The Literary Left in the Era of the Cold War.* Chapel Hill, NC: University of North Carolina Press Books, 2012.

Wallace, Mike. *Greater Gotham: A History of New York City from 1898 to 1919.* New York: Oxford University Press, 2017.

Watts, Jill. *Mae West: An Icon in Black and White.* New York: Oxford University Press, 2003.

Wilcox, Michael. "Cultivating Conformity and Safeguarding Catholicism: The Christian Brothers and their Schools in Ontario, 1851–1962." PhD dissertation, University of Toronto, 2015.

Willemse, Cornelius W. *Behind the Green Lights.* New York: A. A. Knopf, 1931.

Willy, Lawrence R. *The Third Sex.* Urbana: University of Illinois Press, 2007.

Winegard, Richard Clarence. "Thyra Samter Winslow: A Critical Assessment." PhD dissertation, University of Arkansas, 1971.

Yagoda, Ben. *About Town: The New Yorker and the World It Made.* New York: Scribner, 2000.

Yellin, Emily. *Our Mothers' War: American Women at Home and at the Front during World War II.* New York: Free Press, 2004.

Young, Anthony. *New York Café Society: The Elite Meet to See and Be Seen, 1920s–1940s.* Jefferson, NC: McFarland & Company, 2015.

Zerbe, Jerome, and Brendan Gill. *Happy Times.* New York: Harcourt Brace Jovanovich, 1973.

LIST OF INTERVIEWS

Interviews conducted by the author, 2019 via telephone and e-mail

Ronda Cooper, April 14, 2019
Prof. Brandon L. Garrett, May 12, 2019
Prof. Stephen Gillers, July 10, 2019
Prof. Nancy King, July 29, 2019
Ken Lefolii, June 13, 2019
Prof. Richard Leo, June 14, 2019
Justice Gerald Loehr, May 6, 2019
John G. Loehr, July 26, 2019
D. P. Lyle, June 29, 2019
Major William March, May 31, 2019
Gordon Pinsent, April 30, 2019
Leah Pinsent, July 24, 2019
Gerda Ray, April 30, 2019
Prof. Daniel C. Richman, August 2, 2019
Marvin Schechter, May 13, 2019
Beth Schwartzapfel, May 7, 2019
Prof. Christopher Slobogin, July 29, 2019

Index

Italicized page numbers indicate insert photographs.

ABOUT THE AUTHOR

Allan Levine is an award-winning internationally selling author and historian based in Winnipeg, Canada. He has written fourteen books including *Toronto: Biography of a City* (2014) and *King: William Lyon Mackenzie King: A Life Guided by the Hand of Destiny* (2011), which won the Alexander Kennedy Isbister Award for Non-Fiction. His most recent book, *Seeking the Fabled City: The Canadian Jewish Experience*, was published in October 2018.